Canada: The State of the Federation 1985

Edited by Peter M. Leslie

Institute of
Intergovernmental
Relations

Queen's University
Kingston Ontario
Canada

Canadian Cataloguing in Publication Data

Main entry under title:
Canada, the state of the federation, 1985

Includes bibliographical references. ISBN 0-88911-442-0

1. Federal-provincial relations – Canada – Addresses, essays, lectures.* 2.
Regional planning – Canada – Addresses, essays, lectures. 3. Minorities –
Canada – Addresses, essays, lectures. I. Leslie. Peter M. II. Queen's University (Kingston, Ont.). Institute of Intergovernmental Relations.

JL27.C36 1985   321.02'3'0971   C85-099586-8

45,809

The Institute of Intergovernmental Relations

The Institute, part of Queen's University, is the only organization in Canada
whose mandate is solely to promote research and communication on the
challenges facing the federal system.

Current research interests include fiscal federalism, the role of Quebec
in confederation, the reform of federal-provincial relations, aboriginal self-
government, and a wide range of policy issues affected by the structure
and working of federalism.

The Institute pursues these objectives through research conducted by
its own staff, and other scholars, at Queen's and elsewhere; through an
active and growing publications program; and through seminars and
conferences.

The Institute links academics and practitioners of federalism in federal
and provincial governments and the private sector.

Contents

i

Preface

With this volume, the Institute of Intergovernmental Relations launches a new annual series entitled *Canada: The State of the Federation.* Since 1976-77 the Institute has published a *Year in Review: Intergovernmental Relations in Canada* (initially entitled *The Federal Year in Review*), a recap of events on the federal-provincial agenda. To some extent, the new series continues to meet this objective, but its goals have been broadened in two ways. First, it is both retrospective and prospective in character, focusing on the emerging public agenda as well as on the recent past. Second, while federalism and intergovernmental relations remain the primary focus of the book, the phrase 'the state of the federation' acknowledges the impossibility of sharply distinguishing between these aspects of Canadian public life and the more general political situation. At the same time, the new title emphasizes the centrality of federalism and intergovernmental relations to Canadian politics.

As is appropriate to the objectives of the new series, the present volume is the work of several authors. I am grateful to them all for their cooperation in this joint endeavour, and in particular for their readiness to set other projects aside in order to meet a tight publication schedule.

Preparing a book manuscript for publication is always a demanding task. In this case the ordinary difficulties and frustrations were exacerbated by our experimenting with new production technologies which imposed special burdens on the staff of the Institute. In particular, I would like to express my appreciation to Valerie Jarus, who bore the principal responsibility for word-processing and the entry of typesetting codes, and to Andrea Purvis, who took overall charge of the editorial and production process. Additional help in typing and proofreading was provided by Patricia Candido. On the editorial side, the contribution of Bruce Pollard and David

Hawkes was substantial. In short, the production of this book has been very much a collective effort by virtually the entire staff of the Institute. I am more than grateful to them all for the dedication, carefulness, and cheerfulness which they showed through a period of time which was, I am afraid, often stressful.

Peter M. Leslie
Director

Contributors

Gérard Boismenu is a member of the département de science politique at l'Université de Montréal.

Roger Gibbins teaches political science at the University of Calgary.

David C. Hawkes is associate director of the Institute of Intergovernmental Relations at Queen's University.

Peter M. Leslie is director of the Institute of Intergovernmental Relations and teaches political studies at Queen's University.

Bruce G. Pollard is research associate at the Institute of Intergovernmental Relations at Queen's University.

Donald J. Savoie is executive director of l'Institut canadien de recherche sur le développement régional at l'Université de Moncton.

John D. Whyte is a specialist on constitutional law in the Faculty of Law, Queen's University.

I
Introduction

1 The State of the Federation 1985

Peter M. Leslie

In the course of a year (June 1984 to June 1985) Canada has had three prime ministers; Ontario has had three premiers. In both cases a change of party was involved, resulting from an election defeat. In addition, the premiers of Quebec and Alberta are to step down in the fall of 1985; and the Quebec Liberals are confidently expecting victory in an election that must be held no later than April 1986.

How much are such changes in political leadership likely to affect the state of the federation as Canada moves into the latter 1980s and the 1990s? If we look back over the last 20 years, the importance of personality appears to bulk large. Pierre Trudeau dominated Canadian politics through this period, forcing us all to respond to his own political agenda. Now he has returned to private life; his arch-rival, Quebec Premier René Lévesque, is to leave politics as soon as the Parti Québécois can elect a successor.

In 1967 Trudeau wrote: 'By 1962 ... the Lesage government and public opinion in Quebec had magnified provincial autonomy into an absolute, and were attempting to reduce federal power to nothing; and so, to defend federalism, I entered politics in 1965.'[1] In the context of the time, defending federalism meant (to him) asserting and expanding central power. As prime minister, he resorted to unilateralism and confrontation both to curb the power of the provincial governments and to jolt public opinion towards his point of view. In both objectives he enjoyed partial but not complete success. It is unlikely that a conciliatory policy could have done as well as the conflict-generating policy that was actually implemented. In any case, by the time Trudeau left office, Canadians had evidently lost all patience with federal-provincial bickering. They had tired of deliberate polarization of opinion and were fearful of its consequences. 'He's tearing this country apart,' said the critics, many of whom regarded Trudeau as anti-business, anti-'the West', and anti-American. Trudeau's successor as Liberal leader and prime minister, John Turner, appeared to want to change these attitudes, charting a new course. But the country turned instead to the Conservatives under Brian Mulroney. Canadians have welcomed Mulroney's assurances, as regards federal-provincial relations, that the mood will sweeten, that he will consult widely before launching new policy initiatives, and that the operating mode of his government will be cooperation and joint action.

The evidence, a few months after the change in government, is that Mr. Mulroney will do all he can to obtain the good will of the provincial governments. He has ceased treating them as antagonists on matters of policy, and as rivals for the loyalties and affections of the public. Insofar as it is within one person's power to transform the political climate, to elicit collaboration where antagonism reigned before, he will do it. The question is, can it be done? Or, as a follower of Pierre Trudeau might put it, can it be done without selling out to the provinces, or 'giving away the store'?

Two matters are obviously at issue here. One is the extent of conflict in the federation, or (to look at the obverse side of this coin) the ability of federal and provincial governments to search out common ground and to act cooperatively in the pursuit of mutually agreed objectives. A second issue is that of (de)centralization: whether the scope of federal action is expanded while that of the provinces shrinks, or vice-versa. And perhaps more importantly: in areas of joint action, does leadership and control in policy formation tend to be exercised mainly by the federal government; or, conversely, do the provinces primarily hold sway while the federal government plays a helping role? These two issues – conflict/cooperation, and (de)centralization – point also to a third: the policy-effectiveness of government. What most Canadians are interested in is whether government does the things they want it to do, and whether it does these things efficiently and well. The problem, of course, is that the objectives sought by one group are rejected by another.

This chapter presupposes that when one considers the state of the federation, having in mind large issues such as these, explanation must go deeper than to changes in personalities and parties. These matters are not unimportant, but serious enquiry must take account of durable tensions among regions – underlying conditions that do not vanish simply because there has been an election and a change of government. Equally, one must recognize that some basic new factors also are at work, factors quite distinct from the ebb and flow of political fortunes or the entry and exit of players from the stage. Together, the circumstances promoting continuity and change set the parameters within which public figures act. In this respect, six factors would appear to have particular importance.

Two issues keep reappearing in new guises, but reflect conditions that have persisted throughout our history. Their very persistence suggests that it will be difficult to move intergovernmental relations into a less conflictual mode.

Peter M. Leslie

☐ Policies for Economic Development. Canada's historic 'national policies' have reflected, and in the eyes of many Canadians have greatly exacerbated, economic regionalism. In an effort to bind together several loosely integrated regional economies, federal policies have provoked opposition from resource-producing industries and provinces. It seems to have been impossible to devise an economic development strategy that is not regionally discriminatory. On the other hand, abdication of responsibilities for economic development seems unthinkable. No satisfactory solution to this dilemma appears to have been found.

☐ The Provision of Public Services, and Payments between Governments to Finance Them. Controversy persists over the desirable extent of interregional transfers of wealth through the agency of the federal government. The demands of provincial autonomy continue to conflict with notions of citizenship according to which all Canadians are entitled to comparable levels or standards of public services.

Two factors may be bringing about fundamental changes in Canadian public opinion and, as a consequence, in the powers effectively exercised by the federal and by the provincial governments. These factors therefore have the potential for bringing about fundamental changes in the Canadian federal system – probably for strengthening central power relative to that of the provinces.

☐ The Canadian Charter of Rights and Freedoms. The 'equality' provisions of the Charter came into effect in April 1985, transferring important powers from governments and legislatures to the courts – unless public opinion routinely accepts legislative derogation from the provisions of the Charter. This is unlikely to occur in most provinces, though Quebec may continue to do exactly this, reinforcing dualism. Elsewhere the courts will have the duty, subject to express exemption by Parliament and the provincial legislatures, to ensure that citizens have equal benefit of the law. This necessarily allows for continued interprovincial differences in policy. Still, where provincial action complements and applies the federal law (as in the field of criminal justice, and arguably in respect of some cost-shared activities such as health care), the public may appeal to the courts to require policy standardization. Even if the courts do not satisfy such requests, the existence of the Charter may strengthen the concept of Canadian citizenship, building up public pressure for comparability if not uniformity.

☐ Economic Relations with the United States. There is considerable support in Canada for negotiating a Canadian-American Free Trade Agreement (CAFTA). The proponents of such a scheme see it as the basis for an economic development strategy that has the support of all provinces – if only Ontario can be brought on side. Much of the incentive seems to come from fear that the United States is becoming increasingly protectionist, and from the belief that it is urgent to act now in order to gain assured access to the American market. However, the supporters of a bilateral trading arrangement may be overestimating the degree of market access Canada could reasonably hope to gain through a CAFTA. They may also be in for a surprise when they discover what conditions the United States would insist upon, if Congress were to endorse the scheme. It is quite possible, therefore, that if Canada does decide to make serious overtures on the subject, it will be rebuffed or will find the conditions unacceptable. A failed attempt could lead to a new phase of economic nationalism, which in the past has also provoked heightened economic regionalism within the country.

Two factors are 'wild cards': their effects are especially hard to predict. They may serve to reinforce existing patterns in federal-provincial relations, but they may equally well alter, in quite a basic way, the state of the federation.

☐ Economic Stabilization: Controlling inflation, reducing unemployment. If economic conditions do not significantly improve, it is going to be more difficult for governments to break out of their conflictual mode, denigrating and counteracting each others' policies. Not only are there regionally-based conflicts over economic policy, but ideological or philosophical ones as well. A nationalist and interventionist orientation is in tension with a neo-conservative, market-directed approach. Divergent prescriptions for restoring economic health will be, it is safe to predict, championed by the various provinces. None of them will be willing to let Ottawa set an economic course for the country without interference. On the other hand, an impatient public might swing its support behind one order of government, depriving the other of any real capacity to implement its own economic policy.

☐ The Evolving Situation of Quebec and of Francophones Canadians. The question of language rights for English- and French-speaking minorities remains a crucial one for the future development of Canada. Much will depend on how Canadians view themselves and their country – as one where Anglophones and Francophones have equal rights across the land, and play an equal role in national politics and the national economy; or as one where the development of the two major linguistic communities is achieved through the restructuring of the federal system to take account of cultural dualism. The latter view of Canada has been expressed through the Parti Québécois' earlier formula of political sovereignty for Quebec, combined with economic association with the rest of Canada. Now, however, the Parti Québécois has relegated the idea of political sovereignty to the status of 'an insurance policy', something to be resorted to if ever the Francophone minority feels politically or culturally threatened. The Quebec government is now seeking to negotiate a constitutional accord that will enable it to acknowledge the legitimacy of a revised Constitution

Peter M. Leslie

Act. Success in these negotiations, and acceptance of their result by both major political parties in the province, could transform the politics of Canadian federalism. Alternatively, if the attempt fails, the familiar tension between Quebec and Ottawa will reappear, waxing and waning in long, irregular cycles, or leading to a sudden crisis. On the one hand there will be a Quebec government that seeks constantly to expand its powers and its fiscal resources in order to fulfill its special responsibilities as the national government of a Francophone people. On the other, there will be a federal government which views Quebec as a province not greatly different from the others, or regards all provinces as having, each for its own reasons, special interests.

The importance of political personalities is their capacity to act marginally upon events, altering the processes of historical change. To the extent one aspires to understand these processes – both as they unfold, and afterwards – one must attempt to do so with reference to factors such as the six I have just identified. Clarity of vision and the exercise of political will by leading office-holders can be, at times, decisive in affecting their development.

After nine months in office the substance of Mr. Mulroney's vision remains ill-defined; the vigor with which he is capable of exercising political will remains unproven. He has been much clearer about process than about most of the choices he will make when consensus is manifestly absent and unachievable. So far he has been clearest about minority language rights, where he rejected the position taken by the provincial Conservatives in Manitoba. In other areas, especially in all aspects of relations with the provinces, and with the United States, he has mainly insisted that existing difficulties can readily be smoothed over – and indeed, he has done much to accomplish this. The commitment to consensus-building, and to regaining the confidence of the business community, has so far supported what would appear to be his own and his party's ideological leanings, towards a non-doctrinaire, mild form of neo-conservatism. This has been coupled with active support for most aspects of American foreign and defence policy.

Mr. Mulroney's very real gift for consensus-building lends special importance to political changes among the provincial governments.

In Ontario, a 42-year period of unbroken Conservative rule came to an end in a somewhat messy aftermath to the 2 May election. Premier Frank Miller, who entered the election campaign with the support of a clear majority of 'decided' voters, ended up with slightly less popular support than David Peterson's Liberals (37 per cent to 38 per cent) but with 52 seats to the Liberals' 48; the New Democratic Party under Bob Rae held the balance of power with 25 seats (24 per cent of the popular vote). Rae asked the two other party leaders to bid for NDP support on the basis of its intended policies, and a Liberal-NDP agreement was signed on 28 May. It fell short of formal coalition, but the agreement sets out the main features of a legislative program, and the New

Democrats are pledged to support the government for a period of at least two years. Conversely, the Liberals have pledged not to call an election during this period, unless it is defeated in the legislature on an explicit vote of non-confidence, or if its overall budgetary policy is voted down. Defeats on individual bills, including money bills, will not be considered matters of confidence. Once this agreement had been reached it was evident that the Conservatives could not avoid defeat when the new legislature met. Nonetheless, Premier Miller refused to resign, and his government was duly defeated at the first opportunity (18 June). The new Liberal government took office on 26 June.

It is difficult to imagine that in Alberta a change in Conservative party leadership could have an effect anything like what happened in Ontario. Throughout its history Alberta has been a virtual one-party province, but the sudden shifts to a new dominant party have occurred when the governing party was visibly disintegrating. Though the present Conservative party is peculiarly Mr. Lougheed's creation, there is little evidence at present that the party itself is decrepit or internally divided, or that the electorate is searching for an alternative. On the other hand, as Roger Gibbins points out in his commentary on Alberta politics (Chapter 4), the federal Conservative victory may bring out hitherto unsuspected political divisions in the province at large, and within the provincial wing of the party.

In Quebec, the ruling Parti Québécois is to elect a successor to Premier René Lévesque in late September or early October 1985. For the first time in the history of parliamentary government the leader of a governing party will be chosen by direct vote, of party members, somewhat as in U.S. primary elections. There will be no leadership convention. A general election is expected immediately after the vote, or in the spring of 1986. In this case the change in leadership may well have momentous consequences, because over the past year the party has been in turmoil over the constitutional question. The new leader will either confirm the federalist position taken by the party in January 1985 or will induce it to return to its more traditional independence-oriented stance. Whichever way Mr. Lévesque's successor attempts to lead the party, it could easily disintegrate – or, with new-found élan, cheat the Liberals of the electoral victory they now confidently expect. If phlegmatic Ontario could ditch Mr. Frank Miller and the Conservatives, no turnabout of the Quebec electorate could surprise anyone but a pollster.

The future course of the federation will be shaped to some extent by changes in the political fortunes of parties and their leaders; but to understand the events that take place around us, to whose vagaries we are all subject, we must look first to the more impersonal factors of historical continuity and change. I have already identified six such factors, and it is time to look at them again in greater detail. Of the six, three pertain to the economy: policies for economic development; economic relations with the United States; and economic stabilization (controlling inflation, reducing unemployment). We shall look at these issues first. The other three factors are certainly

Peter M. Leslie

not unrelated to economic affairs, but ultimately they are tied in with the concepts of citizenship and community: the provision of public services, and payments between governments to finance them; the impact of the Canadian Charter of Rights and Freedoms; and the evolving situation of Quebec and of Francophone Canadians. The remainder of the chapter will focus on these six topics.

Policies for Economic Development

Canada has always been an exporter of resource products. From pre- confederation days to the present, the Canadian economy has specialized in the exploitation of natural resources, both renewable (fish, forest products, hydro-electricity, farm products) and non-renewable (minerals, coal, oil, gas). The foreign sale of resource products and semi- manufactures, together with the import of foreign capital to finance resource development, has buoyed up the Canadian standard of living. The country remains a net importer of manufactures. In manufacturing, a high percentage of Canadian exports consists of barely processed resources.

It is useful to distinguish between 'primary manufacturing' (the initial stages of processing of raw materials) and 'secondary manufacturing', (the production of more refined products: components, finished goods, and consumer goods). Secondary manufacturing has been pretty much an artificial implant. This sector grew up under tariff protection, especially after the launching of the 'National Policy' of 1879. Protectionism has been called a policy of 'import substitution industrialization',[2] since its aim was to develop a manufacturing sector to supply the domestic market, partially displacing imports. In recent years, with declining tariff protection as a result of multilateral trade negotiations under the GATT (General Agreement on Tariffs and Trade), governments have had increasing recourse to direct subsidies for investment rather than supplying indirect, consumer-paid, support through tariffs. But in either case the benefits of the policy have been channelled to employers and employees in the protected industries, and to other industries clustering around them (construction, finance, etc.); the costs have been borne by the rest of the economy. In effect, the resource sectors have funded the development of manufacturing. The regional impact of the policy has been obvious – and much resented – since manufacturing has been concentrated in southern Ontario and Quebec, while the rest of the country has been almost wholly dependent upon resource production and primary manufacturing.

This is what 'economic regionalism' is all about. The term does not merely indicate that the various regions specialize in different products, or that some are wealthier than others. It means that some regions benefit from national policies while others foot the bill, and that this fact is both understood and resented in the 'hinterland' or primary-producing regions. 'Economic regionalism' means that people in Atlantic Canada, the north, and the west recognize that major economic decisions both in government and in the private sector are taken in central Canada, often to their apparent detriment. They want to gain a greater measure of control over their own economic destiny. In the Atlantic and western regions provincial governments are the instruments at hand to do this, particularly since the constitution confers on the provinces wide (but – especially in Newfoundland – far from unrestricted) powers over resource development.

The federal government's ability to deviate from traditional policies in support of manufacturing is limited. It faces a dilemma, because the protection of secondary industry (by whatever combination of import restrictions and industrial subsidies) may be a political necessity; on the other hand, a protectionist policy may prove increasingly beyond its capabilities, given successive rounds of multilateral reductions under the GATT. It is also an increasingly costly policy, as Asian and South American countries acquire stronger manufacturing sectors.

For any federal government, the ideal economic policy is one that either has no visible consequences for the structure of the economy (and therefore has no discernible regional implications), or even better, finds a way of reconciling sectoral and regional interests which have been in conflict for over a century. In 1981, as will be shown below, an attempt was made to do just this. The date is interesting, because it followed hard on the heels of the National Energy Program (1980), itself an extension and intensification of policies in effect since the mid-1970s. These policies represented in extreme form the traditional tendency to build up manufacturing, based in central Canada, by making the resources sector subservient to it. Beginning in 1973, oil and gas prices were kept below world levels in order to give a competitive edge to domestic industry, and in 1974 the federal government moved to claim a larger share of the increased revenues resulting from OPEC-declared price hikes. This brought it into conflict with the governments of the producing provinces, particularly Alberta; the industry was caught in the federal-provincial crossfire. In 1980, following OPEC's second round of price increases, the same scenario was re-enacted, though this time the federal policies (grouped together as the National Energy Program) were more far-reaching and, in the eyes of both the industry and the producing provinces, more punitive. Continuing price controls were complemented with a new array of tax measures and a system of discretionary grants (Petroleum Incentive Payments, or PIPs). The latter were designed to increase Canadian ownership ratios, and to shift exploration and development activity to the arctic region and the Atlantic seaboard (the 'Canada Lands': areas outside the boundaries of any province, and therefore under complete federal control). The PIPs, being discretionary, would give the federal government sweeping control over the industry. Exploration and development activity in the western sedimentary basin (the oil and gas fields of Alberta, Saskatchewan, and northeastern British Columbia) dropped precipitously. This forced the producing provinces into negotiations with the federal government over prices, royalties, and taxes, making Ottawa the central player in a trio consisting of two orders of government and the industry.

Peter M. Leslie

These negotiations resulted (August 1981) in a set of comprehensive bilateral agreements with the producing provinces, the essence of which was substantially to increase the price of oil and gas. This, it was hoped, would allow both the provinces and the federal government to raise additional revenues, while re-establishing the profitability of exploration activity in the western sedimentary basin, as well as encouraging the development of the oil sands. Thus, over a period of about eight years (1973 to 1981) a policy was put in place that in effect imposed federal controls on provincial revenues from oil and gas production and gave the federal government extensive control over the industry – presumably to be used in the interests of the consumers and the industries of central Canada. However, following the 1981 pricing agreements, it appeared that the stage was set for a new phase of expansion in the oil and gas sector, supported by an interventionist government and with greater Canadian ownership and direction of the industry. This was the context in which the 1981 development strategy was announced.

The policies to reconcile regional and sectoral interests were sketched out in two high-profile reports. The first was the report of the Major Projects Task Force[3] (May 1981), prepared under the direction of Robert Blair, President of Nova Corporation (Formerly Alberta Gas Trunk Line) and Shirley Carr, Vice-President of the Canadian Labour Congress. It was an inventory of 'mega-projects' then on the drawing boards, mostly in the transportation and resource sectors. Its significance was revealed in the second report, a budget paper published in November 1981 under the title *Economic Development for Canada in the 1980s*.[4] It declared that the leading opportunity for economic growth lay in the development of natural resources. This would require massive government-assisted investments in productive capacity and transport systems. Manufacturing industry would supply machinery, equipment, and materials needed for resource development, and would extend the processing of resources beyond the primary stage. In other words, though some expansion of manufacturing would occur in high-technology goods, the principal strategy for strengthening Canadian manufacturing would henceforth lie in building up its linkages with the resource sector. Thus resource development and manufacturing would become complementary rather than competing, harmoniously integrating Canada's diverse regional economies.

It was wishful thinking. Both the energy pricing agreements and the development strategy assumed that raw materials prices, especially energy prices, would continue to rise relative to the price of manufactures. In fact, it was calculated that the scarcity of resources would yield such a large increment in incomes that their development could be encouraged even though governments creamed off large 'economic rents' and used them to provide support for industrial development as well as for general services to the public. This blissful vision dissipated with faltering energy prices. The hoped-for complementarity of resource development and manufacturing has not materialized.

It remains to be seen whether the policies put into effect by the Mulroney government – policies whose first visible accomplishments are the 'Atlantic Accord' and the 'Western Accord' covering a limited range of resources issues – will succeed in buoying up the Canadian economy (including its manufacturing sector) without subordinating the interests of some sectors and regions to those of other sectors and regions.

The Accords, particularly the Western one, will dissolve the remnants of the National Energy Program. (For a description of the Atlantic Accord, see Chapter 3.) The Western Accord, signed April 1985, calls for a return to the pre-1980 system of tax incentives for exploration and development. These will replace the NEP formula of across-the-board taxes coupled with PIP grants and development agreements negotiated between government and operating firms. Price controls will be abolished for the first time since 1961. One vestige of the 1974-1984 policies does remain, however: the Accord commits the producing provinces not to increase their revenues from oil and gas production, implying (according to Energy Minister Pat Carney) a future reduction in royalty rates. (Reductions were announced by Premier Lougheed on 25 June.) An implication may be that if prices rise again, the federal government could tax away some of the resulting increase in profits.

The question now is whether the two energy accords are early signs of a comprehensive economic development policy emphasizing resource development. I am not suggesting that there is a grand scheme worked out in advance, or even that there need be one. The coherence (or tension) among many individual policy initiatives, perhaps undertaken in response to short-run economic pressures and political demands, may become evident only in retrospect. Implicitly, though, a strategy pieced together around the expansion of resource production must wager that – as envisioned in 1981 – the vitality of the primary sector will spill over into manufacturing. Is this likely to happen?

The conditions now appear less favourable than they did in 1981. Under the Atlantic and Western Accords, the federal government gives up substantial revenues, abandons measures to promote the extension of Canadian ownership and control, and eliminates cross-border differences in price (though the possibility remains that in the case of a new oil crisis, price controls and export taxes will again be imposed). It appears that these policy changes were dictated, ultimately, by the softening of world oil prices after 1981. Under these world-economic conditions and the Canadian government's response to them (given their domestic repercussions), can resource production and manufacturing be made mutually supporting? Or will the strength of manufacturing require, as in the past, government protection or support, which in the final analysis must be paid for by the non-sheltered, primary-producing, sectors of the economy?

So far it has been beyond the wit of federal policy-makers to promote the development of manufacturing industry except through a sectorally and

Peter M. Leslie

regionally discriminatory policy. It is politically difficult to dismantle a protectionist policy, leaving industry to compete unaided in both domestic and foreign markets. No federal government can afford to implement policies that reduce the employment-generating effects of manufacturing industry, as this would be politically unacceptable especially in the most populous regions of the country.

The political and economic task at hand is to facilitate the transition to an internationally competitive manufacturing industry while augmenting employment in manufacturing and manufacturing-related industries. It would seem that the resource sector does not, in itself, have sufficient employment-generating potential to compensate for a loss of jobs elsewhere in the economy – and if it did, large inter-regional population flows would probably be required to fit in with a differently-structured economy. No federal government could afford (electorally speaking) to force the necessary adjustments upon the country.

If government support for manufacturing remains necessary (or if the politicians think it is), it is difficult to imagine how economic regionalism can subside. The provinces with resource-based economies – that is, most provinces – will exercise their constitutional powers to direct and control, to the extent they can, their own economic development. Relations with Ottawa will remain harmonious as long as federal policies do not interfere with or restrict 'province-building' policies, or visibly favour one region over others. However, political pressures from Ontario and Quebec may force the federal government (any federal government) to do just this. In that case it would be difficult for Mr. Mulroney, or anyone else, indefinitely to sustain inter-regional and intergovernmental goodwill.

Economic Relations With the United States

The argument in the preceding section assumed that certain historical characteristics of the Canadian economy have persisted into the present, basically unchanged. This may be incorrect. Our trading and investment relationship with the rest of the world, and particularly with the United States, is considered by some observers to have changed substantially in recent years, with the consequence that the old tensions between manufacturing industry and the resource sector – and thus between central Canada and its traditional hinterland – no longer exist in quite the same form. Conflicts between divergent economic interests are still there, but the pattern is more complex. In particular, the regional implications of these conflicts, and thus their intergovernmental consequences, are less clear than in the past.

The major new element in the politics of economic policy is that a much larger segment of Canadian manufacturing industry than ever before is confident that it is now – or, given access to a large market, could become – internationally competitive. Many business leaders are therefore actively supporting a policy of trade liberalization. They see a possible free trade agreement with the United States (a CAFTA, or Canadian-American Free Trade Agreement) as a necessary step towards liberalization on a multilateral basis. Other Canadian manufacturers remain protectionist in outlook, but among this group there are some who are mainly concerned about the challenge posed to high-income countries generally by the 'NICs' or newly-industrializing countries. They are less concerned about competition from the United States. As a defence against the NICs, they want to achieve industrial restructuring on a continental basis. To this end they propose a CAFTA, either sectorally or across-the-board; but they see it as a basis for implementing protectionism on a North American scale (at least above the Rio Grande). Thus they do not regard a bilateral agreement as a stepping-stone to general free trade.

The leading business associations in the country – the Business Council on National Issues (BCNI), the Canadian Manufacturers' Association (CMA), and the Canadian Chamber of Commerce – now endorse far-reaching trade liberalization. The CMA urged, in a letter to the Minister for International Trade (22 April 1985): '... that Canada-U.S. trade discussions [be held] to consider how we could enter into a bilateral trade agreement to secure and enhance each other's market access.' The Chamber of Commerce, in a submission to the Government of Canada (April 1985), notes that: 'The repeated and increasingly frequent assaults on Canadian exports by American protectionist forces are proof that we cannot afford to do nothing ... For these reasons, the Chamber ... recommends the prompt opening of exploratory discussions with the United States over the widest possible range of bilateral trade questions in order to identify what issues are negotiable and in what forms they might best be dealt with.' The clearest statement has come from the BCNI in a letter to the prime minister (24 April 1985):

First, Canada must continue to give strong support to the objective of multilateral trade liberalization and to the General Agreement on Tariffs and Trade (GATT). This will require a commitment to participate in the next round of GATT trade negotiations.

Coupled with this, we are also of the view that Canada should strive to commence, at an early date, discussions with the United States aimed at achieving bilateral trade liberalization and the resolution, where possible, of outstanding trade irritants and disputes between the two countries.

The ultimate objective of these bilateral discussions should be to achieve the broadest possible measure of improved, reciprocal market access, rather than narrow functional or sectoral agreements, although the latter, if the opportunity arises, may well be an important step toward a more comprehensive bilateral trade agreement.

In assessing the views of provincial governments, it is necessary to take account of ambiguities and inconsistencies in the statements made by several of the provinces. At their May 1985 meeting in Grande Prairie the four western premiers called for a 'comprehensive common market arrangement' with the United States, and requested full provincial participation in all stages of the next round of multilateral trade negotiations. However, according to the

Winnipeg Free Press (16 May 1985) Manitoba's Premier Howard Pawley 'said there is a split between Manitoba and the other premiers such as Alberta's Peter Lougheed, who advocates unfettered trade with the U.S.' Pawley seems to have been under the mistaken impression that a common market would be less far-reaching than a free trade area, and endorsed the joint communique on the grounds that it allowed for the protection of sensitive industries.

To the east, Newfoundland is unambiguously in favour of bilateral free trade; Nova Scotia supports an agreement 'broader than a sectoral free-trade approach'; New Brunswick has been ambiguous. Quebec, too, though it is said by some observers to favour a CAFTA, has been less than categorical. Ontario has expressed serious reservations, and with the Liberal government under David Peterson – backed by the NDP – can be taken to be clearly opposed. It seems somewhat paradoxical that the province with the greatest concentration of internationally competitive manufacturing industry should be the most negative of all. Opinion in the province is seriously divided, as can easily be seen in the supportive position of the major business associations, while the trade unions and the NDP are increasingly vocal against a relaxation of protectionism.

The eastern and western provinces' support for a CAFTA reflects their historic reliance on resource production, and their recognition that they cannot prosper if they do not have ready access to the American market. This has recently been a problem in the case of wood products, hogs, and fish. In the case of non-renewable resources industries – minerals and hydrocarbons – the main 'access' problem would appear to be for semi-manufacturers based on Canadian raw materials: metals and petrochemicals.

Some of the proponents of a CAFTA now argue that if Ontario could be brought around to the view that such an agreement would ultimately work to its advantage, then the free trade option would become the basis of *the first national economic development strategy in Canada's history to have the support of all regions*. Everyone recognizes that a CAFTA would entail bankruptcies and loss of employment in certain industries, but the supporters of trade liberalization argue that most of the adjustment costs could be avoided by negotiating a fairly lengthy phase-in period (perhaps as much as 15 years), especially since they expect most of the changes to occur *within individual industries and even within individual plants*. Is free trade now the policy of national unity? If so, and if Canada can negotiate a satisfactory agreement, the conditions exist for a vast reduction in regionalism and in the federal-provincial conflict that incompatibility among regional economic interests engenders.

These are big 'ifs'. To my way of thinking, the puzzle is not why Ontario's attitude is somewhat negative, but why a bilateral trade agreement has so much support among the other provincial governments. One has to suspect that they have not sufficiently considered what sort of agreement the Americans could be induced to sign, and have therefore underestimated the extent to which a trade pact would be likely to restrict both the federal government's and the provinces' capacity to channel and promote industrial development. Both these matters require elaboration.

First, on Ontario's attitude. Its hesitancy can be explained in very simple political terms: it is feared, particularly among trade unionists, that a CAFTA would entail a net loss of jobs. This fear is rejected by CAFTA supporters, who say it is groundless, but electorally speaking the damage done by one job lost outweighs the reward from two jobs possibly or probably gained in the (indefinite) future. More subtly, the unions are concerned that the dismantling of protection will injure the bargaining position of Canadian unionized workers, forcing them to compete with a low-wage, largely non-unionized work force in the American South, and imperilling social benefits (such as medicare and unemployment insurance) that are funded through taxes and employment-related levies. If employment is to be kept up, it may be at the expense of living standards. The political force of these concerns will inevitably be augmented by the Liberals' accession to power in Ontario, with NDP support.

The prospects, therefore, are not bright that Ontario will eventually support the holding of free trade negotiations with the United States. This is ironic because Ontario could be expected to benefit the most, at least in the long run. A CAFTA would result in a restructuring of Canadian industry, probably with further concentration of secondary manufacturing in Ontario. Existing and future obstacles to the export of resource products, an objective obviously dear to those provinces most committed to trade liberalization, could be removed only if the United States agreed not to apply discretionary measures ('contingent protectionism') against Canadian exports. The main devices in question are *countervailing duties*, which are levied at rates calculated to neutralize the effect of any production subsidy in the exporting country, and *anti-dumping duties* whose purpose is to prevent a producer from unloading surpluses abroad at prices below those normally charged in the domestic market.

There is no realistic prospect that the United States would agree under any circumstances tolerable to Canada to forego the right to levy countervailing and anti-dumping duties. It did not do so when it made a free trade agreement with Israel in February 1985, a country which is much less well equipped than Canada to compete against U.S. manufactures. (Perhaps more importantly, there are strong political and strategic reasons impelling the United States to closer ties with Israel.) With Canada, as with Israel, the United States would insist on retaining the right to assess injury to its own producers when foreigners, Canadians included, are deemed to be unfairly subsidizing exports or selling them abroad below domestic prices, or below actual cost of production (dumping). Thus, if we are aiming for 'assured access' or 'guaranteed access' to the U.S. market, meaning that we anticipate being freed from 'the

Peter M. Leslie

tremendous capacity for trade harrassment'[5] inherent in present American legislation, we are simply deluding ourselves. Nor can we, as Canadians, seriously desire to be exempted from threat of countervail and other forms of 'contingent protectionism', since this goal could only be realized on condition that the Americans control our economic policies at both the federal and the provincial levels. As Ron and Paul Wonnacott, who for years have been urging Canada to enter a free trade agreement with the United States, have remarked, the only way we could get in under American administrative barriers is through political union.[6]

Even without obtaining 'assured access' in the rigorous sense just described, it is likely that Congress could be persuaded to sign a CAFTA, if at all, only on condition that we would have to accept quite extensive limitations on our capacity to implement an independent economic policy. Proponents of an agreement have readily acknowledged that benefits to Canada would be much greater than those accruing to the U.S. (the greatest gains are realized in the smallest unit, because its market access is expanded the most). Consequently, our bargaining position is weak. Even if we do not propose, as former federal Deputy Minister of Finance Simon Riesman (one of the principal negotiators of the Auto Pact) has done, to sell the Americans water from James Bay in exchange for access to their markets, we would have to promise not to offer our industry any advantages not equally available to producers south of the border. This would have a very restrictive effect on all forms of industrial assistance and direct government participation in the economy. Prohibited measures would probably include:

- ☐ *Investment subsidies in the form of grants or low-cost loans*, even when the objective is regional development. Not only large projects such as the building of an auto assembly plant or parts factory might be involved –so too might items such as assistance to fishermen to buy or re-equip boats.
- ☐ *Public and mixed public/private enterprise* (i.e., equity participation, for example, as is characteristic of Quebec's Société général de financement). Publicly subscribed capital is equivalent to an investment subsidy. On the other hand, there is no reason to suppose that public corporations such as Hydro Québec could not go on selling power to the U.S.
- ☐ *Export subsidies in the form of low-cost or interest-free loans*, such as are provided by the Export Development Corporation.
- ☐ *Export taxes*, such as were a prominent feature of Canadian oil and gas policy from 1973 to 1985; or *quantitative controls and export licences*, such as remain in effect for long-term contracts for foreign sales not only of oil and gas but also of electricity. If the United States gives Canadian firms unimpeded access to its markets, surely it would insist that American industry should have a chance to compete on equal terms – in other words, that Canadian industry should not have privileged access to sources either in terms of price or of supplies. In effect, the non-discri-

mination provisions of 'the resources clause' or the new Section 92A of the Constitution Act, would now have to apply internationally as well as inter-provincially. For example, neither Canada nor any individual province could attempt to build up a petrochemicals industry by selling it feedstocks at cut-rate prices or by giving the industry priority access if and when supplies are scarce.

☐ Finally, *royalty schedules for resource exploitation* might easily come under scrutiny, as has already occurred in the case of the lumber industry. American producers have (so far unsuccessfully) argued that Canadian royalties are too low, giving Canadian firms an unfair advantage.

As is underlined by the last of these items, Canada will not be exempt from pressures to adapt its policies to American ones simply by pulling away from the idea of negotiating a bilateral trade agreement. Moreover, a foretaste of how the threat of countervail may constrain policy-formation in Canada is provided by the controversial Domtar interest-free loan (April 1985). The $150 million loan, 12.5 per cent of expected construction costs, was granted to assist in building a mill in East Windsor, Quebec. The mill will produce fine papers for export. The Minister of Regional Industrial Expansion, Sinclair Stevens, indicated that a straight subsidy had not been granted because it would have given rise to countervail; the loan, he bravely but unconvincingly said, would not.[7]

The Domtar case, like the lumber royalty case, raises the quite crucial question whether Canadian freedom of manoeuver would actually be reduced or (conversely) augmented if we negotiated a CAFTA. This is too complicated a question to address here; but it is evident that the ground rules for permissible forms of government intervention in the economy would form part of the bargaining. *It is hard to imagine that some of the present supporters of a* CAFTA – *including some of the provinces – could fail to cool as American negotiators (in private) and Congressmen (in public) lay out the conditions upon which they would insist. It is unlikely that those who now view a CAFTA as the cornerstone of a national-unity economic development strategy, if only Ontario could be brought on side, would persist in this opinion.*

A final remark before leaving the CAFTA issue. It is at least worth putting the question, whether a failed attempt to gain 'assured access' to the American market would not cause the pendulum to lurch back towards economic nationalism, as rejection by the Americans has done so frequently in the past. And economic nationalism, it should be remembered, fans economic regionalism too.

Consequences of High Unemployment

For the past four years the unemployment rate in Canada has hovered around 11 or 12 per cent; among some age groups, and in some areas, particularly in winter, rates of 35 per cent or even higher are not uncommon. The pressure on governments, both federal and provincial, to create jobs is enormous.

Peter M. Leslie

However, there is no obvious or broadly-accepted formula for resolving a problem which has now been widespread even among industrial countries for at least a decade, Short-run solutions (industrial subsidies, public sector employment, budgetary deficits) are held by their critics to exacerbate the long-term problem. Long-term solutions (creating a favourable climate for business, and relying on the private sector) are dismissed by *their* critics as ineffective and inequitable.

In the last years of Mr. Trudeau's term of office, the federal government was criticized by the New Democratic Party for lack of compassion and refusal to be more expansionary in its budget policies than it was; it was criticized by the Conservatives for having an anti-business and anti-American bias that scared away investors and undercut the natural (market) forces of recovery. The provinces joined in a single condemnatory chorus. They courteously avoided criticizing each other, at least in public, but when convoked in a First Ministers' conference on the economy in February 1982, together they raised an anthem of vituperation against Federal policies. The experience convinced Mr. Trudeau that such conferences only created a platform for his detractors, and he refused to hold any more of them.

Mr. Mulroney has used different tactics. He has made a public show of consulting the provincial premiers, though for those not included in the process it is too early to tell whether there is real substance to the consultations. A First Ministers' Conference on the Economy was held in Regina in February 1985, an occasion for a public display of cordiality and little else.

The one concrete result of the Regina meeting, apart from reaching consensus on the need for an export promotion drive, was agreement that the First Ministers should gather annually to exchange views on the economy and to attempt to coordinate their efforts to cope with the country's economic problems. What one needs to ask at this juncture is whether, especially if the rate of unemployment does not significantly decline, intergovernmental consensus can be created on so difficult a subject. The First Ministers are, after all, a necessarily disparate group representing rather disparate regional interests.

On what basis might a consensus emerge? In the previous section we discussed whether negotiation of a Canadian-American Free Trade Agreement (CAFTA)could become the centrepiece of an economic development strategy that had the support of all regions. This did seem plausible, though only if the Americans – particularly the Congress – accepted a Canadian proposal without imposing conditions which would be unpalatable to many of us. Now, complementing our earlier discussion of the CAFTA proposal, we should look at the tension between interventionists and neo-conservative strategies for job-creation. However, this does not mean that we should now focus exclusively on the domestic scene where in the previous section we were concerned with the international context. We cannot meaningfully discuss *any* of our economic policies as if Canada were a closed economy. We have to begin by recognizing that we live in a world where mercantalist instincts remain strong even among the most advanced industrial states and even among those countries most committed to liberalization of the world trading environment.

Mercantilism, a policy of limiting imports and promoting exports, is directed towards protecting or creating jobs. Mercantilism is practiced by every modern state within the constraints imposed by its international obligations. Every country's goal in trade negotiations seems to be to ensure that its trading partners are constrained in this respect as effectively as possible, while the limitations on its own freedom of action are kept to a minimum.

The centrepiece of a mercantilist policy used to be tariff protection in order to promote import substitution. Now, however, this traditional form of protectionism is impracticable. Successive rounds of tariff reductions under the GATT have made it so. The question is what is to replace it. One option is interventionism, the creation of a government-and-business alliance (if organized labour is recruited into the alliance, as with an incomes policy, the term 'corporatism' is sometimes used). A second option is neo-conservatism.

An interventionist policy, which may be import-substituting, export-promoting, or both, aims to export unemployment by creating an active partnership between business and government. The distinction between the private and the public sector becomes blurred. Government identifies firms as instruments of state policy and supports them through various forms of subsidy and equity participation (roughly the range of matters surveyed in the previous section, as probable targets for American negotiators if CAFTA talks get seriously underway).

A neo-conservative strategy, like interventionism, concentrates on improving the country's competitive position in the world economy, making it both more resistant to import penetration and better able to capture foreign markets. In other respects it is antithetical to interventionism. Among its hallmarks are that it:

☐ distinguishes sharply between the private and the public sectors, and minimizes the role and the size of government (deregulation, reduced public services);

☐ supports business through writeoffs for investment, for technological innovation, and for exports – various forms of 'tax expenditure', which by their nature are available to all eligible firms without the exercise of bureaucratic discretion; and

☐ strengthens management against labour, with a view to holding down labour costs.

Neo-conservatives, as is everywhere recognized, are noticeably readier than the interventionists to incur high levels of unemployment 'in the short run'. Thus the curbing of inflation typically has priority over immediate job-creation. It is even argued that only when government publicly rejects the Keynesian commitment to high and stable levels of employment, can it succeed in achieving them.[8] This paradox is resolved, according to neo-conservatives, by the fact that deregulation and a reduced fiscal burden unleashes the productive forces of the economy. The private sector, following the signals and obeying the discipline of the market, will create employment far more effectively than an interventionist policy can do.

In Canada there occur, in different parts of the country, differing mixes of the two tendencies. This variation partly reflects regional or provincial differences in resource endowments and economic opportunities. These differences in turn are related to and interact with cultural differences: the richer areas, it would seem, are more attracted to neo-conservatism; the poorer ones, to interventionism. Of course, there are also accidents of personality and partisan fortunes that give rise to differences in the ideological stance of provincial governments. Thus the outcome of the May 1985 Ontario election will probably act as some sort of brake on the neo-conservative tendencies of the present federal government.

Given that interventionism and neo-conservatism are nearly antithetical in their prescriptions, the regionally uneven mix of the two contains much potential for intergovernmental conflict. A federal government that tries to combine elements of both will not only incur charges of inconsistency and drift in the formulation of its economic policies, but will be subject to criticism from provincial governments which in some cases are more interventionist and in others more inclined towards neo-conservatism. Policy cooperation and concertation is possible only when the governments' objectives and strategies are largely congruent. At present, however, agreement does not extend far beyond a mutual desire to reduce unemployment. Agreement is lacking on key issues such as:

☐ the amount of industrial restructuring which will be necessary to significantly improve Canada's international competitive position, or even which industries hold out the greatest promise;

☐ the relative priority to be given to (a) lowering interest rates in order to stimulate investment, (b) restraining expansion of the the money supply to fight inflation and to maintain competitiveness, and (c) propping up the Canadian dollar to prevent a drop in living standards – or depressing it, in order to improve export performance; (one can target interest rates, the money supply, or the exchange rate, but in fixing on any one of these three, government necessarily accepts some loss of control over the other two);

☐ the importance of regional development, and the extent of population movement to be tolerant or sought after; what is at issue here is the definition of goals for regional development policy (see Chapter 5);

☐ to what extent government can afford to burden profitable sectors of the economy by supporting unprofitable ones, or by financing a generous social security system (see next section).

These are issues which will not go away. They have been the subject of controversy within each jurisdiction, and among governments, in the past. It is quite possible that they will continue to sow conflict among political parties, organized interests, and governments, and that such conflict will be sharpened by failure to reduce unemployment levels. Each order of government may continue to criticize the other's policies, and to use the policy instruments at its disposal to counteract or neutralize the other's initiatives. The frustrations produced by the apparently intractable nature of the unemployment problem could well result in a return to the adversarial mode of intergovernmental relations, a style adopted by Mr. Trudeau and fully reciprocated by most provincial premiers.

Conversely, the electorate's impatience over intergovernmental bickering, already high, may discipline the governments, forcing them to cooperate. At the hearings of the Royal Commission on the Economic Union and Development Prospects for Canada (the 'Macdonald Commission') in 1983 and 1984 many witnesses expressed their exasperation over governments' failure to cooperate with each other. Many voices urged governments to stop quarrelling and to get on with the business of governing. On the whole this attitude appeared to support centralization: many witnesses seemed to suggest that the federal government take the lead in the formation of economic policy. If this interpretation is correct, and if public opinion continues to support unified direction of economic policy, this could considerably strengthen central power over the years ahead, eclipsing the role of the provinces.

But this is not the only credible scenario. The federal government may find itself increasingly constrained to follow the U.S. lead in economic policy (and indeed in other spheres as well). Ottawa, pressured by Washington, may find itself incapable of taking initiatives displeasing to the American administration, other than on the basis of a strong interprovincial consensus. It is possible to imagine that the federal government could become, more and more, reduced to the role of an agency for the interregional redistribution of wealth through intergovernmental and interpersonal fiscal transfers. The prime initiative for the formulation of economic and perhaps even social policy may lie basically in Washington, with adaptations to it being made mainly by provincial governments. Their role may be, as J.A. Corry wrote nearly 30 years ago, that of 'playing variant melodies within the general theme'.[9] But what of the theme itself? Will it be played in Ottawa or in Washington?

Public Services and Intergovernmental Transfers

The next general revision of federal-provincial fiscal arrangements will go into effect in 1987; the crucial decisions will be made in 1986; the major thrust of any changes may well be blocked out in 1985. Given the size of the federal budgetary deficit (upwards of $35 billion – that is, almost eight per cent of GNP, or a third of federal tax revenues), it is hard to imagine that the process can be completed without a good deal of acrimony. Indeed in a document

Peter M. Leslie

released with the budget on 23 May 1985, federal Finance Minister Michael Wilson warned the provinces that, while there would be no change to provincial transfers during the current fiscal year:

The federal government is proposing to limit the rate of growth of transfers to provincial governments in order to effect savings amounting to about $2 billion in 1990-91. The same principles of restraint will be applied to transfers to provinces as to other expenditures to spread the burden of expenditure reduction as broadly and fairly as possible ... The place and manner of achieving these savings will be the subject of discussions with the provinces commencing this fall.[10]

The subject of intergovernmental transfers may turn out to be a hot issue in 1985/86 for an additional reason: the federal spending power is being challenged in court, and the case may well come to trial in later 1985 or in 1986. Even a limited degree of success in this challenge could profoundly change the character of the Canadian federal system, and of Canada itself. At stake is a large part of the system of *interregional redistribution* of wealth and income, and the capacity of the federal government to take the lead in inducing the provinces to work towards the establishment and observance of *national standards in public services.*

THE CONSTITUTIONALITY OF THE SPENDING POWER   Most aspects of education, health care services and social assistance (i.e., means-tested income support) lie within exclusive provincial jurisdiction. This means that the Parliament of Canada cannot legislate in these areas except in very specific ways. For example, if a province fails to observe constitutionally guaranteed rights of religious minorities, Parliament may enact 'remedial legislation'. But in most respects the provinces alone have legislative power. The power is explicit in the case of education, and exists by inference in the other two fields, where the provinces are allocated exclusive jurisdiction over 'Hospitals, Asylums, Charities, and Eleemosynary [i.e., alms-supported] Institutions in and for the Province, other than Marine Hospitals.' Some uncertainty may arise from the phrase 'in and for the province', a phrase which also occurs in relation to legislative power over education; but so far as I know there is no judicial decision that has drawn on these words to limit provincial power or to extend federal power.

Notwithstanding the nominally exclusive role of the provinces in the three fields just mentioned, the federal government is heavily involved in all of them through the exercise of its 'spending power'. This is the power, generally thought to be constitutionally sound, to make payments out of general revenues (the Consolidated Revenue Fund) (a) to individual persons, (b) to institutions, and (c) to provincial governments, in order to achieve national goals even in areas where the provinces have exclusive legislative power. A qualification on this power is that it must not constitute a regulatory scheme. That, at least, would seem to be the inference to draw from the words of Lord Atkin, speaking for the Judicial Committee of the Privy Council, in the 1937 *Social Insurance* case:

That the Dominion may impose taxation for the purpose of creating a fund for special purposes and may apply that fund for making contributions in the public interest to individuals, corporations or public authorities could not as a general proposition be denied ... But assuming that the Dominion has collected by means of taxation a fund, it by no means follows that any legislation which disposes of it is necessarily within Dominion competence. It may still be legislation affecting the classes of subjects enumerated in section 92, and, if so, would be *ultra vires*. In other words, Dominion legislation, even though it deals with Dominion property, may yet be so framed as to invade civil rights within the Province: or encroach upon the classes of subjects which are reserved to provincial competence.

One infers that Parliament may offer support for activities in areas of provincial jurisdiction so long as it does not restrict or control them.

The aspect of the spending power that is of greatest current concern is the intricate and extensive system of payments to provincial governments ('intergovernmental transfers'). Some are unconditional, some conditional, and some 'semi-conditional', as will be explained below.

☐ *Unconditional transfers* consist overwhelmingly of the *equalization payments*, which are now mandated under the Constitution Act, 1982. Their purpose, as stated in section 36(2) of the Act, is 'to ensure that provincial governments have sufficient revenues to provide reasonably comparable levels of public services at reasonably comparable levels of taxation.' (The exact formula is modified or recast every five years, with other amendments sometimes occurring between the quinquennial revisions. For a thorough discussion, see Thomas Courchene: *Equalization Payments: Past, Present and Future*, 1984.) The distinguishing feature of the equalization payments, other than their very uneven distribution among the provinces – four receive none at all – is that the payments are absolutely untied to any object of expenditure. The receiving provinces can spend the money on whatever purposes they wish, or use it to reduce taxes.

☐ The federal government may also offer the provinces conditional grants or specific-purpose subsidies to induce them to adopt certain programs in areas of their exclusive jurisdiction. This both alters provincial spending priorities and influences program standards. Under conditional grant schemes, or shared-cost programs, the federal government exercises supervision over the design and implementation of provincial programs. In addition, the size of the grant to which a province is entitled depends on how much it spends on the program (the federal government contributes a stipulated share of eligible costs). At present, by far the most important of the conditional grants program is the Canada Assistance Plan.

☐ Cash payments to provincial governments under the 'established programs financing' or EPF scheme might appropriately be labelled *semi-conditional transfers*. These grants are a successor to 'mature' shared-cost programs in the field of health care (hospital insurance and diagnostic services, and medical care) and in postsecondary education – though the latter was never, in a strict sense, a shared-cost program. EPF payments are conditional in the sense that the amount of money a province receives may be affected by the design of the programs they are intended to support. Thus the Canada Health Act (1983) imposes penalties on those provinces that allegedly infringe basic principles of medicare (universality and comprehensiveness) when they permit doctors to collect a fee from patients in addition to what they receive from the public treasury ('extra-billing'), or impose user-charges for hospital services. On the other hand, under the EPF scheme, the size of the transfer is not affected – or has not hitherto been affected – by the amount of money the receiving province spends in the areas concerned. In other words, EPF payments may be conditional in one sense, but are unconditional in another.

☐ Conditional and semi-conditional grants are now being challenged in court. In November 1983 Winterhaven Stables Limited, an Alberta company, filed a statement of claim in the Court of Queen's Bench in Calgary. The statement, which cites the federal Attorney-General as defendant, alleges that:

The [federal] Income Tax Act is *ultra vires* the Parliament of Canada as it constitutes 'direct taxation within a province in order to the raising of a revenue for provincial purposes', which is within the exclusive legislative jurisdictions of the provinces by reason of section 92(2) of the Constitution Act, 1867.

The basis of the case is that federal income tax revenues are used in part to pay for conditional grants and the EPF scheme, that is, to finance programs that are 'for provincial purposes'. By attacking the Income Tax Act, Winterhaven Stables sought to challenge large parts of the federal spending power. A June 1985 amendment to the claim directly challenges also 'the EPF Act, the Canada Health Act and the Canada Assistance Plan Act', stating that 'the conditional spending authorization contained in the statutes ... has established a scheme to regulate and thereby indirectly legislate within areas of provincial jurisdiction'.[11] The case is likely to come to trial in 1986 if not before. Assuming subsequent appeals, it will be years before the Supreme Court of Canada makes a final determination of the matter, though the process could be speeded up if the federal government referred the whole matter to the Supreme Court. This would effectively leap-frog some stages in the usually drawn-out process.

To obtain an impression of the significance of the *Winterhaven Stables* case, it is necessary to take note of two major underlying issues. One is the extent of interregional redistribution. A federal system makes redistribution among the regions more obvious in a unitary state because much of it is highlighted in intergovernmental transfers. On this subject, two principles contend: *equity*, which arguably supports extensive transfers, and *efficiency*, which (together with the principle of fiscal responsibility) has frequently been invoked to support a reduction in intergovernmental transfers and consequently in interregional redistribution. A second underlying issue is how to reconcile respect for diversity – regional differences in needs and preferences – with the concept of citizenship. Citizenship calls for equality of sacrifice in support of the community, and also suggests equal entitlement to public services. The latter objective is often taken to require standardization, or at least the setting of national standards. Thus, for some people, the idea of citizenship (and the goal of nation-building on the basis of common citizenship) justifies vigorous use of the federal spending power in a way that limits and constrains provincial autonomy.

The issues of interregional redistribution, and of citizenship and national standards in public services, are also being continuously fought out in the political arena. The *Winterhaven Stables* case simply adds a judicial dimension to a fundamentally political set of controversies – something, as will be emphasized below, that is likely to become increasingly common in Canada as a result of the entrenchment of a Charter of Rights in the constitution.

INTERREGIONAL REDISTRIBUTION   Tax revenues are drawn unequally (on a per capita basis) from the various provinces, and federal payments to provincial governments also vary on a per-capita basis. Broadly speaking, the wealthy provinces pay more in taxes and receive less in fiscal transfers. In consequence, there occurs a readily-observable redistribution of incomes among regions. Interregional redistribution also occurs through wholly federal programs such as unemployment insurance.

Probably many people would be surprised to learn how much interregional redistribution occurs in Canada. To obtain a comprehensive view, one must go back to 1981, because full data are not available for later years. Table 1.1 shows the extent of redistribution for that year. Part of it occurs through transfer payments to provincial governments, paid for out of federal tax revenues.

Peter M. Leslie

Table 1.1
Interregional Redistribution, 1981
All figures are dollars per capita

	Federal Cash payments to provincial governments[a] (1)	Federal Expenditures in the province[b] (2)	Subtotal (1) + (2)[c] (3)	Federal government[b] revenues (4)	Net Redistribution (4) − (3)[c] (5)	Personal Income Per Capita[d]
Nfld.	1292	2574	3866	1036	2831	7528
P.E.I.	1504	3379	4884	1189	3695	7829
N.S.	1080	4096	5176	1919	3257	9041
N.B.	1134	3287	4421	1891	2530	8272
Que.	663	2143	2806	2071	735	10611
Ont.	373	2511	2884	3018	− 134	12386
Man.	814	2380	3194	1919	1212	10806
Sask.	554	1921	2475	2515	− 40	11583
Alta.	353	1498	1851	3763	− 1912	12779
B.C.	407	1830	2238	2713	− 476	12538
Canada	574	2366	2940	2616	324[e]	11520

Notes:
(a) fiscal year ending 30 April 1982
(b) calendar year 1981
(c) figures may not add up exactly due to rounding
(d) includes impact of redistribution (column 5)
(e) reflects the size of the federal deficit.
Sources: Calculated from Statistics Canada: *Federal Government Finance 1981* (Cat. 68-211), *Provincial Economic Accounts 1966-1981* (Cat. 13-213), *National Income and Expenditure Accounts 1967-1981* (Cat. 13-201), *Canadian Statistical Review* (Cat. 11-003).
Acknowledgement: I am grateful to Keith Brownsey for doing the calculations.

A great deal of attention has deservedly been directed at the fiscal equalization scheme. Table 1.1 illustrates how important it is to avoid the error of thinking of interregional redistribution uniquely in terms of equalization payments or indeed federal-provincial transfers generally – unconditional, semi-conditional, or conditional. Keith Banting, in his magisterial study of *The Welfare State and Canadian Federalism*, notes that federal payments to individual persons through various income support measures also redistribute tax dollars interregionally, and he suggests that the sums involved in this sort of redistribution are probably as great as those dispensed to the provinces through the equalization program.[12] This explains some of the variation in levels of federal expenditure by province, observable in Table 1.1. Other relevant factors are: the extent of federal public works spending, the number of federal employees, and the volume of federal government procurement by province. The figures in Table 1.1 (column 2) suggest that there is a rough inverse correlation between the wealth of the province and the volume of federal spending, though if this were consistently the case one might expect rather more spending in Newfoundland and less in Ontario and Nova Scotia.

Table 1.2
Provincial Reliance on Federal Cash Transfers
1984/85 (Estimates)
All figures except percentages are in dollars per capita

	Equal-ization	EPF	CAP	all cash transfers[a]	provincial-local own-revenues[b] sources	(4) as a per cent of (5)[c]	provincial-local expenditure excluding debt charges
	(1)	(2)	(3)	(4)	(5)	(6)	(7)
Nfld.	1017	352	138	1725	2115	82	3375
P.E.I.	1021	344	177	1768	2035	87	3182
N.S.	705	345	131	1333	2441	55	3470
N.B.	748	384	194	1481	2178	68	3522
Que.[d]	465	349	232	1148	3542	32	4225
Ont.	0	322	107	497	3363	15	3466
Man.	453	346	118	1041	3081	34	3871
Sask.	0	359	143	561	3987	14	4125
Alta.	0	255	178	561	6526	8.6	5916
B.C.	0	310	202	537	3668	15	4053

Notes:
(a) The figures in column 4 are slightly greater than the sum of those in columns 1,2, and 3, which report only the major categories of federal grants.
(b) Excludes cash transfers from the federal government; includes value of tax points transferred to the provinces under EPF. Includes revenues of school boards and hospital authorities.
(c) This column indicates the percentage by which provincial-local own-source revenues are augmented by federal cash transfers.
(d) Figures in columns 2,3,4,5, and 6 are adjusted for value of tax points associated with contracting out, as follows: EPF, 8.5; CAP, 5; Youth Allowances, 3 (total of 16.5).

Other aspects of interprovincial (and hence interregional) redistribution are illustrated in Table 1.2. The Table does three things.

☐ First, it shows the relative importance of the major categories of cash transfers to provincial governments. It should be noted that the data on established programs financing (EPF) refer to slightly less than half the total fiscal transfer, which is partly in cash (the portion reported in the Table) and partly in 'tax points' – i.e., a sum representing revenues foregone by the federal government and collected by the provinces,

Peter M. Leslie

because a share of the personal income tax was handed over to them to help them pay for health care services (about two thirds of the total) and post-secondary education (the remaining third).

☐ Second, by comparing (a) the sums transferred to the provinces with (b) total revenues of provincial governments and local authorities, the Table demonstrates the extent to which the various provinces rely upon federal grants. The aggregated revenues form a better basis of comparison than provincial revenues alone, since the municipalities, school boards and hospital boards are created by the provincial governments. Taxing powers and spending responsibilities that are assumed directly by the provincial government are, in other provinces, delegated to municipalities and other local authorities. It is therefore useful for our purposes to use consolidated data on provincial-local finance. It will be observed that reliance on federal transfers varies widely. They augment provincial 'own-source revenues' (taxes, resource revenues, etc.) by an amount that varies from nine per cent to 87 per cent.

☐ Third, the table supplies information (column 7) that enables one to guess at the overall impact of intergovernmental transfers. They evidently go a long way towards enabling the poorer provinces to provide services at a standard comparable to the standards obtaining in the richer ones. Still, the transfers do not eliminate interprovincial discrepancies or even succeed in bringing up the poorest provinces to the average level. In short, there remains – with two critically important exceptions – a rough correlation between a province's wealth and its expenditure per capita. The exceptions are Quebec, which has expenditure levels second only to Alberta, and Ontario, which spends less than any other province except Prince Edward Island and Newfoundland. Even disregarding these two cases, which deviate from an otherwise intelligible ranking, the data give a more favourable impression of the impact of intergovernmental transfers than is probably warranted. 'Tax effort' varies widely (i.e., rates are higher in some provinces than in others), with the poorer provinces taxing more heavily than the richer ones. Moreover, a province where incomes are low and unemployment rates are high has to spend a lot more per capita if standards of service are to be comparable. Some hint of this is provided in the figures on federal transfers under the Canada Assistance Plan, where expenditure levels (the federal government pays half the total) simply do not correlate, positively or negatively, with wealth.

In short, the data in Table 1.2 seem to indicate that the surest way to obtain equal standards in public services across the land would be to hand over spending responsibilities (and corresponding fiscal resources) to the federal government. But of course that would prevent the adaptation of programs to regional or local needs. That is the rationale for decentralization together with the present, rather extensive, system of intergovernmental transfers. One may easily deduce that without them, or if they were significantly reduced in the future, the poorer provinces would have appallingly low standards of public services (education, health care, roads etc.). Already the extent of inter-regional redistribution that is accomplished through the equalization program is very high. Any further reliance on this policy instrument, such as would be required if EPF or the CAP were reduced or eliminated, would be extremely dangerous for those provinces that receive large sums in equalization. They are already very vulnerable to any change in the formula used to determine the overall size of equalization grants, and their allocation among the provinces.

The provinces most dependent upon equalization have ample reason for disquiet. Voices are now being raised suggesting that the system of intergovernmental transfers – and hence interregional redistribution – is too generous. For example, Tom Courchene, the Chairman of the Ontario Economic Council, argues that in today's difficult economic circumstances we must give priority to improving the competitiveness of our industry, and, in the tradeoff between equity and efficiency, tip the balance now towards efficiency.[13]

This is simply one aspect of a larger controversy over the extent and future of the welfare state in Canada. One should note its similarity with the controversial decision announced by federal Finance Minister Michael Wilson in his budget of 23 May 1985, – but withdrawn a month later – to partially de-index the old age pension. If the federal government had proceeded with its plan to withdraw indexation for the first three percentage points of inflation, the effect would have been to halve the real-dollar value of the pension every 23 years.

Perhaps the important lesson to learn from the pension de-indexing incident is that trimming back the welfare state is well-nigh impossible, politically speaking. But another possible conclusion, no doubt preferred by those dismayed by the size of the budgetary deficit, is that government will have to learn to impose cutbacks more selectively and with greater political finesse. If the 1985 budget is an indication of a more general and lasting policy, in future people will be expected to take more responsibility for their own welfare, and to rely a lot less upon the state. Income inequalities will be greater. The partial withdrawal of a public safety net will force those who work in the wrong industries or who live in the wrong regions to adapt more quickly to the vagaries of the market. Conservative doctrine, which seems to be gaining strength in Canada (notwithstanding the government's retreat on the pensions issue, and the Ontario election results), holds that people will hurt less – and it will be better for us all – if they are made to realize where there is no future for them. Too soft a welfare net inhibits economic adjustment, and is bad for its supposed beneficiaries. As the American neo-conservative George Gilder puts it, 'The poor most of all need the spur of their own poverty.'[14]

The future of the welfare state in Canada cannot be dissociated from the future of the fiscal transfers system. The provinces' ability, over the years, to

Peter M. Leslie

continue providing public services on the existing scale, or to improve them, will depend on future federal government decisions regarding its payments to the provinces. It was possible, in the quarter century that followed the second world war, to construct a welfare state in Canada only through the joint enterprise of federal and provincial governments. Without an extensive system of fiscal transfers, implying considerable interregional redistribution, the poorer provinces would have lacked the means to put existing programs in place. Similarly, if in future the federal government decides to cut back on payments to the provinces, or to hold any increases to a level below the increase in program costs, those provinces that rely heavily on federal transfers will be forced to allow their services to deteriorate. And if the federal government cuts back on its own programs – as in the pensions proposal, or in any reduction in unemployment insurance benefits – it will thereby shift costs to the provinces, because more people will be forced to rely on provincially-supplied (though cost-shared) public assistance programs.

Intergovernmental transfers and the quality of public services are linked in another way also. If in the past the poorer provinces could not have afforded to provide adequate services by relying wholly upon their own fiscal resources, some of the wealthier ones would have lacked the incentive to do so. The incentive came to a large extent from federal conditional grants. Through the 'fifties and 'sixties the federal government played a major role in inducing the provinces to expand public services. It sought, through conditional grants, to work towards implementing national standards in public services. Naturally, this objective was in tension with the principle of provincial autonomy in social affairs, and so it remains. This is our next subject.

NATIONAL STANDARDS AND PROVINCIAL AUTONOMY   In 1977 full financial responsibility for hospital insurance, medical insurance ('medicare'), and post-secondary education, all of which were financed in part through federal conditional grants, was transferred to the provincial governments under the EPF scheme. As already noted, these programs are supported through what I have described as a 'semi-conditional' fiscal transfer consisting of a mixture of tax points and cash. The federal government's supposition at the time, which turns out to have been a grave miscalculation, was that the provinces would be forced by public opinion, to continue providing the services at existing levels or better. When some provinces introduced hospital user fees or permitted supplementary billing by doctors – both actions being consistent with a 'user-pay' principle, and presumed to have some deterrent effect against abuse of public services – the then federal Health Minister Monique Bégin took the view that the health care programs were no longer truly universal. She sponsored the Canada Health Act (1983) to impose financial penalties upon provinces that acted in this way. The initiative was supported by the Leader of the Opposition, Brian Mulroney.

The federal government has also clearly been dissatisfied with the level of provincial funding of post-secondary education (PSE). Here no principles of program design have been set, by which provincial programs may be judged, but the federal government is demonstrably bearing an increasing share of the costs. Since there is no agreed way of calculating the federal contribution, especially as a share of program costs, it is difficult to be precise about this, though the trend is clear. According to A.W. Johnson, who submitted a public report on the subject to the Secretary of State in March 1985, there are now five provinces that receive more money from Ottawa (tax points plus cash) than they actually spend on PSE (see Table 1.3). Johnson has proposed that grants to some of the provinces be cut back,[15] essentially because he considers that they have not lived up to their half of an implicit bargain. The provinces, for their part, insist that no such bargain ever existed; they are simply fulfilling their responsibilities to the provincial taxpayers: to manage public funds carefully.

Table 1.3
EPF/PSE Fiscal Transfers as a Percentage of Provincial Operating Grants to Universities and Colleges

| | EPF/PSE Transfers as a % of Provincial Operating Grants | | Increase in EPF/PSE Fiscal Transfer 'Share' or Reduction in 'Purely Provincial Share' |
	1977-78	1984-85	
Canada	68.9%	79.6%	10.7%
Newfoundland	83.3%	106.9%	23.6%
Prince Edward Island	101.5%	106.9%	5.3%
Nova Scotia	87.5%	91.6%	4.1%
New Brunswick	98.1%	101.8%	3.7%
Quebec	56.1%	59.6%	3.5%
Ontario	73.7%	88.7%	15.0%
Manitoba	80.3%	102.9%	22.5%
Saskatchewan	81.6%	90.3%	8.7%
Alberta	63.9%	73.1%	9.2%
British Columbia	78.9%	104.3%	25.4%

Sources: Reproduced from A.W. Johnson, *Giving Greater Point and Purpose to the Federal Financing of Post-Secondary Education and Research in Canada,* a Report prepared for the Secretary of State of Canada, 15 February 1985, 12.

Whether or not the federal government accepts the recommendations of the Johnson Report, it will have to decide whether its role will continue to be what it has been in the recent past: to work towards the development and implementation of national standards in public services. If this is its choice, and if the spending power survives legal challenge, it can choose among several approaches or instruments.

Peter M. Leslie

- The federal government can subsidize designated provincial services through a shared-cost program. The subsidy induces provinces to spend more money in the area, and enables Ottawa to set implicit program norms. A province that operates below the norm foregoes part of the subsidy it might otherwise receive. A province may, of course, do better than the norm: it may provide unsubsidized services.
- The federal government can transfer monies to the provinces, as under EPF, such that the size of the transfer does not depend upon the volume of provincial spending. On the other hand, conditions may be set: for example, under the EPF Act and the Canada Health Act, a province's eligibility for the transfer may be made to depend on program design. A further possible step, which has not been taken in Canada, might be to impose penalties (reduced transfers) on a province for substandard performance. In other words, the federal government might formulate, and through a system of penalties attempt to impose, national program standards.
- The federal government can legislate national standards by setting up a basic program of its own with the possibility that some or all provinces might establish their own programs as supplements. Briefly: provinces could top up a basic federal grant by operating their own programs in parallel with the federal one. (This is a feature of agricultural price support programs.)
- Finally, there is equalization. The three methods already discussed involve varying degrees of respect for provincial autonomy. Compared with these three, equalization is least constraining on the provinces, but it is also least effective in ensuring minimum levels of service across the country. The purpose of equalization is to make it possible for provinces to provide public services to a national average standard, without making any such standard mandatory.

Through various combinations of these devices the federal government may, if the courts do not restrict the scope of the spending power, continue to work towards the definition and implementation of national standards in public services. But to do so is costly. If it chooses to spend fewer tax dollars in support of provincially-supplied public services, the consequences are clear: a deterioration in overall standards of service, and increased discrepancies among the provinces in the quality of services provided. Indeed, it is possible that the federal government may lead the way, in combination with the provincial governments, towards retrenchment – in effect, reversing the tendency of its earlier policies.

In an era of slow economic growth and continuously rising life-expectancy, such as are currently being experienced, the tension between maintaining public services and regaining control over public sector finances cannot but continue, and may well increase. As the population ages, costs of health care rise sharply, and dependency ratios (those without paying jobs relative to those who have them) also increase. In other words, to maintain current standards of public services the share of GNP devoted to paying for them will probably have to increase. To avoid a fiscal crisis governments will have to raise additional revenues, which by recent experience seems very difficult to do, especially for countries with right-of-centre governments.[16] The spectre of fiscal crisis looms in every country with even a rudimentary welfare state.

In a federal country, especially one where (as in Canada) the provinces/states are responsible for a high proportion of public spending, the fiscal situation is complicated by the sharing of responsibility for funding public services. It is impossible to dissociate the system of intergovernmental transfers from the issues of program design and national standards.

Thus, beyond the technical intricacies of formulas for revenue sharing and the financing of joint programs, lie very fundamental questions of community, citizenship, and social solidarity. What is the extent of responsibility that members of a community have towards each other, and what is to be the role of government in providing the mutual support that the concept of 'community' implies? And, crucially, what are the boundaries of community? In our own case, how do the Canada-wide and the provincial communities interlace, and how do they relate to each other? How will they evolve in relation to each other over the next few years, or decades? In thinking about this, two factors especially stand out: the significance of the Canadian Charter of Rights and Freedoms, contained in the Constitution Act of 1982; and the place of Quebec in the wider Canadian community, which some see as pluralist, others as bilingual and multicultural, and others again as dualist.

Equality Rights

On 17 April 1985, the 'equality rights' clause of the Canadian Charter of Rights and Freedoms came into force. The main part of it reads:

15. (1) Every individual is equal before and under the law and has the right to the equal protection and equal benefit of the law without discrimination and, in particular, without discrimination based on race, national or ethnic origin, colour, religion, sex, age or mental or physical disability.

There are three possible escapes from the clause. One is the section immediately following, which permits affirmative action laws and programs. A second is the general exemption clause (Section 1 of the Charter) allowing infringement of its principles within 'such reasonable limits prescribed by law as can be demonstrably justified in a free and democratic society.' The third is the 'override' or *non obstante* clause (Section 33) allowing Parliament or a provincial legislature to declare that a given law 'shall operate notwithstanding a provision included in Section 2 or Sections 7 to 15 of this Charter.' (Section 2 covers 'fundamental freedoms'; and Sections 7 to 14, 'legal rights'; no legislative override is permitted for language rights, though of course here the general exemption in Section 1 continues to apply.)

The equality rights clause is of very sweeping significance, for it imposes upon the courts – as do also some other sections of the Charter, notably those pertaining to language rights – a duty to supervise the action of Parliament and the provincial legislatures with a view to determining the *adequacy* and *fairness* of the laws and of policies based on them, according to the principle of *equal benefit*. Previously the courts had authority to declare that Parliament or a legislature had overstepped the bounds of its authority, notably in the division-of-powers sections of the Constitution Act of 1867. But the courts could not instruct a legislature to use its powers in particular ways; now they are enjoined to do so, upon action by any person claiming that others receive greater benefit of the law than (s)he. Possibly reinforcing any such claim is the 'equalization and regional disparities' clause (Section 36), which – besides formulating a goal for equalization payments – declares that 'Parliament and the legislatures, together with the government of Canada and the provincial governments, are committed to ... (c) providing essential public services of reasonable quality to all Canadians.'

It is not known at this time how vigorously the courts will exercise the power that is potentially theirs under the equality rights clause. One cannot yet tell whether the courts will become, as in the United States, another avenue for the injection of political demands into the system, a potent instrument of policy innovation. The possibility is there. It may take a decade or a generation for the possibility to become a reality – or it may not happen at all.

If the courts do assume a more forthright policy-supervisory role, the mutually reinforcing character of the equalization clause and the equality rights clause may turn out to be significant. Clearly, the courts would not use Section 15 to tell one provincial government to follow the lead of another, bringing about the uniformity of provincial laws. On the other hand, they might justifiably look at policy areas such as health care, post-secondary education, and social assistance and, in view of the role of the federal government in funding services in these areas, begin to support the idea of national standards. After all, federal laws are involved; and a taxpayer might justifiably claim that his federal tax dollars are being unfairly expended if his province does not provide the services in question to the same standard as in a neighbouring province.

It is also quite conceivable, though, that the primary significance of the equality clause – indeed of the Charter as a whole – will not lie in the shift in power from the legislative to the judicial branch of government. After all, the override clause is there for Parliament and the legislatures to use. What may matter most of all is the impact that the Charter has on the way Canadians think about themselves and about Canada as a political community. If people come to take for granted that, *as* Canadians, they have certain rights in common or can justifiably make claims on each other through the agency of government, it will become increasingly difficult for a government to invoke the override clause. In other words the Charter may have its greatest effect on the structure and working of the political system, *through its impact on public opinion*. The more it strengthens the concept of Canadian citizenship, the more it may strengthen the power of the central government vis-à-vis that of the provinces. We are speaking here (as, again, J.A. Corry spoke 30 years ago) of a 'nationalizing of sentiment' and its effect in stimulating the federal government to action while restraining the provinces from demanding full respect for their autonomy.

The big exception, as in much else, may be Quebec. The National Assembly has invoked the override clause, not to make specific laws or clauses of laws exempt from the effects of the equality provisions of the Charter, but to create a blanket exemption for all Quebec laws. This action, if not subsequently reversed, will reinforce the idea of dualism. Already the tendency is strong among Francophone Quebecers to regard the Quebec community as primary and the Quebec government as the national government for that community, whereas elsewhere 'the nation' means Canada.

'Federalism and the French Canadians' After Trudeau – And Lévesque

Among the factors influencing the future evolution of the Canadian federal system, none is more important or more unpredictable than the situation of Francophone Canadians and of Quebec. Two subsequent chapters deal with particular aspects of these issues: Bruce Pollard on minority language rights (Chapter 8), and Gérard Boismenu on the constitutional status of Quebec and the May 1985 proposals of the Lévesque government (Chapter 2). Our task in this section is to distinguish alternative conceptions of the Canadian political community, or *polity*, thus establishing a framework within which to consider the significance of the events described and analyzed by Boismenu and by Pollard. Specifically, it is useful to recognize that for some the Canadian polity is *bicommunal* or *dualist*, while for others it is *bilingual and multicultural*, and for others yet again, simply *pluralist*. These concepts are both empirical and normative: they both describe the Canadian political community, and identify goals for how it should develop in the future.

CANADA AS A BICOMMUNAL POLITY   In certain societies the structure of governmental institutions, the allocation of public offices, and the exercise of public power are primarily shaped by the relationship among two or more ethnic or territorial communities. In such cases the polity is structured to reflect and to accommodate differences among 'subcultures' or among territorially-focussed national groups. Where societies are thus divided into distinct groups politics becomes understood by all to be an activity primarily concerned with perpetuating, regulating, or modifying the inter-relationship among the groups. A major task of political leadership, perhaps its most important task, is to maintain harmony among them.

When political debate highlights the relationship between two ethnic or territorial communities, but not more than two, the polity is bicommunal. Not that the society contains two and only two groups defined by territory or ethnicity (which is seldom if ever the case). Rather, the essence of bicommunalism is that historical and contemporary conditions in some way give particular visibility to the relations between two such groups while downplaying the political significance of other entities. Each of two major groups acquires the character of a community whose members are aware of the bonds among themselves and are conscious, too, of their distinctiveness relative to other communities, or peoples. The feeling of belonging to a particular community need not, of course, imply the exclusion of other groups or intolerance towards them, but it does foster a sense of solidarity based on shared cultural attributes.

Some of our historians, sociologists, and political scientists – not to mention our politicians, including contemporary ones – have viewed Canada (though not in so many words) as a bicommunal polity. The essence of Canadian politics has seemed to them to lie in attempts to reach workable compromises that satisfy the essential interests of, respectively, English-Canadians and French-Canadians. From this perspective the most important feature of the arrangements put into place in 1867 was the creation of a constitutional regime where the French-Catholic population would be in a majority in at least one province (Quebec). Under the Canadian form of federalism, the provinces –and most importantly Quebec – would have sufficient autonomy to establish and maintain a distinctive set of institutions. These would be consonant with the value-system of its own population. Provincial autonomy was both written into the British North America Act, and in succeeding years was supported by a cohesive 'Quebec bloc' within the governing party and cabinet. Even so, the system broke down at least three times: with the hanging of Louis Riel, and with the conscription crises in both world wars.

The process of accommodation between English-Canadian and French-Canadian elites is generally acknowledged to have established a partnership which was visibly unequal in two important respects: first, Anglophones enjoyed rights in Quebec that Francophones either never had, or quickly lost, elsewhere in the country; and second, even within Quebec, Anglophones enjoyed economic dominance. Quebec was thus an instance, perhaps not uncommon in bicommunal polities, where a disfavoured majority obtains certain political rights in exchange, so to speak, for acquiescing in their condition of economic inferiority.

From the mid 'fifties onwards, however, the defence of provincial autonomy increasingly appeared to Francophone Quebecers to be an inadequate basis for cultural protection. In addition to resenting their economic inferiority, they became aware of the assimilationist pressures stemming from this condition. Thus, towards the end of Premier Duplessis' rule (he died in September 1959), French Canadian nationalism, with its emphasis on withdrawal and the defence of provincial autonomy, was transformed into a more positive, Quebec-centred 'nationalism of growth' which demanded the *extension* of Quebec's policy responsibilities and fiscal resources, and constitutional powers. The modernization of Quebec society, which Anglophones greeted as heralding a new era of cooperation between Quebec and the rest of the country, turned out to produce new tensions and to demand new institutional adjustments. An earlier pattern of elite accommodation was revealed to be inadequate to satisfy the heightened aspirations of those who began, during the 1960s, to call themselves *Québécois*. These aspirations were captured in the 1962 Liberal election slogan, 'Maîtres chez nous': 'Masters in our own house'.

The changes brought about by the shift from 'French-Canadian' to 'Quebec' nationalism may be summarized in the following way: the bicommunalism of majority and minority, Anglophone and Francophone, was transformed into a bicommunalism of two majorities, French-speaking Quebec and English-speaking Canada. The Quiet Revolution of the 1960s, and the political, constitutional, and financial demands formulated by successive Quebec governments since that time, expressed a new form of bicommunalism. It placed rather more emphasis on territory in the definition of the two communities. The English language and Anglo-American culture would predominate outside Quebec; within it, the French language would become the primary language of work and business as well as of all other social activities. Ottawa and Quebec City would be, respectively, the political centres of the two majorities. A distinctive Quebec culture would grow and flourish. Some of the new nationalists made an attempt to gain for this project the support of immigrant groups and the traditionally dominant Anglophone minority, but their efforts were meagrely rewarded.

It was generally presumed by the new nationalists that Quebec needed, in order to realize its cultural goals, wider powers and greater fiscal resources than the other provinces had any reason or desire to claim. Hence the demands that arose, beginning in the mid 'sixties for 'special status', and later for 'sovereignty-association'. Both projects envisioned redefining Quebec's relationship with the rest of Canada as a new form of bicommunalism, a bicommunalism of two majorities. The concept implies that the two communities would enjoy *coordinate economic, social, and political status*. Its logical extension, of course, was full political independence, untrammelled by economic association. But few Quebecers proposed to go that far, fearing the cost.

The failure of the sovereignty-association project in the referendum of May 1980, and the subsequent passage of the new Constitution Act (1982) marked a severe set-back for the idea of Canada as a bicommunal polity on the two-majorities model. Quebec emerged much weaker, politically and constitutionally, than it had been before. However, before pursuing this theme any further, it is important to consider views of Canada as either pluralistic (in the particular sense to be described) or as bilingual-and-multicultural.

CANADA AS A PLURALISTIC POLITY   The bicommunalist view of Canada does not go unchallenged. For many Canadians, probably a sizeable majority, linguistic and cultural differences have no greater political significance than other forms of political cleavage. They regard the Canadian polity as *pluralistic* – that is, in their view no single personal quality, whether region of residence, ethnicity, income-level, or any other, has political significance overshadowing the rest. To the extent that they regard differences of language and culture as important, it is not dualism but multiplicity of cultures that they see. But such diversity does not stand in the way of political unity. Theirs is 'one Canada', pluralistic and multicultural.

The pluralist-multicultural view of Canada downplays the notion that language symbolizes and supports overall culture, viewed as a distinctive set of attitudes, beliefs, and values, and a distinctive way of conceiving the relationship between the individual and the collectivity. As one Anglophone politician recently said of Francophone Quebecers (trying to be sympathetic), 'They want to do the same things as we do, but they want to do them in French.' The statement caught the spirit of what John Porter wrote in *The Vertical Mosaic* in 1965:

> ... as Quebec becomes more industrialized it will become culturally more like other industrialized societies. At that time the similarities in social characteristics which its urbanized population will share with other provinces may be far more important in terms of future social development than whatever differences remain.[17]

Such attitudes are probably typical among members of a cultural majority, suggesting incomprehension of minority group demands. Incomprehension easily shades off into intolerance. Moreover, a sizeable proportion of those belonging to minority groups may come to share the materialism that underlies the attitudes of the majority. This is what promotes assimilation. The likelihood of cultural haemorrhage, so to speak, causes leaders of the minority group(s) to seek to strengthen the culture by supporting the institutions through which it is expressed. This requires political instruments. Thus constitutional revision has been of continuing and especial importance to Quebec. Its failure to make any progress at all in this respect (indeed, the weakening of its earlier claim to special recognition) explains why Quebec has been unable to accede to the constitutional accord that was struck in November 1981.

CANADA AS A BILINGUAL AND MULTICULTURAL POLITY   The November 1981 accord implicitly rejected the view of Canada as a bicommunal polity (especially the two-majorities variant), but did not embrace the pluralist view either. It was largely inspired by Mr. Trudeau's opinion that, 'In terms of *realpolitik*, French and English are equal in Canada because each of these linguistic groups has the power to break the country.'[18] Considerations of *realpolitik* were mixed together with an individualist social philosophy to support the principle of equal partnership of the two major language groups in Canada, or the 'two founding races' (as was said in the terms of reference of the Royal Commission on Bilingualism and Biculturalism). Mr. Trudeau saw the federal government as the preferred instrument for achieving the economic and political equality of Anglophones and Franco-phones; the Quebec government, whose pretensions to special status he rejected out of hand, was treated by him as a rival for the political affections and loyalties of Francophone Canadians.

Trudeau, acting consistently with the views of nationalism and nationality expounded by the nineteenth century British historian Lord Acton, did all he could to weaken the principle 'one people, one state'. To him the principle, which he called the 'theory of nationality' implied that the state exists to support the interests of one ethnic or national grouping at the expense of others; the nation-state promotes intolerance and is itself, ultimately, totalitarian (in the sense that its activities may be extended into all aspects of social life).

To counteract the force of ethnic nationalism in Quebec, Trudeau sought to expand opportunities for Francophone Quebecers to participate fully in all aspects of social life in Canada – not just in Quebec. He reinforced the earlier policy of official bilingualism, defining and protecting the rights of official-language minorities; his goal was to make those language rights effective, and to extend them geographically, establishing full equality between Anglophones and Francophones in politics and business. Thus the French and English language required a constitutionally-entrenched status, which they partially obtained in the Charter of Rights. (As is demonstrated by Pollard below, much remains to make those rights fully effective, as to a large extent it is the provinces that have jurisdiction and the relevant policy responsibilities.)

Trudeau's emphasis on individual rather than collective rights is consistent with a policy of multiculturalism, which is essentially a policy of supporting traditional artistic attainments and forms of recreation against assimilationist pressures. Support for traditional languages is part of this policy, but no one suggests that – in this context – such languages will have much use outside the home or the ethnic communities concerned, particularly when they are at play. This is very different from supporting a language as one (or *the* one) in which a society does its business. The latter has been the objective of Quebec's language legislation, as has the policy of official bilingualism at the federal level.

AFTER TRUDEAU AND LEVESQUE   Where Trudeau sought the full integration of Francophones into Canadian society, under conditions that would enable them to withstand assimilationist pressures, the Parti Québécois has sought national self-determination for the Quebec people, initially as a sovereign state associated for economic purposes with the nine remaining provinces, and more recently (officially, since January 1985) within the federation. The route to economic equality and cultural *épanouissement* has been through the affirmation of Quebec's character as a distinct society. The difference between

Peter M. Leslie

their objectives is captured by the contrast between a policy aiming to strengthen bicommunalism (on the two-majorities model), and a policy of bilingualism and, though only incidentally, multiculturalism. The two projects are, conceptually speaking, like oil and water.

From 1976 to 1984 (excepting the Clark interregnum 1979-80) political action by both governments sought to polarize the Quebec electorate on the bicommunalism issue. Whereas Quebec policy sought to restructure the Canadian state in a way that would both respond to and reinforce the ethnic/cultural cleavage, federal policy aimed for institutional and constitutional reform of a character that would reduce its salience, and would weaken bicommunalism.

Now the two generals have retired from the battlefield. On the federal side, the new government has an overall perspective not noticeably different from Mr. Trudeau's – though with one vital difference. Mr. Mulroney does not overtly treat the provincial governments as opponents and rivals; this approach applies as much to Quebec as to any other province. He pretends that differences do not exist, or can easily be accommodated.

Over the next year it will probably become a lot clearer whether the desired accommodation can be achieved. The basis for achieving it seems to lie in extending and protecting the rights of official-language minorities, especially in the four provinces where sizeable minorities exist, and in achieving such changes to the Constitution Act of 1982 that Quebec can be induced to accept its legitimacy. Neither will be easy, because behind the immediate issues lie quite different images of what Canada is, and should be.

Conclusion

What overall assessment can one make of the present-day state of the Canadian federation? The picture that emerges from our survey of six factors affecting the development of the federal system and the character of the country itself is not bleak, but nor is it serene.

On the economic side, the search continues for a development strategy that is capable of obtaining the support of all regions. This is a problem that has been close to the centre of political controversy in Canada since Confederation. Our national economic policies have been, by and large, regionally divisive. A solution may lie, as many appear to believe, in negotiating a closer economic association with the United States, that is, a Canadian-American Free Trade Agreement or CAFTA. However, the difficulties confronting this project are substantial. Some of them have to do with the political attitudes that find expression in the Congress, where protectionist forces are vocal and perhaps dominant; others derive from the nervousness and outright opposition of important political forces in Canada. The opposition to a CAFTA is partly regional, being centred in Ontario; but the issue is also one that tends to divide management and labour, and ranges various industries or sectors against each other. Trade liberalization is one aspect of a more general policy of support for a market-directed economy, and thus resonates with neo-conservatism. The labour movement is more and more clearly against the CAFTA initiative. Thus the questions of economic development strategy, trade relations, and the role of government in the economy are all closely linked to each other. The most tangible of them is the trade issue, which becomes a touchstone of attitudes on the other two.

Since issues that are only partly regional in nature tend to find expression in Canada through the working of the federal system, federalism affects the course of action eventually taken on major economic issues. On the other hand, decisions on economic policy stand to alter, over the longer term, the structure of the federation. A momentous decision is clearly at hand. If the federal government decides to press for a bilateral trade deal, it will necessarily do so against strong opposition. Conversely, if it decides against this course of action, it will disappoint a large body of opinion, including the very core of its own political constituency. Either way, the provincial governments will seek to involve themselves in the decision; some will be critics, others will voice their support. Even if the Mulroney government decides not to press for anything more substantial than a goodwill agreement, aiming vaguely for 'trade enhancement', provincial governments will necessarily be involved in Canada's future trade policy. They will have to be involved because future rounds of discussions (bilateral and/or multilateral) will focus on non-tariff barriers, many of which are put in place by the provincial governments.

Economic issues tie in closely with issues of culture (value-systems), sovereignty, and political community. Can a country whose economy is closely integrated with that of a large and powerful neighbour continue to develop in its own way, in accordance with its own preferences? One of the fears expressed about achieving closer integration with the United States, particularly through an agreement that restricts the capacity of governments (both federal and provincial) to implement a preferred economic development strategy, is that it will diminish Canada's political independence. Political independence is what enables a country to give expression, through distinctive policies, to a distinctive culture.

Of course, concern with cultural distinctiveness or diversity arises not only in relation to the Canadian political community, given its close economic and political (defence-related) ties with the United States. The same concern lies at the root of debates over (de)centralization within the federal system itself. This issue is raised in several different ways, all of which will be the focus of attention over the next few years. This essay has pointed to three aspects of the issue: the achieving of national standards in public services (and related questions of intergovernmental transfer payments), the equality rights provisions of the Charter of Rights and Freedoms, and the situation of Quebec and of Francophone Canadians. In all three respects Canadians continue to ask themselves about the character of community, the claims of Canada and

Peter M. Leslie

of the provinces upon their political loyalties, and the obligations and entitlements bound up in the idea of citizenship. That these questions continue to underpin political debate is testimony to the still-unsettled state of the federation.

Notes

1. Pierre Elliott Trudeau, *Federalism and the French Canadians* (Toronto: Macmillan, 1968), xix. The citation is taken from the Foreword, which is dated August 1967.
2. The term is used especially by Glen Williams. See his *Not for Export: Toward a Political Economy of Canada's Arrested Industrialization* (Toronto: McClelland and Stewart, 1983).
3. *Major Canadian Projects, Major Canadian Opportunities, A Report by the Major Projects Task Force on Major Capital Projects in Canada to the Year 2000,* Ottawa, 1981.
4. *Economic Development for Canada in the 1980s,* Government of Canada, November 1981.
5. The phrase was used by Richard Cooper at the Ontario Economic Conference entitled 'Canadian Trade at a Crossroads: Options for New International Agreements', Toronto, 16 April 1985.
6. '... it is hard to see how – short of out-and-out political union – Canada can hope to achieve anything like complete success in getting behind the entire US administrative wall.' See their 'Free Trade Between the United States and Canada: Fifteen Years Later', in *Canadian Public Policy,* Vol. 8 supplement (October 1982), p. 415.
7. *The Globe and Mail,* 6 April 1985, p. 2.
8. John H. Goldthorpe, 'Problems of Political Economy after the end of the Post-war Period'. Paper prepared for the Committee of Western Europe of the American Council of Learned Societies, mimeo at Nuffield College, Oxford, August 1982, pp. 5-6.
9. J.A. Corry, 'Constitutional Trends and Federalism', in J. Peter Meekison (ed.), *Canadian Federalism: Myth or Reality* (Toronto: Methuen, 1968 [1958]), p. 57.
10. Canada Department of Finance, Budget Papers, 23 May 1985, p. 72.
11. 'Agreed Statement of Facts, filed with the Court of Queen's Bench of Alberta, Judicial District of Calgary' [1985], p. 4.
12. Keith Banting, *The Welfare State and Canadian Federalism* (Kingston and Montreal: McGill-Queen's University Press, 1982), p. 176.
13. Thomas J. Courchene, 'The Fiscal Arrangements: Focus on 1987', in Thomas J. Courchene, David W. Conklin, and Gail C.A. Cook (eds.), *Ottawa and the Provinces: The Distribution of Money and Power,* Vol. 1 (Toronto: Ontario Economic Council, 1985), p. 19.
14. Quoted by Andrew Hacker, 'Welfare: The Future of an Illusion', in *New York Review of Books,* 32:3 (28 February 1985), p. 37.
15. A.W. Johnson, *Giving Greater Point and Purpose to the Federal Financing of Post-Secondary Education and Research in Canada,* February 1985, pp. 29-31.
16. This suggestion was made by David A. Wolfe at the 1985 annual meeting of the Canadian Political Science Association (Montreal). See also his forthcoming study for the Royal Commission on the Economic Union and Development Prospects for Canada ('The Macdonald Commission'), on 'the politics of deficits'.

17. John Porter, *The Vertical Mosaic, an Analysis of Social Class and Power in Canada* (Toronto: University of Toronto Press, 1965), pp. 382-3.
18. Pierre Elliott Trudeau, *Federalism and the French Canadians* (Toronto: Macmillan, 1968), p. 31.

II
Focus
on the
Provinces

2 Backing Down or Compromising the Future: Quebec's Constitutional Proposals*

Gérard Boismenu

Introduction

In this brief evaluation, I will focus on the Quebec government's assertion, as set out in its Draft Agreement on the Constitution,[1] that 'Quebec's proposals are designed to generate a new impetus for profound change in the Constitution.'

First of all, I will try to describe the related proposals by the Quebec government in relation to the Canada Bill and Quebec's official statement opposing it. [*Editor's note: 'Canada Bill' is a term frequently used in Quebec to refer to the Constitution Act of 1982, or to the Resolution of the Canadian Parliament in December 1981, which contains the text of the Constitution Act. Neither the Government of Quebec nor the official opposition has ever acknowledged the legitimacy of the Constitution Act.*] The phrase 'to sign the Canada Bill' refers to Quebec's acknowledging at some future time, the legitimacy of a revised Constitution Act. Then I will briefly summarize the structure of the draft agreement. Of course, any change to the constitutional framework must be considered in the context of the entire political picture. This leads one to ask what significance Quebec's proposal will have for other governments in Canada, and what pertinence, or even political usefulness, it may have in the sparring between the government and the official opposition.

Lastly, I will consider whether reaching an agreement would mean that

*The Institute of Intergovernmental Relations is grateful to the Federal-Provincial Relations Office, Government of Canada, for assistance in translating the text from the French. The final version of the translation is the responsibility of the Institute of Intergovernmental Relations.

English Canada was backing down – or that Quebec was giving in on basic principles. On the whole, the least that can be hoped for is a guarantee that Quebec's future position will not be compromised.

A 'Fine Risk' and a Crumbling Government

For the moment, the constitutional proposal by the Government of Quebec marks the latest phase in the development of the Parti Québécois' policy on sovereignty, which has been the PQ's main objective since its creation.

In response to the staggering blow of the Canada Bill, the Parti Québécois, as a partisan organization, announced its commitment to hold the next provincial election on the issue of independence.[2] In such a 'referendum election', a vote for the Parti Québécois would be a vote for independence. This position, which immediately lined up the PQ troops against Trudeau's federalist vision of Canada, did little to hide internal conflict over the conclusions to be drawn from the government's defeat in the May 1980 referendum. The provincial election to be held in 1985, or 1986 at the latest, the Mulroney government's election to power in September 1984, and the lack of support for sovereignty in the opinion polls were among the factors which fanned into flame an opposition which had been smouldering for a long time within the party.

In his speech opening the 1984 fall session of the National Assembly, Premier René Lévesque announced an abrupt reversal of party policy. Rather than emphasize the structural conflicts within the federal system, he focused on the mood of federal-provincial relations and the attitudes of the individuals involved. It was an analysis of the key players of federalism. Alluding to the new Conservative federal government, Lévesque stated that the new era that was beginning resulted from the atmosphere he anticipated: 'All this,' he said, 'gives us hope that we can finally find government leaders in Ottawa who will discuss Quebec's demands seriously and work with us for the greater good of Quebecers.'[3] With this statement, René Lévesque invited his party to take a chance on the 'fine risk' of federalism. This support would best be expressed by accepting the Canada Bill provided certain conditions could be met. This position was confirmed in a serious, personal statement by Lévesque to the Parti Québécois executive on 20 November 1984.

Of course, in affirming that sovereignty was not an issue in the election or even in the foreseeable future, and that in the meantime, a major task would be to firm up Quebec's constitutional status, the PQ leader was far from receiving unanimous support. The 'orthodox' members opposed the henceforth dominant position of the party executive, labelled 'revisionist'. This opposition consisted of several key government figures (Jacques Parizeau, Camille Laurin and Gilbert Paquette, to name a few) as well as a significant number of party members and organizers. Moreover, a special party convention held 19 January 1985[4] drove a solid wedge between the two sides and caused a government crisis: five ministers resigned and left the National Assembly or sat with the opposition, while two backbench members crossed the floor and one other resigned.

These defections, coupled with Liberal victories in the four resulting by-elections (June 1985), greatly reduced the government majority and strengthened the official opposition to the point where it could threaten the PQ majority in the National Assembly. After the by-elections the National Assembly was composed of 61 PQ members, 53 Liberals and seven independents who had left the Parti Québécois ranks. Furthermore, another by-election will have to be held by the fall of 1985, owing to the resignation of J.-F. Léonard.

For the first time in nine years, the PQ government is threatened by a motion of non-confidence. Its situation is made more precarious by the fact that the former PQ members would not hesitate to bring down the government, as they proved on 18 June 1985, when they supported a Liberal non-confidence motion.

All actions by this wing of former Parti Québécois MNAs are guided by their desire to have their position on sovereignty triumph within the party. Although they no longer sit with the government, they remain party members. With their supporters, they have formed a political movement called the Rassemblement démocratique pour l'indépendance (RDI). This 'internal caucus' will likely serve as a rallying point for any overt or covert attempt to steer the course of the Parti Québécois. The party is now in the midst of a leadership campaign in which the party's position on the constitutional question is generating heated controversy.

Divisions within the party and poor performance in the opinion polls brought the question of René Lévesque's leadership to a head in the spring of 1985. On 21 June, faced with a crushing defeat in an election which could not (by law) be delayed beyond 20 April 1986, Lévesque announced his decision to step down. However, a pitched leadership battle does not augur well for the party. The new leader might be able to bring about a swing in voter support. However, the fate of the government would probably depend on the former PQ members who now sit with the opposition. They probably would not allow the new leader to continue in office long enough to shape an image of continuity accompanied by change.

In opposition is Robert Bourassa, newly elected as an MNA, who controls the Quebec Liberal Party with a firm hand. He is being somewhat patient, convinced that he will make a massive sweep in the next election. Although defeated in 1976, Bourassa intends to pluck power back from the PQ like a ripe plum in the coming election. His task is to draw together the disparate factions of the opposition; to do this, he must avoid making any major errors, gradually develop political credibility, compromise himself as little as possible on major issues, and build up his image with an 'exotic' second James Bay hydro-electric power project. The final deadline is 20 April 1986. Time marches on.

But in order to judge the significance, scope and pertinence of the PQ government's constitutional proposal, more than a brief background analysis is required. Major changes to the constitution are important moments in a country's history, affecting the basic power structure; the changes will be confirmed by the realignment of the political system and the exercise of power. Therefore, we must assess the meaning and scope of the PQ proposals, taking into consideration both the 1982 constitutional reform, which it is intended to address, and the current political relationship between Quebec and the federal government.

1982: A New Deal for the Use of Provincial Powers

The 1982 Constitution Act established a new framework for the exercise of provincial powers. This framework was not created through a massive transfer of responsibilities, but rather through constraints on the exercise of acknowledged provincial powers.[5] For the sake of brevity, we can say that the main constraints are contained in the Charter of Rights and Freedoms, especially its clauses on language policy and on the economic union.

To begin with, the Charter of Rights and Freedoms entrenched two complementary principles: the federal government is recognized as having exclusive responsibility for the collective interests of the Canadian people; and constitutional revision must be based on the sovereignty of the individual. The basic unit in the Canadian Charter is the citizen. Thus, despite the fact that Quebec nationalism was at the root of the principal constitutional debates, the Charter makes no reference to this distinct society and its collective rights. By contrast, the 'aboriginal peoples of Canada' are mentioned (sections 25 and 35), and the promotion of Canadian multiculturalism is given as a criterion for interpreting the Charter. It also deserves mention that the federal government finally agreed to allow legislative derogations from the fundamental human rights contained in the Charter; however, two areas involving the exercise of provincial powers were excluded from the override clause: language rights and mobility rights.

The sections concerning language rights, particularly language of instruction, do not allow a provincial government to determine its own language policy exclusively and independently. Exercise of this power may properly be considered to be a political condition essential to the continued existence of Quebec as a national community. The immediate effects of the principles set out in the Canadian Charter were to impose radical changes on the Quebec Charter of the French Language and to reduce provincial control over language policy to the mere formulation of means to apply these principles.

Lastly, the section on mobility rights (the right to move residence and gain a livelihood) which is a primary factor in maintaining the Canadian economic union, directly interferes with provincial powers because it affects policies, legislation, institutions, programs and so on which restrict the circulation of goods, services, persons, capital and businesses. However, regionally restric-

Gérard Boismenu

tive measures are permitted if there is a higher-than-average unemployment rate in the area and if the measures are aimed at helping disadvantaged individuals. Notice that individuals needing help are given priority, and not measures to improve the socio-economic conditions that lead to regional underdevelopment.

All in all, the 1982 Constitution Act significantly modifies the framework of provincial power by placing constraints on initiatives to tackle regional and national issues. Most of the key points are familiar ones:

□ government actions are subject to judicial review;
□ the rights of the individual take precedence, and the collective rights of the Quebec people are not recognized;
□ the federal government is given exclusive responsibility for the collective interests of Canadians;
□ provincial constitutional powers are subordinate to the inviolable principle of Canadian economic union;
□ in matters of language provinces must conform to the principles imposed.

All of these points gravely impair the status of the Quebec government. The backdrop to this situation is Quebec's loss of the power, which it thought it possessed and indeed had exercised in the past, to veto constitutional amendments.

Two Incompatible Constitutional 'Logics'

In December 1981 the Government of Quebec proposed a constitutional option that was irreconcilable with the underlying principles of the Canada Bill. In a motion passed by the National Assembly,[6] the government put forth a counterproposal to eliminate constitutional restraints on the exercise of provincial powers, which limit effective action by the provincial government.

In response to the theory that Canada absorbs and integrates its minorities, the Quebec government argued that there were two founding peoples and that Quebec must be recognized as a distinct society within the federal system. Consequently, the collective rights of the Quebec people must be respected, and the Quebec government is the primary, if not exclusive, legitimate guarantor of these rights.

Whereas the central government regards itself as representing the general interests of Canadians and as guaranteeing the integrity of the economic union, the Quebec government proposes instead that it should have primary responsibility for the province's socio-economic development, and that it should be the political expression of the Quebec community. This proposal combats the two elements in the Charter which infringe upon (Quebec) provincial power. In a version of the Canadian Charter of Rights and Freedoms that would be acceptable to Quebec, there would be no section 6 concerning Canadian economic union. In this way, the practices related to provincial regional policies could not be restricted in the name of free circulation of factors of production in an economic area that is unfettered by internal barriers. On language issues, there is no question of compromise.

For the federal government, constitutional reform began with an emphasis on 'individual sovereignty', which in effect strengthens federal authority. Quebec cannot accept any constitutional reform that does not confirm its exclusive responsibility in areas under its jurisdiction. At issue is the idea that only the Quebec government can claim to represent the collective rights and interests of the Quebec people. Thus, in the amending formula, for example, the only majority that would count would be a majority in the Quebec National Assembly.

These two 'logics' leave little middle ground: either the federal government has to back down considerably, or Quebec has to compromise its principles in order for the province to accept the Canada Bill.

Conditional Acceptance: Quebec's Special Status

In its recent Draft Agreement on the Constitution,[7] the Quebec government agrees to accept the Canada Bill and the federal system on the condition that special constitutional provisions guarantee Quebec a distinct status reflecting the distinctiveness of the Quebec people.

Recognition of Quebec as a distinct society is given as a prerequisite, since it is the cornerstone on which to build an agreement with Quebec.[8] For this recognition to have a significant constitutional impact, it cannot be limited merely to culture; it must comprise also socio-economic and political dimensions.

Historically, this explicit or implicit claim by Quebec governments has not had any of the desired results. We are told that Mulroney will change all that. However, if we look closely at his statements, this does not appear to be true. On 21 May 1985, in Winnipeg, he declared: 'Quebec is, of course, distinct.' 'Quebec has,' he stated, 'unique responsibilities in the areas of language and culture.' It is not that the Prime Minister was expressing himself carelessly; this qualification is a repetition of an earlier remark, made on 18 January 1985, when Mulroney stated that it was a well-known fact that Quebec was different, and that he considered it quite reasonable for Quebec's cultural and linguistic wealth to be recognized and respected within the Canadian system.

There is a long tradition of Conservative thought which suggests there will be clear differences within the party concerning recognition of the Quebec people. These differences are certain to widen when Quebec's conditions for an accord are discussed.

An implicit order of priority is apparent in these conditions. During the constitutional negotiations of the summer of 1980, the federal government divided the issues into those concerning the people and those concerning governmental powers. It was a way of dealing with, in order of priority, the Charter of Rights and Freedoms, equalization, the amending formula, and repatriation of the Constitution – the main components of the Canada Bill.

Gérard Boismenu

There are two sets of issues in Quebec's draft agreement as well: those concerning the people, which are urgent priorities; and those concerning government, which cover a much broader field and which, it is acknowledged, cannot be quickly resolved. Obviously, the first set, which essentially aims to neutralize the Canada Bill,[9] is to receive attention first.

Rather than attempt to work within the Canadian Charter of Rights and Freedoms by proposing that it recognize the collective rights of the Quebec people, Quebec prefers to call for primacy of the Quebec Charter of Human Rights and Freedoms.[10] Such primacy would ease many of the Quebec government's concerns:

- to recognize the Quebec people without treating this collectivity as an ethnic minority within Canada;
- to officially identify the Quebec people with the provincial government;
- to have Quebec laws prevail in areas of provincial jurisdiction, and thus maintain responsibility for language policy (especially language of instruction) and nullify the federal Charter's section on the mobility of citizens and goods.

I will come back to these last two items, but first I would like to clarify one point. It has been said recently that there cannot be two charters and two categories of Canadian citizens. As previously noted, the Canadian Charter contains an override clause (or 'notwithstanding clause') which suspends application of section 2 and sections 7 to 15 when expressly indicated in federal or provincial law. The Quebec government took advantage of this clause in general for an initial five-year period.[11] During this time, the Quebec Charter of Human Rights and Freedoms was in effect; moreover, the Anglophone group Alliance Quebec invoked the Quebec Charter before the courts in order to invalidate the provisions of Bill 101 requiring the posting of commercial signs in French only. As we can see, the Quebec Charter already normally takes precedence over other Quebec statutes in areas of legal guarantees and equality rights.

We could compare the advantages and guarantees provided by the two charters, but for the moment, I would like to emphasize two consequences that the predominance of the Quebec Charter would have. In return for legislative authority over language of instruction, Quebec promises to make two amendments to its own Charter:[12]

- The 'Canada clause' of the Canadian Charter would apply in Quebec;
- Minority Anglophones would be guaranteed the right to their own cultural and educational institutions, and to receive health care and social services in their own language.

It should be pointed out that the mobility clause regarding persons and goods would not be included – the Quebec Charter is certainly not going to affirm Canadian economic union!

The first set of constitutional issues also contains the proposal to modify the amending procedure, giving Quebec a veto over changes to federal institutions, and either a veto over amendments to the Constitution or the right to opt out with full compensation. Quite apart from other issues,[13] the right of veto once again raises the problem of legal inequality among the provinces, and the right to opt out with compensation nullifies the suggestion that Quebec is distinctive in a merely cultural sense. It opens the door to special status, which would confirm the actual situation of Quebec.

All in all, about 15 of the 60 sections of the Canada Bill would remain in force; we can thus say that the basic aim of the first set of proposals is to substantially modify the general structure or coherence of the Canada Bill as it applies to Quebec. Accordingly, with respect to the dilemma of which I spoke earlier, the Quebec proposals give ground to some extent but do not fundamentally compromise its position.

The second set of proposals goes beyond the Canada Bill. It calls for the redistribution of powers both by eliminating Parliament's unilateral powers (i.e., controlling the use of the spending power and abolishing the powers of reservation and disallowance) and by increasing Quebec's powers.

The Draft Agreement on the Constitution states: 'The present constitutional division of powers in economic matters must be reviewed and certain powers already held by Quebec in the social and cultural domains as well as the international domain must be increased' (see Appendix A). The proposals seek primary responsibility for Quebec over manpower and economic development. Quebec should also have the right to take part in appointing Quebec judges to the Supreme Court and the exclusive right to appoint judges to the Quebec superior courts.

In my opinion, this second set of proposals establishes a long-term political agenda, identifying major objectives which would reinforce the concept of special status.[14] The distinct status for Quebec, which would be acknowledged if the primacy of the Quebec Charter of Rights were accepted, would be complemented by a special distribution of legislative powers favouring Quebec. In this way, the special status of the Quebec government would be affirmed. Thus the distinctiveness of the Quebec people would underpin a special constitutional status encompassing socio-economic and political areas and not simply cultural affairs.

A few comments should be made here. As a political agenda, this second set of proposals includes issues which are certainly subject to negotiation. However, I really cannot foresee discussions beginning on these points, much less being brought to conclusion. Moreover, I am uncertain of the nature of this special status; certain terms used in the Quebec proposals are ambiguous. For example, Quebec is described as the 'maître d'oeuvre' in the economic realm. Normally 'maître d'oeuvre' means a foreman or project manager. One wonders whether a genuine decentralization of decision-making authority is envisaged, or merely the delegation of administrative responsibilities.[15] The difference is a significant one. Lastly, there is reason to wonder why negotiations would ever take place on the second set of proposals, and, more importantly, why Quebec would receive what it wants.

The Great Delusion

These constitutional proposals seem very abstract in relation to current political life in Canada; they appear intangible, no doubt because they are based on a great delusion. Quebec's hopes are vain in at least two respects.

To begin with, the proposals ignore the distribution of political power which is inevitably at the heart of all constitutional negotiations. This is made even more absurd by the fact that the PQ government focused the 1980 referendum campaign on this issue of the political strength of Quebec in Confederation. The referendum was supposed to change the power relationship. The Quebec government's 1979 document, entitled *Québec-Canada: A New Deal*,[16] stated that a 'yes' in the referendum would be 'an element of greater consequence, more decisive than all the files and protest meetings and public statements' (p. 76), and that '... recourse to the referendum technique will change the bases and conditions of the Canadian political debate' (p. 76). This major new weapon seems to have backfired; however, all previous Quebec governments saw the need to arm themselves with additional ammunition, whether by mobilizing public opinion or playing the card of separatism.

At first glance, one would think that the current urgency of the constitutional question, as well as the apparently more favourable political climate stemmed from a few statements by Prime Minister Mulroney. This would be a rather naive conclusion. It's as if such general statements could really commit the federal government to specific changes. Or as if a number of provinces, just because they have Conservative governments, could be bound by such declarations.

Initial reactions outside Quebec are fairly revealing. To use an analogy, the Canadian family does not appear ready to kill the fatted calf at the return of the prodigal Québécois son. Even the federal government, while making noises to the effect that anything is possible, is not in much of a hurry to get the process started. In reality, a provincial government that is expected to lose in the next election carries very little weight.

In short, I do not see what, from Canada's perspective, could impart a sense of urgency to the constitutional question, or what could compel Canada to open negotiations with the present Quebec government. Nor do I see why the federal and other provincial governments should accept the proposals made by Quebec. In conclusion, I find it hard to believe that these governments will back down significantly regarding the Canada Bill either before or after the next Quebec election.

The second respect in which Quebec's approach is based on self-delusion is that not much attention has been paid to the treatment given in the past to Quebec's traditional constitutional position. In the draft agreement, the government states that it has refrained from reviewing the background to the constitutional debate so as not to add fuel to the fire. But this also prevents the government from saying why its proposals, which 'follow in the tradition of all previous Quebec governments',[16] should be greeted more favourably.

Overall, the draft agreement supports the proposal for special status, completely in line with the Pépin-Robarts Commission, almost as if this concept were new to the constitutional disputes. However, in *Québec-Canada: A New Deal* (1979), this same government criticized special status as an illusion: 'The idea, fashionable during the 'sixties and taken up again with certain variations, seemed to have the advantage of answering a good many of Quebec's aspirations. ... But this solution was quickly rejected by English Canada, which was opposed to Quebec's possible acquisition of powers denied to the other provinces.' (p. 45). The latest idea seems to be the same old illusion under a different name!

The bubble of illusion under which the Quebec government is labouring, and which it maintains, has not been punctured by the federal government. Probably it will not be at least until after the next election, although nothing concrete will likely be done about it in the meantime. After all, Prime Minister Mulroney stated on 29 May 1985 that negotiating the proposals with Quebec would be a long and complicated process, that he was not sure now would be the most propitious time to begin and that, for the time being, he preferred to react to them only in a general way.

In view of this, I wonder to whom the Draft Agreement on the Constitution is addressed.

An Appeal to Quebec Voters

The Quebec government's draft agreement is a political manoeuvre intended mainly for domestic consumption and scheduled for pre-election release. Although this paper is addressed to the federal and provincial governments, it is also intended for the people of Quebec. It has both an external objective – the constitutional negotiations – and an internal objective – the definition of a constitutional program, with the stamp of federalism, to beat the official opposition on its own turf.

Since the Parti Québécois decided officially in January 1985 that sovereignty was a remote political possibility, its constitutional program has been full of holes. But the May 1985 proposals do give the government the program that it has been missing and, as a result, a coherent political platform. It has two advantages: first, the approach is federalist ('These proposals ... fit into the federal framework of the present Constitution'); and second, it is in keeping with the government's traditional position. It stresses nationalism while transposing it into a claim for provincial autonomy.

This 'federalist option-provincial autonomy' mixture, which has always been effective within the province, threatens the position of the Quebec Liberals and attempts to put the official opposition on the defensive. The government has taken malicious pleasure in borrowing several Liberal policies, although in many cases giving them a different perspective. This has led Mr. Bourassa to declare that he agrees with 18 of the government's 22 proposals.[18]

However, appearances can be deceiving. To begin with, similarity of form does not mean similar content as well.[19] For instance, the Quebec government claims that recognition of the Quebec people involves not only cultural but socio-economic and political considerations as well; therefore the province requires special status. The Quebec Liberals, on the other hand, insist primarily on cultural powers. The difference between the two parties is that they have different ideas about what is necessary to safeguard Quebec's distinctiveness. There are also, fundamentally, points of actual disagreement. The differences between the two parties are more pronounced in the main points of the first set of proposals, aimed at neutralizing the Canada Bill. In effect, for the Quebec Liberal Party: the Quebec people are a cultural entity; the Canadian Charter should have primacy (the Liberals thus support its articles on language of instruction and the principle of the Canadian economic union); concerning the amending formula, the right of veto should be granted for all matters. In the second series of proposals, there seem to be more areas of agreement between the two parties. But this is an area that does not compromise, to the same degree, the idea of Quebec's distinctiveness.

It seems obvious that the debate the PQ wants to launch either in the National Assembly or in the public forum aims to accomplish two things: first, to portray the Liberals' stance against federalism as a timid one; and second, to ask the Quebec public which brand of federalism it would rather have (that of the Liberals or of the Parti Québécois). The PQ must therefore give itself some ammunition to deal with the constitutional problem while making it a major theme of the election campaign. Mulroney cannot very well reject the Quebec proposals in the coming months, and the Quebec government will be looking for a sign from Canada to give their initiative some credibility.

Compromising the Future?

By way of conclusion, I must admit to being deeply sceptical and fairly pessimistic. It is difficult to imagine that the other provincial governments and the federal government will back down significantly over the Canada Bill, whether by agreeing to exempt Quebec from it or in any other way. It would be just as surprising if the other governments agreed, with goodwill or otherwise, to give Quebec special status, particularly when the distribution of political power has never been as unfavourable to Quebec.

If it becomes possible to discuss an agreement, and if the Quebec government officially signs the Canada Bill, it will certainly not be the result of Canada's giving in, as is presently hoped. The principles that have historically been defended by the Government of Quebec will probably have to be abandoned; this is the concession that it is feared Quebec will be forced to make. A Bourassa government would feel more at ease in making such a concession since, aside from supporting Quebec's claim of a universal right of veto, the Quebec Liberals have attached fewer conditions to their acceptance of the Canada Bill.

The provincial Liberals[20] view Quebec's identity from a cultural standpoint; they speak of a distinct society, much like Trudeau's vision of a sociological nation. Thus, the first condition for acceptance set out in their platform (recognition of Quebec as a distinct society) is accompanied by a demand for control over immigration, intended primarily as a cultural safeguard. With respect to federal institutions, the Liberals call for participation by Quebec in selecting Supreme Court judges and they support a limit on the federal spending power. As for the amending formula, they naturally demand a full veto, but they have said that it will not be easy to regain lost ground, and have hinted that the right to opt out with compensation is a lesser evil. The Liberals could give in on this issue and cover themselves politically by alleging that it was impossible to regain the veto lost by a heedless PQ government. Exclusive jurisdiction over language policy is not one of their conditions for signing the Canada Bill, and acceptance of the Canadian Charter of Rights and Freedoms means approval of the principle of Canadian economic union. The Liberals are keen to improve interprovincial relations, particularly with respect to strengthening the Canadian economic union. One way would be to prepare an interprovincial code of ethics.[21] The Liberals have definitely attached fewer conditions for acceptance of the Canada Bill!

However, a PQ government could also end up making comparable concessions. We have become used to twists and turns of Parti Québécois policy and to reversals on major issues.

In the face of this political duel which is dominating public affairs, a number of organizations have banded together to state their opposition to the government's proposals and insist on the need to have the Quebec people's right to self-determination formally recognized. This group, the Coalition pour l'indépendance du Québec, consists of the three major union organizations – the Confederation of National Trade Unions, the Teachers' Federation, and the Quebec Federation of Labour – the Mouvement national des Québécois, the Mouvement socialiste, the Rassemblement démocratique pour l'indépendance and others. This opposition group is based outside the National Assembly and includes organizations that are not essentially political in nature. Even though the election system leaves little room for small political groups, perhaps they will make their dissenting voice heard through the social visions of various political theories and express a current of thought deeply rooted among Quebecers, which ranges from an essential and substantial increase in the real power of the Quebec government right up to independence.

In conclusion, many people feel that to avoid compromising the future position of Quebec, whichever party negotiates a constitutional settlement should tie the recognition of Quebec's character as a distinct society to the right of self-determination, in such a way that a link is officially established between this guarantee for the Quebec people and the UN Declaration of Human Rights. This basic demand, which the PQ government has left by the wayside, would guarantee the possibility of someday breaking free of the mortgage that the political parties, concerned primarily with political opportunism, are prepared to accept without receiving much in return.

Notes

1. Government of Quebec, *Draft Agreement on the Constitution*, Quebec, May 1985, p. 32.
2. At the PQ convention held in June 1984, a resolution was passed to fight the next election mainly on the issue of Quebec sovereignty. A vote for the Parti Québécois would mean a vote for Quebec sovereignty.
3. National Assembly, *Journal des débats*, Vol. 28, No. 1, 16 October 1984, p. 23.
4. The June 1984 resolution was amended to state that the fundamental objective of the Parti Québécois was to achieve sovereignty for Quebec.
5. My articles: 'Vers une redéfinition des lieux d'exercice du pouvoir d'Etat au Canada', *Cahiers d'histoire*, Vol. II, No. 1, Université de Montréal, 1981, pp. 11-30; 'Le Québec et la centralisation politique au Canada, le 'beau risque' du Canada Bill', *Cahiers de recherche sociologique*, Vol. 3, No. 1, Université de Québec à Montréal, April 1985, pp. 119-139.
6. In the official letter from Premier Lévesque to Prime Minister Trudeau, stating that he intended to exercise his 'veto' over the constitutional accord from which Quebec was excluded, Mr. Lévesque pointed out that the motion put before the National Assembly represented the absolute minimum Quebec required to protect its special nature and its rights. National Assembly, *Journal des débats*, Quebec, Vol. 26, No. 9, 25 November, 1981, p. 463; Vol. 26, No. 12, 1 December 1981, p. 605. We are analyzing the principles of this motion here. In the next section, we will compare the motion with certain aspects of the present Quebec proposal; our observations will also be included in these notes.
7. *Op. cit.*, p. 35.
8. Several changes were made to the motion of 1 December 1981. Initially, the motion was based on the principle of the Quebec people's right to self-determination; however, in the present draft agreement, the Lévesque government states in the introduction – not in the proposals themselves – that the proposals do not alter the inalienable right of the Quebec people to self-determination. Until 1981, the Lévesque government stated that recognition of this right had to figure in any preamble to the constitution. The wording also changed: two basically equal founding peoples became a Canadian duality with special needs; reference to Quebec as a distinct 'nation' disappeared, leaving only the concept of the Quebec people, as integrators of their own minorities.
9. Quebec governments had traditionally insisted that an agreement on the division of powers be reached before the constitution was repatriated. The momentum which began to grow in the summer of 1980 at the time of Trudeau's initiative, and which the Lévesque government grudgingly accepted, was in the opposite direction from this longtime Quebec requirement. In its proposals, the present Quebec government adopts the order of items imposed previously by Trudeau; therefore, the division of powers seems to figure in the second stage of discus-

sions. It is certainly no longer the starting point for an agreement to accept constitutional reform.

10. In 1981, the government accepted a Canadian Charter after opting out of parts of it and subordinating it to Quebec laws in areas of the province's jurisdiction.

11. The constitutional validity of this law is now being challenged before the Court of Appeal.

12. These are two major concessions which would involve making Quebec's exclusive responsibility over language policy subject to conditions and constraints that concern the operation of institutions and minority language education.

13. Claude Morin, 'Retrait ou veto: de quoi s'agit-il?', Le Devoir, 13 February 1985, and 'Veto ou retrait: quelques considérations pratiques', Le Devoir, 14 February 1985; Gérald-A Beaudoin, 'Le veto et le retrait: esquisses d'une solution', Le Devoir, 23 January 1985; Louis Dussault, 'Le droit de veto et le droit de retrait', Le Devoir, 20 February 1985; Gil Rémillard, 'A quelles conditions le Québec peut-il signer la Loi constitutionnelle de 1982 (2) La formule d'amendement', Le Devoir, 27 February 1985.

14. A close comparison with Quebec's traditional claims would show that the proposals of the Lévesque government are far from extreme; they are much more moderate in many respects.
For documentation useful in making this comparison, see the study of Quebec's demands from the Duplessis era to 1982 by Andrée Lajoie, Pierrette Maluzzi and Michelle Gamache, 'Les idées politiques au Québec et l'évolution du droit constitutionnel canadien, 1945-1985', in La Cour suprême du Canada comme instrument du changement politique, Vol. 47 in the appendixes to the report by the Macdonald Commission, published in the fall of 1985.

15. There seems to be some ambiguity in the proposals regarding 'maître d'oeuvre' and 'responsabilité première': 'First, the Government of Québec insists that it should have the primary responsibility [être maître d'oeuvre] for the formulation and implementation of general economic policy in Québec.' Later, the document states: 'The Government of Québec insists, therefore, that its primary responsibility [responsabilité première] be recognized in the matter of the general direction of its economic development and that of its regions.' Government of Quebec, op. cit., p. 28.

16. Government of Quebec, Québec-Canada: A New Deal (Quebec: Service des publications officielles, 1979).

17. Government of Quebec, Draft Agreement on the Constitution, p. 6.

18. 'Constitution: tout n'est pas négociable', Le Devoir, 22 May 1985, p. 1. This was a generous assessment by the Liberals. The reaction outside Quebec was the opposite: the document was labelled crypto-separatist. Two points should be added. First, this assessment (agreement with 18 of the 22 proposals) is generous and free. Second, it was not necessarily based on a careful comparison of the texts produced by the government and the opposition, and ignored the notable differences illustrated in the following paragraph.

19. Parti libéral du Québec, Maîtriser l'avenir, Programme politique, Montreal, 1985.

Gérard Boismenu

Appendix A

Draft Agreement on the Constitution: Proposals by the Government of Quebec
[Released May 1985]

Quebec was not a party to the constitutional accord of November 1981, which led to the patriation of the Canadian Constitution and to its amendment in some essential respects.

Quebec rejected this Accord and refused to acknowledge its legitimacy, because it was negotiated and concluded without its participation.

The Canada Act 1982 would be acceptable only if we could reach a new constitutional agreement with the rest of Canada, restoring to us our rights, recognizing the distinctiveness of our people and launching an in-depth review meeting our aspirations and our needs.

The present situation is viable neither for Canada nor for Quebec. A federation cannot operate for the benefit of its citizens without the active participation of one of its major partners, just as Quebec can never be satisfied with the diminished status imposed upon it. We must seek an opportunity to remedy this situation.

We believe that this opportunity has been afforded us by the election last September of a new government in Ottawa. It will be recalled that during the election campaign, the now Prime Minister of Canada not only recognized the reality of the problem, but also solemnly committed himself to resolving it:

I know that, in the province of Québec, there are wounds to be healed, worries to be calmed, enthusiasms to be rekindled, and bonds of trust to be established. (...)
I know that many men and women in Québec will not be satisfied with mere words. We will have to make commitments and take concrete steps to reach the objective that I have set for myself and that I repeat here: to convince the Québec National Assembly to give its consent to the new Canadian Constitution with honour and enthusiasm. (Notes for an address by the Honourable Brian Mulroney, P.C., M.P., Sept-Iles, 6 August, 1984.)

This undertaking was reaffirmed at the opening of the Canadian Parliament last 1 November:

Ultimately such a new consensus must be reflected in the fundamental law of our land, for it is obvious that the constitutional agreement is incomplete so long as Québec is not part of an accord. While their principal obligations are to achieve economic renewal, my Ministers will work to create the conditions that will make possible the achievement of this essential accord. In this work, the cooperation of all partners in Confederation will be necessary.
(Speech from the Throne, Hansard, 5 November 1984, p. 6)

The Government of Quebec, which had already insisted that the question be reopened, saw in these commitments an expression of good faith leading to new dialogue with real opportunities for both correcting the past and brightening the future. It thereupon agreed to reassess its attitude and formulate its requirements – and since then, has worked diligently to that end.

The Government of Quebec has sought to fulfill that task faithfully and realistically. Its proposals follow in the tradition of all previous Quebec governments and go beyond party lines; they are intended to respond to the concrete needs of our fellow citizens, yet without ignoring the future. These proposals take into account the new Canadian political environment. They are substantive proposals, submitted initially for consideration by Quebecers and also for consideration by the other governments with the objective of concluding an agreement resulting from negotiations conducted in good faith.

These proposals, it will be seen, fit into the federal framework of the present Constitution. They are intended to improve it in such a way that the people of Quebec may, as long as they so decide, find in it the most favourable conditions possible for their development. It goes without saying that they in no way alter the inalienable right of the people of Quebec to democratic self-determination with regard to its constitutional future.

In developing these proposals, we have taken into account the requirements formulated by the National Assembly in its Resolution of 1 December 1981. We have also taken into consideration the recommendations of those who, as with the Pépin-Robarts Commission, have made an in-depth study of this question, as well as recommendations made recently by other interested parties in Quebec.

Finally, we have based ourselves on requests made by our predecessors who, for over 20 years, have taken part in the long exercise of constitutional review – unfortunately, without much success.

Over and above redressing the wrongs caused Quebec in 1981, in reopening this question, we are, as has been the case for almost 20 years, seeking constitutional structures adapted as much as possible to the changing reality of Quebec and Canada.

In order to seize the new opportunity provided us to get things moving again, in initiating this process, the Government of Quebec has duly noted the changes that have taken place in Quebec and Canada. However, it is of the greatest importance that it be clearly understood what constitutes, today as yesterday, and regardless of the government of the day, the very essence of Quebec's concern: the distinct character of the people of Quebec and the legitimacy of the legal and institutional instruments derived therefrom.

PART ONE
Recognition of the Existence of the People of Quebec

The recognition of the existence of a people of Quebec is an essential pre-requisite in Quebec's agreement and participation in a new constitutional relation. The present constitution acknowledges the Canadian duality only through the concept of institutionalized bilingualism. It makes no mention of the particular needs that flow from the differences between the people of Quebec and the population of the rest of Canada.

During recent years, constraints have quickly appeared when Quebec wanted to ensure the conformity of its development with the legitimate aspirations of its population in the fields of manpower, income security, communications, international cooperation, or the protection, affirmation and development of the French fact, to name but a few. It is necessary to understand fully that the Quebec positions on these matters (which we shall discuss later) have been drawn up in accordance with the needs and aspirations peculiar to the people of Quebec. These positions embody the various ways whereby the men and women of Quebec express the conditions they consider essential for their fullest development.

The Pépin-Robarts Commission recommended not only that the distinctiveness of Quebec be recognized, but also that Quebec be permitted to determine its particular responsibility with respect to the French heritage within its own territory.

The recognition of Quebec's distinctiveness alone is meaningless, unless it is matched with provisions that give it substance; it must also be reflected in content, which is the basis of the following chapters. This recognition of Quebec's distinctiveness constitutes an essential step in the coherence of the undertaking.

To sum up, the Government of Quebec proposes:

☐

that the Constitution explicitly recognize the existence of a people of Quebec.

PART TWO
The Conditions for an Agreement

Once the existence of the people of Quebec is recognized in the Canadian Constitution, Quebec stands ready to conclude a new accord, insisting upon certain conditions. Quebec will consider itself party to the agreement if its primary authority in the matter of rights and freedoms is recognized, if the rest of Canada agrees to modify the amending formula to grant Quebec satisfactory guarantees, and if agreement is reached on the terms of Quebec's participation.

CHAPTER I
Recognition of the Primary Authority of Quebec in the Matter of Rights and Freedoms

Quebec can take pride in being the guarantor of individual rights and freedoms through its institutions. The Government of Quebec intends to protect the integrity of its jurisdiction in this matter. This applies to language rights which are so intimately linked to the personality of the people of Quebec: it is Quebec that must assume primary responsibility for these rights. This is also true in the domain of civil, political, economic and social rights codified by the Quebec Charter of Human Rights and Freedoms, which should alone take precedence over Quebec statutes.

1. Quebec's Responsibility for Language Rights
The distinctiveness of the people of Quebec goes far beyond the question of language, but language is at the origin and the heart of that distinctiveness.

For nearly four centuries, there has existed along the shores of the St. Lawrence a people of French origin which, under two colonial regimes and many constitutional systems, has progressively affirmed itself through its institutions and, with the contribution of other communities, has developed to the point where it has acquired all the characteristics of a distinct society.

This people spread into the greater part of the continent and contributed to its development, but, in the course of time, the English language gained ascendancy everywhere except in Quebec. This is how the Canadian duality came about.

The advent of mass communications, the spectacular expansion in the dissemination of sound and pictures, books and ideas, and increasingly, the movement of commercial goods and services, both along the north-south and east-west axes, lead us to consider North America as the point of reference of the linguistic, cultural and economic reality in which we are evolving. French-speaking persons today constitute scarcely two per cent of the North American population. At a ratio of 50 to one, specific measures are required to protect French as the everyday language. This fact is self-evident if we consider the case of the French-speaking communities outside Quebec and it also holds true in Quebec, even though more than 80 per cent of its people are French-speaking.

The interests of French-speaking Quebecers are akin to those of French-speaking communities outside Quebec. For Quebecers, the assimilation of French-speaking communities outside Quebec is a loss to, and a dangerous weakening of, the French-speaking cultural mainstream. For their part, the French-speaking minorities in the other provinces recognize the importance of the vitality of the Quebec French fact for the maintenance of their cultural and linguistic identity.

Although there are interests common to both, the means required to promote them differ according to the context. The Quebec context is quite different from that of the other provinces with regard to language. Recognition of this reality is a prerequisite to the development of solutions which penalize neither group.

Thus, in the opinion of French-speaking communities outside Quebec, Section 23 of the Canada Act 1982 offers a means, insufficient in itself though it be, for protecting their rights. That section was designed to ensure protection of the linguistic rights of a minority and is, therefore, suited to their reality. On the other hand, the effect of Section 23 in Quebec is to neutralize certain measures adopted by the National Assembly of Quebec to ensure the survival, affirmation and development of the French identity in the face of the enormous linguistic pressure placed upon it by the North American environment, and to which these measures were designed to act as a counterweight.

Quebec is the only North American territory where the linguistic, cultural and economic concerns of the French-speaking population are predominant. Therefore, Quebec legitimately claims confirmation of its powers in linguistic matters.

We take into account, however, that the people of Quebec is not entirely composed of French-speaking citizens. The English language community, the ethnic communities and the native peoples have rights and, over and above their individual and particular rights, they have a more general right of access to all the resources society makes available to everyone.

In the past, Quebec experienced certain periods of tension with regard to language matters. That tension bespoke the concern of the French-speaking population over its future, particularly in regard to the means of ensuring the survival of French over the long term which appeared to be clearly insufficient. In spite of these periods, a climate of tolerance and respect in the treatment of minorities has generally prevailed in the search for affirmation of the French character of Quebec. In that respect we quote from the Pépin-Robarts Commission Report:

We also expect that the rights of the English-speaking minority in the areas of education and social services would continue to be respected. These rights, and this should be stressed, are not now guaranteed by the Canadian constitution. Yet they are recognized under Bill 101, the charter of the French language, a law passed by a Parti Québécois government. Thus, we already have proof that the rights of the English-speaking community in Quebec can be protected, without any constitutional obligation, and that the governments of Quebec are quite capable of reconciling the interest of the majority with the concerns of the minority.

(The Task Force on Canadian Unity, A Future Together, Observations and Recommendations, January 1979, pp. 52-53)

Quebec intends to fulfill its responsibilities to its minorities: to continue to actively promote their rights and to give them the means necessary to exercise them.

With regard to the English-speaking community, the Government of Quebec is ready to undertake, within this new framework, to enshrine in its laws the right of the English-speaking minority to receive health care and social services in its own language, as well as its right to its own cultural and educational institutions.

The Government of Quebec is also ready to amend the Charter of the French language to secure access to the English school system for the children of those who have received their primary instruction in Canada in English; it expects in return that throughout Canada those who benefit from Section 23 can in actual fact avail themselves of access to the French school system.

Quebec also intends to fully support the French-speaking communities outside Quebec. The Government of Quebec is prepared to cooperate actively with any provincial government that wishes to improve the services it provides to its French-speaking minority. It is rather by way of intergovernmental cooperation than by the sole authority of the Constitution that progress can be achieved.

To sum up, the Government of Quebec proposes:

- That the Constitution recognize that Quebec has the exclusive right to determine its official language and to legislate on any linguistic matter within its jurisdiction.
- That Quebec secure the right of the English-speaking minority to its cultural and educational institutions, as well as the right to receive health care and social services in its own language.
- That the Quebec Charter of the French Language be so amended that the children of those who have received their primary instruction in Canada in English be guaranteed access to the English school system, regardless of their number.
- That throughout Canada, those who are eligible for instruction in French may in fact avail themselves of the rights guaranteed by Section 23 of the Canadian Charter of Rights and Freedoms.
- That to support the development of the French-speaking minorities outside Quebec, agreements of mutual assistance be signed between the governments concerned.

2. Acceptance of the Primacy of the Quebec Charter of Human Rights and Freedoms

In 1975 the people of Quebec gave itself a Charter of Human Rights and Freedoms which is one of the most complete and generous there is.

A charter of rights and freedoms is the finest instrument for the affirmation of the values held by a people. It reflects both its most fundamental beliefs and the often difficult choices and decisions that a society is called upon to make. It secures to each person the minimal conditions for the exercise of his freedoms. It reflects, therefore, the framework in which individuals evolve as a collectivity. As such, and taking into consideration the distinctiveness of the people of Quebec, it is not a matter of indifference as to whether it should be the Quebec Charter or the Canadian Charter that should apply to the laws of Quebec.

The Quebec Charter is more generous than the Canadian Charter. It provides not only for civil and political rights, as does the Canadian Charter, but also for economic and social rights. Furthermore, the Quebec Charter applies not only, as does the Canadian Charter, to relations between the State and the citizen, but also to relations between private persons. Moreover, it grants the right to equality and protection against discrimination in a way that is explicitly more extensive. Citizens have accessible and effective means of remedy against infringement of their rights through the Quebec Charter. It recognizes the recourse of action for damages as well as injunctions. It also innovates in allowing the Courts to grant exemplary damages. The Charter also allows citizens to address the Commission des droits de la personne (Human Rights Commission) in the case of discrimination, one of the most important sources of litigation when it comes to rights and freedoms.

In reality, there is no essential difference between the Charter included in the Canadian Constitution and the Quebec Charter as to the level of protection they both grant. Both charters prevail over the laws of Quebec and, in this sense, both have a special status. Also, each includes an exception clause ('notwithstanding' clause) conferring on both the federal Parliament and the National Assembly the power to expressly override their fundamental provisions by a majority vote of their members. The power to override the constitutional Charter is the same, therefore, for all the Canadian legislatures with respect to the Canadian Charter and is exercised in essentially the same way as for the Quebec Charter.

In the event of its being amended, the Canadian Charter is subject to the constraints and uncertainty of the constitutional amendment procedure in which the other provinces play a preponderant role.

As for the Quebec Charter, it has a quasi-constitutional status and gives the ultimate responsibility in the affirmation of human rights and freedoms to the Quebec legislature, elected by and responsible to the population for the proper functioning of society. The people of Quebec is fully aware of its own distinctiveness; it possesses its own democratic institutions. It must take responsibility for rights and freedoms and ensure their evolution and extension within Quebec without being constrained by a structure over which it has very little control. The inclusion of a charter in a constitution entails certain guarantees, but it is meaningful only to the extent where it is the people immediately concerned who determine its content and scope, which, for instance, would be the case if the Quebec Charter were to be included in a Quebec Constitution.

That is why the only Canadian constitutional limitations to which Quebec has never objected and by which it agrees to be bound relate precisely to the political rights which ensure the proper functioning of our democratic system.

To sum up, Quebec proposes:

☐ That only Sections 3 to 5 of the Charter included in the Canadian Constitution which guarantee democratic rights continue to bind Quebec without the National Assembly being able to make exceptions thereto.

☐ That Quebec be empowered to subordinate its own laws only to the Quebec Charter of Human Rights and Freedoms.

CHAPTER II
Modification of the Constitutional Amendment Procedure

1. Recognition of a Power of Veto over Federal Institutions and the Creation of New Provinces

With respect to federal institutions, namely the Senate and the Supreme Court, and the creation of new provinces, with the exception of the composition of the Supreme Court, which cannot be modified without the unanimous consent of the provinces the consent of seven provinces representing at least 50 per cent of the Canadian population is required to modify key elements of the Senate and the Supreme Court, and the representation in the House of Commons, as well as the establishment of new provinces.

This formula is a major improvement over what previously existed because most of these matters were formerly within the exclusive jurisdiction of the federal Parliament. The Government of Quebec believes, however, that it must hold a power of veto over any change that could affect the role of Quebec in these federal institutions, particularly over the composition of these institutions and their powers, as well as over the method of appointment of the persons called to be members thereof, and also over the creation of new provinces.

To sum up, the Government of Quebec proposes:

☐ That Quebec be recognized as having a power of veto over modifications of federal institutions and the establishment of new provinces.

2. Modification of the Division of Powers

The Resolution adopted on 1 December 1981 by the National Assembly requested that the method of constitutional amendment be modified either to grant Quebec a power of veto or to secure to it a reasonable and mandatory compensation in all cases of non-participation in a constitutional amendment. The Government of Quebec believes that this alternative must be maintained and it is ready to discuss it with the other governments.

Government of Quebec

In fact, each of these two formulas guarantees what is essential for Quebec: that none of its powers can be taken away from it without its consent. The formula of non-participation with compensation, however, offers the additional advantage of flexibility.

To sum up, the Government of Quebec proposes:

☐ That the present method of constitutional amendment be modified either to grant Quebec a power of veto or to secure it a reasonable and mandatory compensation in the event of non-participation in a constitutional amendment.

CHAPTER III
Conditions for Participation

If redress of the wrongs caused Quebec by the enactment without its consent of the Canada Act 1982 is imperative, it is also a prerequisite to the real participation of Quebec in the Canadian federation. That participation will be ensured if the legitimate claims of Quebec are satisfied as an outcome of constitutional negotiations which Quebec intends to pursue in good faith, as it has done in the past, with its partners in the federation.

One cannot expect to achieve a new in-depth constitutional arrangement overnight. But, based on the numerous constitutional discussions of the past, it would be possible to reach a significant constitutional consensus which would result in agreements. On several points, these would settle the constitutional dispute between Quebec and the rest of Canada and open the way to better participation in the work of the federation as well as to a continuous adaptation to the changes thereto which are bound to occur.

For Quebec, the division of powers has always been and still is at the center of the constitutional debate. The proposals which follow envisage a better division of powers. Such a division will be fair only if there is an adjustment, indeed an elimination of certain excessive powers of the federal Parliament. Furthermore, the division of constitutional powers should be adapted to the particular needs of the people of Quebec. Certain judicial institutions should be reformed to better suit them to the new context.

1.   The Revision of the Distribution of Powers
To ensure that its citizens have the services best suited to their needs, to avoid costly duplication and guarantee the efficacy of its actions, Quebec must be able to exercise its existing constitutional powers without limitation and it must obtain increased powers in order to freely ensure its economic, social and cultural development.

a)   The Restriction and the Elimination of Certain Unilateral Powers of the Federal Parliament
The unlimited use made by the federal Parliament of its spending power has distorted the division of powers codified in the Constitution.

The successive governments of Quebec have always denounced the unrestrained use of this excessive power which has become one of the main causes of the dissatisfaction of Quebecers with Canadian federalism.

However, Quebec does not dispute the legitimacy of certain uses of the federal spending power and has particularly supported the use of it to combat disparities between the regions of Canada through unconditional grants. On the other hand, Quebec has always opposed the use of spending power when the federal government has used it to intervene in areas outside its jurisdiction, such as in municipal affairs, health and education.

The Government of Quebec proposes a two-tier structure for the limitation of the exercise of the spending power. First, conditional grants to the provinces should be, as the federal government itself suggested in 1969, subject to the prior consent of a majority of provinces. In addition, any province that refuses these grants should receive fair compensation.

In matters of education and culture, the federal government has used its spending power to create State corporations and make grants to individuals and institutions, thereby intruding in areas that are characteristic of Quebec's distinctiveness.

Limits should be imposed on such interventions by major readjustments. Starting immediately, payments to individuals and institutions should not be made unless they have been the subject of prior agreement with the Government of Quebec.

If the spending power can thus remain, the contrary holds true for the powers of disallowance and reservation still constitutionally held by the federal government. They are the residue of a colonial heritage whose obsolescence is today universally recognized. These powers no longer have any place in the Constitution. Moreover, the federal government committed itself in the past to abolishing them once the Constitution had been patriated, and Quebec considers their abolition overdue.

To sum up, the Government of Quebec proposes:

☐ That the federal spending power be limited in such a way that conditional grants to the provinces be subject to the consent of a majority of provinces, that any non-participating province be entitled to compensation, and that grants to individuals and institutions working in the areas of culture and education be submitted for approval by the Government of Quebec.

☐ That the powers of disallowance and reservation be abolished.

b) Adapting the Division of Powers to the Needs of Quebec

The benefits that will result from the limitation of the spending power and the abolition of the powers of disallowance and reservation are not sufficient. The special responsibilites of the Government of Quebec in the economic, cultural and social fields can only be fulfilled if the division of powers is suited to the needs of Quebec and its population. The present constitutional division of powers in economic matters must be reviewed and certain powers already held by Quebec in the social and cultural domains as well as in the international domain must be increased.

Gérard Boismenu

The Government of Quebec believes that policy-making authority in economic development and manpower must be defined in greater detail.

First, the Government of Quebec insists that it should have the primary responsibility for the formulation and implementation of general economic policy in Quebec. Quebec considers itself responsible for its economic progress as well as the direction it can give to its overall development and especially that of its regions.

The economy in general will always remain a shared responsibility in a federation; however, as the Government of Quebec stated at the economic conference held in Regina, the federal government should recognize that it is up to the provinces to first define the type of development which best suits them. General prosperity will be enhanced if the provinces are more dynamic. The Government of Quebec insists, therefore, that its primary responsibility be recognized in the matter of the general direction of its economic development and that of its regions.

The same holds true for manpower policy which includes the placement, retraining and vocational training of workers. In the implementation of its policy on adult training, its apprenticeship policy, its back-to-work programs and its job creation policies, Quebec has felt as never before the urgent necessity of achieving a better integration of manpower related activities, a goal which at present eludes it. Even though efforts have been made to minimize the disadvantages, there is a duplication of services in this area which is costly and inefficient. Quebecers would be better served by a better integrated system; that, in effect, is what the great majority of organizations representing workers, employers and other concerned groups in Quebec consulted on this subject believe. And that is why the Government of Quebec insists on holding the powers and resources such responsibility entails.

Furthermore, powers should be added which, even though they pertain to culture, will nevertheless have important economic repercussions. These are powers dealing with immigration and communications.

The Constitution should enlarge upon the Cullen-Couture Agreement of 1978 by confirming the paramountcy of Quebec's powers in the matter of selection, and by extending that paramountcy to the integration and settling of immigrants. These powers are of fundamental importance because it is upon their exercise that, among other things, the preservation and consolidation of the distinct character of the people of Quebec depends.

With respect to communications, an increase in the powers of Quebec in this area is in line with the common position taken by the Canadian provinces, a position in which the present federal government might wish to concur. Indeed, the negotiation of a redistribution of powers in this area would likely find support among the various governments. It should extend to the communications sector in general which would be of singular importance to Quebec in terms of identity as well as cultural security.

Another field on which there has been a provincial consensus as to jurisdiction is the area of marriage and divorce. This jurisdiction should be transferred to Quebec given its evident local and private nature.

The Government of Quebec also reiterates certain long-standing claims in the field of international relations. It, therefore, asserts the following claims which it considers to be justified in view of the distinct character of the people of Quebec.

The presence of Quebec as a participant government in international organizations of the 'Francophonie' is essential. This status of participant government is already granted to Quebec within the framework of the 'Agence de coopération culturelle et technique' and should be envisaged in the case of the planned 'Sommet Francophone' and in what will result therefrom. Quebec's presence in other international organizations relating to its jurisdictions should also be provided for in a suitable way.

To sum up, the Government of Quebec proposes:

☐ That the primary responsibility of Quebec over the general field of manpower with all the powers and resources such responsibility entails be confirmed.

☐ That the primary responsibility of Quebec for the formulation and implementation of its general policy of economic development, including regional development, be recognized.

☐ That the paramount jurisdiction of Quebec in the matter of selection and settlement of immigrants in Quebec be recognized.

☐ That Quebec be granted a significant increase in powers pertaining to communications.

☐ That Quebec be granted exclusive jurisdiction in the matter of marriage and divorce.

☐ That in international matters, recognition be given to the specific situation of Quebec in all that relates to its jurisdictions and its identity, particularly within the framework of the 'Francophonie'.

2. Reform of the Judicial System

The importance of the judicial process makes it necessary that Quebec play a decisive role in the process of appointment of the judges of the Supreme Court of Canada. With regard to Quebec Courts and administrative tribunals, the exercise of Quebec's jurisdiction over the administration of justice is hampered by Section 96 of the Constitution Act of 1867 which must be reassessed in further constitutional talks.

With the increased importance of the Courts in recent years, and in particular since the advent of charters of rights and freedoms, Quebec's traditional stand in this matter takes on an even greater legitimacy.

a) Quebec's Participation in the Appointment of Judges to the Supreme Court of Canada

The Government of Quebec considers that it must be consulted in the appointment of the three judges from Quebec. Even though the power of appointing Quebec judges to the Supreme Court may in principle belong to the federal government, consultation with the Government of Quebec should be formalized and its consent required.

The representation of Quebec on the Supreme Court already provided for by federal statute as well as the principle of alternation in the appointment of the Chief Justice should be explicitly entrenched in the Constitution.

Apart from the composition of the Supreme Court, the distinctiveness of Quebec should also be reflected in the jurisdiction of the Courts and of their judges. Specifically, the Government considers that questions of civil law should only be decided by judges from Quebec, trained in its law.

To sum up, the Government of Quebec proposes:

☐ That the Constitution explicitly recognize that three of the nine judges of the Supreme Court of Canada come from Quebec, as well as the principle of alternation in the appointment of the Chief Justice.

☐ That the Constitution recognize the right of the Government of Quebec to participate in the appointment of Quebec judges to the Supreme Court of Canada and that its consent be obtained before their appointment.

☐ That judges from Quebec trained in its law have sole authority in matters of civil law.

b) The Attribution of Authority over the Appointment of Judges to the Quebec Superior Courts

While Quebec does not require exclusive jurisdiction over the process of appointment of its judges on the Supreme Court, it requires such jurisdiction over the appointment of judges to the Quebec Court of Appeal and Superior Court.

It is important to correct forthwith the anachronism of a constitutional procedure whereby the federal government appoints judges who are part of the Quebec judicial system and are subject to the authority of Quebec under Section 92 (14) of the Constitution Act of 1867.

This situation should be remedied by instituting a procedure of appointment whereby Quebec would have the authority over the appointment of judges with the obligation of prior consultation with the federal government. Indeed, it is desirable that the latter be part of the appointment process in view of the fact that the Quebec superior Courts must apply many federal statutes.

It is therefore expedient to amend Section 96 of the Constitution Act of 1867 to grant the Government of Quebec the power to appoint judges to the Quebec superior Courts.

To sum up, the Government of Quebec proposes:

☐ That Section 96 of the Constitution Act of 1867 be amended so as to recognize the authority of Quebec to appoint judges to the Quebec superior Courts following consultation with the federal government.

3. The Need for an Ongoing Process of Constitutional Negotiations
Constitutional discussions should be reopened with the clear understanding that a comprehensive review of the Constitution must eventually be proceeded with. The process that is beginning will only be truly meaningful if it includes key elements which evidence a new spirit of dialogue.

Quebec's propositions are designed to generate a new impetus for profound change in the Constitution.

The Government of Quebec believes that over and above the conditions of a new accord, the solemn commitment of the governments to pursue constitutional review must be obtained forthwith.

During this review process, Quebec would like to see, in addition to the proposals set out in this document, other aspects of the division of powers addressed, particularly the residual and declaratory powers of the federal Parliament, as well as questions relating to income security and certain other dimensions of international relations. Quebec also would want the reform of the central institutions, especially the Senate, to be proceeded with.

Conclusion

In preparing these proposals, the Government has first been mindful of the people of Quebec, its aspirations and its needs. The Government, therefore, will be particularly attentive to its reactions and comments.

All these proposals are aimed at enhancing the ability of Quebec's institutions to fully assume their responsibility to promote the general well-being.

Among these institutions, the National Assembly is of paramount importance. It must be involved.

These proposals also concern the whole of the Canadian population. The willingness for redress expressed by the Prime Minister of Canada has given rise to hope on both sides. The people of Quebec and its Government respond to this willingness. We firmly believe that through mutual respect, good faith and frank negotiations, there exists a real possibility of creating the conditions leading to a better future.

Government of Quebec

Appendix B

Extracts From *Mastering our Future*, by the Quebec Liberal Party's Policy Commission (February 1985)

Intergovernmental relations in a federal system are always inseparably linked with the task of governing, for one simple reason. As the governing 'tools' are shared by two separate levels of government, each with its own sphere of jurisdiction, as a rule the overall objectives can be achieved only if the two partners agree to share their efforts and resources. In other words, there is no substitute for intergovernnental cooperation and coordination.

This is true in a great many areas, especially those involving the economy such as taxation, manpower, research and development, energy, interprovincial trade and natural resources. This is why the Parti Québécois practice of boycotting federal-provincial meetings is such a futile attitude, detrimental as it is to Quebec's interests.

Nevertheless, we must keep in mind that at times Quebec must wage a vigorous defence of its interests within the federal system, and assert the autonomy of the National Assembly in the face of over-zealous intrusions by the central government. Yet we must rise above simply defensive reactions, and reject the idea that Canada is nothing more than a fruit to be squeezed dry.

In a federal system, it is essential for each partner to contribute towards the common good before claiming specific benefits for itself. It would be easy to show that, in the past, Quebec succeeded in asserting its views in a number of key areas: the division of tax powers; the equalization formula; the creation of cost-sharing programs and the opting-out formula applying to their financing; provincial adjustments to family allowance payments; the Quebec Pension Plan, etc.

Mastering Our Future   75

Whenever Quebec succeeded in asserting its views, it was invariably the result of clearly-set and realistic objectives, of well-documented dossiers, and of being able to convince its Canadian partners that its proposals had merit. In short, Quebec was able to affirm its leadership on the Canadian intergovernmental scene by adopting a pragmatic and positive approach in intergovernmental relations. That was the approach used successfully by the Liberal governments of Jean Lesage and Robert Bourassa, an approach which will be restored to a place of honour without delay by the next Liberal government.

We also intend to revive interprovincial relations, which have been sadly neglected in recent years. There is no intention on our part of urging the provinces to form a common front against the central government, but we seek rather to find practical solutions to the concrete problems we share.

Two projects of prime importance can serve as testing-grounds for this new form of cooperation: the strengthening of our economic union and the creation of interprovincial norms in higher education. The Quebec Liberal Party has already made its views known on the first point, in a brief it presented to the Royal Commission on the Economic Union in February 1984. We suggested an interprovincial code of ethics to prevent discriminatory practices by the provinces in such matters as interprovincial trade and the mobility of businesses, services and capital.

As for the second point, we believe that a specialized interprovincial organization in the education field, such as the Council of Education Ministers, should be entrusted with the mandate of drawing up interprovincial standards for higher education, and of enforcing them. Both of these are fields in which the provinces must assert their jurisdiction and, at the same time, demonstrate their ability to work towards common goals and coordinate their action.

It will undoubtedly be necessary to create some form of permanent organization for concerted federal-provincial dialogue and action. Such a forum would improve the efficiency of government action in numerous fields, particularly those of economic development and job creation. That is one of the two principal objectives sought by the Beige Paper in its proposal to transform the Senate into a Federal Council. [*Editor's note: The official name of the 'Beige Paper' (January 1980) was A New Canadian Federation.* In it were expounded, in detail, the Quebec Liberal Party's constitutional proposals in the pre-Referendum period.] The other is to place certain limits on the central government's overriding powers, especially the spending and emergency powers.

Although this proposal still retains its original merit, the recent idea of Canada's new Prime Minister that First Ministers' conferences could be made institutional, might prove an interesting substitute. Naturally, the concept would have to be explored in greater detail.

Conditions for Accepting the New Constitution

Nothing less than Quebec's dignity is at stake in future constitutional discussions. The Quebec Liberal Party intends to negotiate a constitutional agreement which will restore Quebec to its proper place in the Canadian federation. These negotiations will be based on three main objectives:

- write into the Canadian Constitution an explicit recognition of Quebec as a distinct society, homeland of the francophone element of Canada's duality;
- obtain solid guarantees for Quebec's cultural security;
- preserve Quebec's existing powers, while restoring its ability to influence the future evolution of the Canadian federation.

Explicit Recognition of Quebec as a Distinct Society

It is high time that Quebec be given explicit constitutional recognition as a distinct society, with its own language, culture, history, institutions and way of life. Without this recognition, and the accompanying political rights and responsibilities, it will always be difficult to agree on the numerous questions involving Quebec's place in Canada. This recognition should be formally expressed in a preamble of the new Constitution.

Guarantees for Quebec's Cultural Security

Population growth and demography, both within the province and in Canada as a whole, are questions of paramount importance for French-speaking Quebec's cultural security. Inside the provinces, Quebecers want to be assured that the demographic balance will be maintained in such a way that Quebec's unique French character will be permanently preserved. At the same time, they are anxious to maintain their present percentage share of the overall Canadian population, a crucial factor of their political influence within the federation.

Fears about Quebec's internal demographic balance are hardly justified in the foreseeable future, at least as far as the French-speaking majority is concerned. But the same cannot be said about the external balance, since current trends point to a slow but inexorable decrease in Quebec's share of the overall Canadian population.

In a developed society such as ours in Quebec, migratory movements determine demographic growth even more than birth rates. Such movements depend in large measure on the state of the economy and, conversely, economic growth depends on them. That is why Quebec must have the tools it needs to influence the patterns of migratory movements – international immigration, in particular – so that it can establish a true population policy. It is not only a question of internal and external population balance, or of cultural security. It is also a question of building our economic growth and the future of our society on sound demographic foundations.

Jurisdiction over immigration is now shared between the provinces and the central government, which has the final authority. But for some years now, Quebec has had an important say in selecting immigrants who want to settle here. A federal-provincial administrative agreement was worked out in this area of key importance for the future of Quebec.

Thanks to this agreement, Quebec is now better able to preserve its current linguistic balance and to counterbalance, or even reverse, the demographic trends which seem to indicate a gradual reduction of Quebec's relative importance within Canada. A Liberal government will go even further in this direction to safeguard Quebec's future. We will seek the constitutional right to have an equal say with Ottawa as regards the selection and the number of immigrants settling in Quebec each year. Solidly based on the principle of Canadian duality, these constitutional guarantees will make it possible for us to define a real and workable general policy for population and immigration, and better ensure Quebec's cultural security whilst however maintaining our tradition of openness and welcome towards refugees.

Preserving and Reinforcing Quebec's Powers

This involves three matters which must be seriously studied: appointments of judges to the Supreme Court, the federal spending power and the constitutional amending formula.

APPOINTMENT OF JUDGES TO THE SUPREME COURT There are several still unresolved aspects to the issue of the Supreme Court. The Constitution contains no specific clauses regarding its status, composition, jurisdiction, or the procedure by which its members are to be appointed. The Constitution Act, 1982 did, however, establish that these subject are, in principle, subject to the normal amending procedure, with the exception of the composition of the Bench, which falls under the rule of unanimity.

While the Quebec Liberal Party remains by and large firmly committed to the proposals for reform of the Supreme Court contained in the Beige Paper, we are aware of the difficulty of introducing the entire complex package into the shorter-term negotiations on the conditions for Quebec's acceptance of the present Constitution. One preliminary step to reform is considered essential, however, and that is the recognition of Quebec's responsibilities with respect to selection of members of the Bench. Therefore we shall request that our Canadian co-signatories acknowledge the principle of Quebec's right to participate in the selection of judges from Quebec – presently three in number – to sit on the Supreme Court.

LIMITING THE FEDERAL SPENDING POWER Under existing legal interpretation, Canada's central government has the power to make direct payments to individuals, institutions and to provinces, relative to matters within provincial jurisdiction. Although the extent of this power has never been defined by the courts, it has proved extremely useful in developing the present system of equalization payments. This latter aspect was actually enshrined in the Constitution Act of 1982. This power has been of equally great use in establishing provincial programs for health and social services, social assistance and post-secondary education. On the other hand, it has become a source of discord every time the federal government uses it as a lever to impose relatively rigid conditions on the provinces, especially Quebec, regarding the use of transfer payments.

By its nature, the federal spending power for specific provincial purposes is a 'fluid' power with an unpredictable evolutionary pattern. However, experience has proven that it can bring about substantial changes in the actual division of responsibilities between the two levels of government. Therefore, we continue to believe that for the use of the federal spending power to conform to the spirit of true federalism, it would have to be exercised within the framework of a permanent federal-provincial institution such as the Federal Council proposed in the Beige Paper, or of institutionalized First Ministers' meetings.

Meanwhile, however, two preliminary steps must be taken in order to clarify, in the Constitution itself, both the scope of the spending power and control over its expansion. Firstly, we will request that the creation of new federal programs involving conditional subsidies to the provinces be submitted for the latters' approval, such approval to be sanctioned through a procedure similar to the constitutional amending formula. Secondly, we will require that the Constitution more clearly define the nature of the conditions that can be imposed on the provinces regarding shared-cost programs. In order to be acceptable, these conditions should cover only the broad norms to be respected by the provinces as regards the programs they set up. In no way should they prescribe regulations relative to the administration of such programs.

These steps would leave intact the federal spending power in the case of equalization payments and any other form of unconditional transfers. At the same time, Quebec would be protected adequately against any new exercise of the federal spending power deemed to be unacceptable, as well as against difficulties of the kind encountered lately regarding the financing of health programs under The Canada Health Act (Bill C-3).

THE AMENDING FORMULA   By signing the 'group of eight' agreement on 16 April 1981, the Péquiste Government threw away Quebec's historic opportunity of enshrining into the Constitution the right to a political veto which it had successfully exercised twice in the past. It was first used in 1965 by the Lesage government during discussions on the Fulton-Favreau Formula, and again by the Bourassa Government following the Victoria Conference, in 1971. Formal recognition of its right of veto would have made it possible for Quebec to oppose any constitutional amendment which it deemed contrary to its interests – not only regarding the division of powers, but also concerning federal institutions or any other constitutional question.

And what did Quebec actually receive in exchange for the Péquiste renunciation of its veto power? Along with all the other provinces, Quebec obtained the consolation prize of an opting-out formula: in the event that provincial jurisdiction should be transferred to Ottawa – a decision to this effect must be made on the strength of a vote of two-thirds of the provinces representing at least 50 per cent of Canada's population – the dissenting provinces have the right to opt out and retain the particular powers involved. In return, they receive full financial compensation from the central government.

The renunciation by the Parti Québécois government of a universal veto power in exchange for the opting-out formula proved a dramatic setback for Quebec, which is now left with very limited means to prevent centralizing measures which might occur in the future. Quebec thus became a province like all the others, with no explicit recognition of the distinct nature of its society. At best, it obtained the very imperfect guarantee that the powers exercised by its Parliament and government since 1867 will be preserved.

Sadly, the Quebec government carried its blundering and recklessness even further. Devoid of any strategy for defending our rights and interests within the federal system, it neglected to demand a specific right of veto in crucial areas where the opting-out formula obviously does not apply: namely, the powers of the Senate, the principle of proportional representation in the House of Commons, the role and powers of the Supreme Court, the creation of new provinces, and the addition of new territories to existing provinces. Worse still, the PQ government agreed that these matters were to be decided according to the rule of a vote of two-thirds of the provinces representing at least 50 per cent of Canada's population, thus conceding that, on such matters of crucial importance to us, Quebec's future can be decided by a majority from which we might be excluded.

The PQ government thus took the ultimate gamble on an opting-out formula which was deficient from the start, since it applied only to half of the constitutional field. Furthermore, at the crucial juncture in the negotiations, it was unable to mobilize the support of its allies to preserve the indispensable element of the opting-out formula: financial compensation. It was only at the very last minute, and then only because of pressures exerted by the Quebec Liberal Party and the Official Opposition in the House of Commons, that the principle of financial compensation was reinstated but, unfortunately, only for matters involving education and culture.

It will not be easy to regain the lost ground. Indeed, the new Constitution provides that any changes to the amending formula requires unanimous consent. This means that, to amend it, it will become necessary to convince the new federal government, as well as the nine other provincial governments. Only a truly federalist government of Quebec acting without ulterior motives will have the necessary credibility to achieve this, especially since changes to the amending formula are far from superficial.

A Liberal government will spare no effort in bringing about changes that will allow Quebec not only to retain its existing powers, but also play a key role in the evolution of the Canadian federation. These two aspects of the equation are inseparable in our view: protection of Quebec's powers and participation in Canada's future. They must be fully respected in any amending formula.

Two approaches are worth exploring when seeking an amending formula acceptable to Quebec. The first, in the spirit of the present opting-out formula, would be to extend the principle of financial compensation to all matters involving the sharing of jurisdictions, and to include a formal right of veto on matters listed in Section 42(1) of the Constitution Act, 1982 (representation in the House of Commons, Senate, Supreme Court, creation of new provinces and addition of new territories to existing provinces.)

The opting-out formula as it applies to the transfer of provincial powers to Ottawa is an arrangement under which the province can opt to retain only the powers in question. It is false to claim that making the system of financial compensation general would lead to unbridled decentralization and the balkanization of Canada. Quite the opposite, in fact. For Quebec in particular, it would offer a minimal measure of protection ensuring that the 1867 agreement on the sharing of powers would continue to apply for as long as we would want it to. A veto on the matters listed in Section 42(1) is needed so that Quebec can play its full role in maintaining the principle of Canadian duality.

The second approach to be considered is that of a universal Quebec veto on all matters of a constitutional nature, including the sharing of powers. In fact, this would mean the constitutional recognition of a right which Quebec has exercised in the past. Through this formula Quebec would be expressly recognized as a major partner in the federation, thus reflecting the duality of Canada in a much fairer manner. It would also protect Quebec adequately against any undesirable changes in its rights and powers, while restoring to the province an effective means of participating in the overall evolution of Canadian federalism. In practice, this veto would apply to any question of a constitutional nature, including the Charter of Rights and Freedoms.

Taking everything into consideration, the second approach offers the most advantage. It is a much better reflection of Quebec's history, and corresponds more closely to our vision of federalism. That is why a government run by the Quebec Liberal Party intends to ask its Canadian partners to enshrine into the new Constitution the veto power which had been offered to Quebec prior to 1982.

The following are the main conditions which would enable a Liberal government to seriously consider Quebec's acceptance of the Constitutional agreement of 1981: a preamble recognizing Quebec as a distinct society; a constitutional right in the matter of immigration; a stipulation providing for Quebec's participation in the appointment of judges to the Supreme Court; limitation on the federal spending power; and a full veto for Quebec, written into the amending formula.

3 Newfoundland: Resisting Dependency

Bruce G. Pollard

Introduction

In 1984, there was a dramatic shift in the approach of the Newfoundland government towards the federal government. During the Trudeau years, Newfoundland had adopted a hardline and abrasive approach to federal-provincial relations. Interaction during the early part of the 1980s was generally marked by suspicion, distrust and a lack of communication. Relations were cold and acrimonious.

The election of a federal Progressive Conservative government under Brian Mulroney on 4 September 1984, had a major impact on Newfoundland-Ottawa relations. The tone of Newfoundland's interaction with the federal government underwent a remarkable change, as the provincial government adopted a very conciliatory attitude. Premier Brian Peckford now speaks of a 'new atmosphere of federal/provincial co-operation.'[1]

Newfoundland's shift in approach to the federal government reflects the extent of its dependence on the central government. In Canada, inter-governmental relations are an integral part of most policy formulation. There are few areas where a government can act without coming into contact with the activities of another government. However, because of various historical, natural and economic factors, Newfoundland is perhaps the most constrained of all governments in Canada in its ability to implement policy autonomously.

Newfoundland is heavily reliant on federal government transfer payments, thereby making its economy more susceptible than other provincial economies to shifts in federal policy. Much of the resource base exploited by Newfoundlanders is not fully under the control of the provincial government. While all provinces own the resources on crown lands, much of New-foundland's resource base is offshore and, by court decision (1984) is under federal ownership. Second, the bulk of the province's hydro resource is located in Labrador. Therefore, for this power to be exported, it must be transmitted through another province (Quebec). As such, Newfoundland does not have the clear control over its hydro resources that most other provinces do. Jurisdiction over a third major sector of the Newfoundland economy – the fishery – lies with the federal government, though Newfoundland does have constitutional authority over processing operations. In sum, the provincial government does not exercise full control over the resources which are of critical importance to the Newfoundland economy. Intergovernmental relations, and especially relations with the federal government, are critical to policy-making in Newfoundland.

Federal action has tended to dictate Newfoundland's approach. When the federal government has appeared intransigent towards the province, adopting a centralist position, the Newfoundland government has tended to be defiant and to blame Ottawa for its economic woes. Newfoundland does not carry much political weight on the national scene. Hence, if the federal government is uncooperative, Newfoundland can only try to assert its constitutional powers – which it unsuccessfully did in the last years of the Trudeau era.

Newfoundland's response to the Trudeau regime may have been the politics of desperation and powerlessness: a natural reaction to the so-called 'new federalism' tendencies which the Trudeau government had exhibited since 1980. Newfoundland was particularly vulnerable to this approach, which was marked by unilateral action, cutbacks, little consultation among governments, and an emphasis on programs delivered directly rather than jointly. Federal cutbacks in transfer payments and in funds for regional development programs had hurt Newfoundland. Federal fisheries policy had a major impact on Newfoundland because it was the main industry in the province. In fact, a federal-provincial agreement on restructuring the fishing sector took place only after the federal government had threatened unilateral action.

Newfoundland's desire for at least an equal share in the control of off-shore resources collided with a stubborn federal government that feared being 'blackmailed' by a determined provincial government. That had happened in 1981 when the Alberta government cut oil production in reaction to the federal government's energy policy, thereby reinforcing the premise underlying Pierre Trudeau's new federalism, that the provinces had become too powerful. This may, at least partly, explain the Trudeau government's intransigent position on management of the offshore resources. The adversarial nature of federal-Newfoundland relations was also heightened by the personalities of the two main actors – Pierre Trudeau and Brian Peckford – which consistently clashed.

With Mr. Trudeau's departure, Newfoundland's approach changed drastically. It has responded to Mr. Mulroney's overtures for cooperation.

Newfoundland has everything to gain from being cooperative with a sympathetic government in Ottawa.

Policies of the Newfoundland government in virtually all sectors have been geared towards the development of a strong economic base, which it now conspicuously lacks. The government regards its poor performance to be due, at least partly, to its dependence on others: therefore, it needs greater control and management over its own resources.

There is a cultural element here, as well. Newfoundlanders feel themselves to be distinct from other Canadians and even from those who reside in the other Atlantic provinces. They feel their history, their culture, their social fabric, and even the nature of their economy is unique. Moreover, they believe their distinctiveness is neither appreciated nor understood in the rest of Canada, including the national capital. The Newfoundland government argues that its interests are too often in conflict with or irrelevant to those of central Canada, such that they are ignored in federal policy-making. Hence, it objects to external control over the major decisions affecting it.

It has often been suggested that poorer provinces in Canada tend to be centralists. They are the most dependent on the goodwill of the federal government for equalization payments, contributions to regional development programs, and other federal policies. This view has been implicitly held by Newfoundland's maritime neighbours: Prince Edward Island, New Brunswick and Nova Scotia.

Newfoundland, however, bucks this trend. While unquestionably a poor province, Newfoundland's stance is more akin to the historical positions of Quebec, Alberta, and to some extent, Saskatchewan. Quebec's appeal for greater decentralization is based on its historic desire for autonomy in social and cultural policy as well as in economic affairs. Alberta's stance is rooted in the desire to manage and control its natural resource wealth, in order to diversify its resource economy. Similarly, in the 1970s, Saskatchewan saw resources as a means to rise above its 'have not' status, and to diversify its economy. The Newfoundland government shares this objective, seeing greater provincial control to be essential if it is to extricate itself from its position of economic dependence and deprivation.

For Newfoundland, as for several of the other provincial governments, this is an entirely acceptable view of the federation. Diversity is an integral part of that perspective. In granting to the provinces control and ownership over natural resources, the Constitution Act, 1867 enabled them to have a certain measure of control over the basic building blocks of their economy.[2] It provided for the primary production and development so critical to the existence of many Newfoundland communities to be guided by the order of government closest to the activity. This view is consistent with a 'provincialist' approach to Canadian federalism, an affirmation of a major role in policy decisions for provincial governments because they are perceived to be better able to understand the needs of the people and the implications of policy decisions.

While acknowledging an important role for the federal government in defending the national interest, Newfoundland's version of 'balanced federalism' means greater provincial control over those powers most important to provincial economies. As such, Newfoundland's battles are not unlike those that have been waged by other provinces. Bruce Phillips of CTV's Question Period suggests that the offshore and hydro issues in Newfoundland are, in a sense, 'a reflection of many of the problems affecting the whole state of Confederation and the relationship between the central and provincial governments.'[3]

The position of the Newfoundland government appears to be ambivalent. On one hand, it is asking to be treated in a fashion similar to the way other provinces have historically been treated. On the other, it is asking that federal policy-makers recognize and make special provision for its unique situation. In a federal state, both goals in this seeming contradiction may be legitimate.

With respect to the first, Newfoundland claims that it has been treated differently from other provinces, and that its poor economic position is partly due to the federal government discriminating against Newfoundland. As far as the provincial government is concerned, much of what it has been seeking is no different from what has been granted to other provinces at various points in their development: 'the same right to the use of [its] resources – whether hydro, oil or fish – as other provinces enjoy.'[4]

Yet, implicit in the Newfoundland perspective is the belief that it should be treated differently. Clearly, Newfoundland feels its poor economic status in relation to the other provinces demands some special attention. Moreover, its uniqueness should be recognized in the way in which the federal government deals with and in the way other Canadians perceive the province.

These broad objectives underlie Newfoundland's goals in most policy sectors. This chapter will examine four of the key sectors in the Newfoundland economy: fisheries, offshore oil, hydro-electricity, and regional development. Issues in these sectors have tended to dominate the intergovernmental agenda. The chapter will begin, however, with a quick look at the province's economy.

The Newfoundland Economy

An examination of three dimensions of the Newfoundland economy can aid in better understanding the principles guiding the policy objectives of the provincial government. First, various economic indicators, such as rate of unemployment and gross domestic product per capita show that the economy is in poor health relative to the rest of Canada. Second, an examination of economic activity reveals the extent to which the Newfoundland economy is dependent on natural resources. Third, a breakdown of provincial government income reveals the extent to which Newfoundland relies on federal government transfer payments.

Bruce G. Pollard

Table 3.1 lists some of the key indicators of the Newfoundland economy; these were included in the provincial government's submission to the Royal Commission on the Economic Union and Development Prospects for Canada in 1983.

Table 3.1
Economic Indicators

		Newfoundland	Canada	Newfoundland as a % of Canadian average
personal income/capita	1981	7,549	11,810	63.9
earned income/capita	1981	5,486	10,365	52.9
GDP (GNP)/capita	1981	7,354	13,929	52.8
avg earnings/family	1980	20,971	26,748	78.0
unemployment	1982	16.9%	11.0%	

Source: Statistics Canada, Newfoundland Statistics Agency, Census of Canada. Reported in *Submission of the Government of Newfoundland and Labrador to the Royal Commission on the Economic Union and Development Prospects for Canada*, September 1983.

On nearly every indicator of economic well-being, Newfoundland trails all other provinces in Canada. Moreover, most statistics show that Newfoundland is far below the Canadian average. For example, its earned income per capita is only 52.9 per cent of the national average. Premier Peckford has often pointed out that this figure is barely an improvement over the pre-confederation state of the Newfoundland economy when, in 1949, Newfoundland's per capita earned income was 47 per cent of the Canadian average.

With respect to the Newfoundland economy's dependence on resources, 9.2 per cent of Newfoundland's labour force is in primary resource development (that is, fishing, trapping, mines, quarries, oil wells, forestry), as opposed to 2.8 per cent for Canada as a whole.[5] This statistic hides the fact that the social fabric of the province is such that numerous communities throughout the province are almost entirely dependent on the resource industries. In addition, many Newfoundland communities are dependent on 'primary manufacturing' industries, such as fish processing, which are directly related to the resource sector.

A third dimension concerns the extent to which the Newfoundland government relies on federal funds. Almost half of the provincial government's total current revenue is from the federal government (49 per cent, or 921 million dollars for 1984-85). The sources of the federal contribution are outlined in Table 3.2.

Table 3.2
Source of Federal Contribution to Newfoundland Government 1984-85

Equalization payments	60.0%
Established Programs Financing grant	24.1%
Canada Assistance Plan	7.8%
Other	8.1%

Source: Government of Newfoundland and Labrador. *1985 Budget*, p. VI.

The situation in Newfoundland demonstrates that regional disparity, described at times as a threat to Canadian unity, persists and that the policies of recent decades have done little to alleviate it. This examination of the Newfoundland economic situation raises the question of whether the provincial government even under the best of circumstances would be capable of correcting the imbalances which have put the province in such a disadvantaged position.

The principal objective of the Newfoundland government in recent years has been to overcome this disadvantage. This goal has permeated virtually all of Newfoundland's interaction with other governments. The Newfoundland government has argued that control over its own resources and over their development is the key to the realization of this goal. It may still be, however, that the province lacks the economic base, – the 'development potential' – to support, and fully employ, the Newfoundland population. As the developments in four key sectors – fisheries, offshore oil, hydro-electricty, and regional development – are examined, this issue will never be far beneath the surface.

The Fishery

The fishery sector is the single largest employer in Newfoundland, and numerous small communities are dependent on the industry for their survival. However, most aspects of the industry, including harvesting, are under federal jurisdiction; provincial jurisdiction is limited to on-shore fish processing.

Newfoundland believes that it has not controlled the fishery since 1934; since that time the fishery has been in disarray: stock depletion, incursions of foreign fleets; erosion of world markets because of quality and price problems, and serious financial problems have plagued all major firms.[6] The province considers itself powerless to intervene effectively because the levers of power controlling the fishery are not in its hands.

The provincial government has argued that it ought to have more control over the management of the fishery because it is 'closer to the people' and and more sensitive to the implications of policy and the needs of local communities. Since the extension of the offshore 'economic zone' to 200 miles in 1977, the Newfoundland government has argued for greater control over fisheries management to ensure that its coastal communities receive the primary benefit from resources adjacent to the province.

Bruce G. Pollard

Newfoundland believes that it should control the resources upon which it depends. The provincial government argues that it is the only province where the major industry, in terms of employment, is beyond its control. This argument is debatable. The provincial government of Ontario, for example, does not 'control' the key policy levers affecting the manufacturing or services sectors, which are the major employers in that province. It can be argued, however, that Ontario, because of its population size, has substantial political weight at the national level, thereby ensuring that its views will influence the formulation of national policy. Newfoundland lacks this weight. This debate raises an interesting normative question: Should every province control its most important industries?

There exists a precedent for provinces having greater control over the fishing industry, although this is not the basis of the Newfoundland argument. In 1922, the federal government devolved to the Quebec government responsibility for the fishery in that province. However, in 1983, on the recommendation of a federal task force, power over the fishery in Quebec was reassumed by the federal government.[7] The rationale was the need for an integrated and coherent policy for the entire Atlantic fishery.

Newfoundland has not argued for a complete devolution of powers, as took place in Quebec in 1922. Rather, it is seeking some sort of joint management. It wants some input into federal decisions affecting this industry which is central to Nefoundland society. The provincial government sees concurrent jurisdiction over fisheries as a reasonable objective. This option was endorsed by eight other provinces at the 1980 constitutional talks, although Nova Scotia later withdrew its support. Newfoundland appears to have conceded, however, that a constitutional amendment to change the jurisdiction over fisheries is a long-term rather than an immediate objective.[8] In the short term, the Newfoundland government seeks more consultation concerning federal policy over the fishery. It argues that the national policies have often conflicted with provincial objectives. For example, a federal government decision in November 1984 to allocate to the Soviet Union an additional 17,000 tons of caplin was said to hurt Newfoundland interests. According to Premier Peckford, this denied Newfoundland fishermen access to a resource they needed:

This agreement demonstrates both in form and substances how important it is that this province have a real say in the management of its resources. If thousands of tons of fish can be traded off without any regard for provincial objectives and without concern for the needs of our people, it follows that the same kind of decisions will be made if we do not get a 'real say' in the management of the offshore.[9]

An important development in the Newfoundland fishery took place in 1983. A federal task force, headed by Michael Kirby, had been established in 1982 to recommend a long-term strategy for the Atlantic fishery. The task force's report, *Navigating Troubled Waters*, was released in February 1983. At that time, Mr. Kirby stated that substantial restructuring of the major fish processing firms in both Newfoundland and Nova Scotia would be required. (Three of the largest firms in these provinces had applied to the federal government for financial aid.)

Negotiations commenced between representatives of the Newfoundland and federal governments, but were broken off in June 1983. The federal government, blaming the Newfoundland government for ending the talks, announced on 4 July a plan to restructure unilaterally the province's fishery. The plan called for the creation of one large fish processing company, built on the assets of three financially-troubled Newfoundland firms. This endeavour was to be financed by the federal government and the Bank of Nova Scotia. The federal proposal was widely opposed in Newfoundland.

The fishery was in dire economic straits during the summer of 1983. Many trawlers sat idle and several plants were closed. All major companies in the province were on the brink of receivership. In this situation, and in the shadow of the federal government's unilateral proposal, the provincial government returned to the bargaining table in August for a series of secret negotiations with the federal government. Power tactics by the federal government, public pressure, and economic conditions were all factors in forcing the Newfoundland government to reach some sort of agreement. That was accomplished on 26 September 1983. The new plan was better than the 4 July proposal if for no other reason than the province was party to it.

The agreement was similar to the federal plan. Three financially-troubled companies were restructured, leading to the creation of one giant fish processing company, later named 'Fishery Products International'. Although this is the largest company in Newfoundland, there remain numerous small and medium-sized independent operations. The 'super company' was created largely with funds from the federal and provincial governments, and the Bank of Nova Scotia. Federal Fisheries Minister Pierre DeBané hailed the agreement as 'the most important bilateral agreement signed since Newfoundland joined Canada in 1949'.[10] (A similar agreement was reached among the Federal and Nova Scotia governments and the banks to bail out and stabilize the largest company in Nova Scotia.)

Newfoundland had won some concessions from the federal government. All fish processing plants were given the opportunity to operate, at least temporarily, in an attempt to prove their viability. This was an important change from the original federal plan, which had left the fate of all plants to the management of the new company, implying that certain of the unprofitable plants would be closed.

The Newfoundland government boasted that, for the first time since 1934, it had a major say in the fishery, including a veto over major decisions that would affect the province. Any plant closures, mergers, increases in mechanization, or trawler transfers which resulted in a permanent change in employment for more than 100 people, or for half the work force in a single plant location, would be subject to the approval of both governments.

Bruce G. Pollard

Clearly, though, the victory was incomplete. Despite its claim to having 'a significant presence on the Board of Directors' of the restructured company, the province held a minority position. Five of the 11 members were appointed by the federal government and only three by the province. This largely reflected shareholder equity. Whereas the federal government put up 75 million dollars in direct equity capital, the Newfoundland government converted 30 million dollars of loan guarantees to equity as its contribution. (The Bank of Nova Scotia also converted 44 million dollars.)

Despite the optimism of politicians at both levels of government in September of 1983, the Newfoundland fishery remains in serious difficulty – more the result of world economic conditions than federal policy. International demand for Canadian fish has decreased partly because Canadian fish exports have become more expensive in countries, especially in Europe, that have devalued their currencies in the past two years, and because these countries have gained a competitive edge in exporting fish to the United States, Canada's primary market.

Offshore Oil and the Atlantic Accord

Of all the fronts on which Newfoundland has been engaged in battle, the offshore is the most important. Premier Peckford has stated on several occasions that the only real hope for Newfoundland to shed its 'have not' status lies in the province being able to reap the benefits from the mineral and hydrocarbon resources off its shores. As far as the Newfoundland government is concerned, offshore oil production will enable Newfoundland to overcome its economic disadvantage within Canada only if the development is carried out with regard for ensuring maximum benefit to the province's economic development.[11] The only way this can come about is if the provincial government has an equal say in the management of offshore oil and if the funds from the oil are divided between the governments 'as if it were on land'.

On 11 February 1985, Prime Minister Brian Mulroney and Premier Brian Peckford signed the 'Atlantic Accord'. It was a very significant moment in the rather turbulent history of federal-provincial relations with respect to offshore mineral resources. That history has been dominated by confrontation between the Governments of Newfoundland and Canada. The conflict has alternated between attempts at reaching a negotiated settlement and courtroom battles over ownership of the resources.

While these two routes – the political and the judicial – have been separate, developments in one have clearly affected the course of events in the other. As well, developments outside the federal-provincial arena have had important implications for the Newfoundland-Ottawa debate over offshore resources. One such external development was the signing of an accord in 1982 (and its subsequent drafting into legislation two years later) between the federal government and the Province of Nova Scotia concerning the oil and gas resources off Nova Scotia's shores. That provincial government chose to reach a political agreement with the Trudeau government rather than fight the issue of ownership in the courts. A second crucial development was the election of the Mulroney government in September 1984. The following summary briefly looks at developments since 1982 – but focuses on events in 1984 and 1985 – which led to the signing of the Atlantic Accord.

Negotiations were under way in late 1981 and early 1982 between federal Minister of Energy Marc Lalonde and Newfoundland Energy Minister William Marshall when a labour relations issue came before a Federal Court. That case dealt with which union would represent the workers offshore and, therefore, had implications for which government had jurisdiction over labour relations in the offshore region. The federal government, however, requested the Court to widen the question to include the whole question of ownership of the offshore minerals. This posed a tactical problem for Newfoundland. If the Court accepted the federal request, the case would go directly from the Federal Court to the Supreme Court of Canada; hence the Newfoundland Supreme Court would not get a chance to rule on the issue. Uncertain as to how the Federal Court would react to the federal request, the Newfoundland government immediately referred the ownership question to the Supreme Court of Newfoundland. Brian Peckford later told a national television audience:

We were forced into court by the federal government ... We thought the risks were too great that the Federal Court would rule upon the jurisdiction and ownership since they had decided to hear it, so then we referred to our Supreme Court of Newfoundland.[12]

In the end, the federal court chose not to deal with the ownership question.

Upset at the way the federal government was negotiating and at its move with respect to the Federal Court, Premier Peckford called an early election in the province in April 1982. He campaigned almost solely on the question of Newfoundland's position on the offshore. His party was returned to power with an even greater mandate (61.2 per cent of the popular vote) than it had received in the election of 1979.

Just prior to the Newfoundland provincial election, the federal government and the Government of Nova Scotia signed an agreement concerning the management of the offshore resources off Nova Scotia's shoreline. Although the agreement was signed on 2 March 1982, it was not given legislative effect until over two years later. Mirror legislation was introduced in the House of Commons and the Nova Scotia Legislature on 31 May 1984, and given royal assent 11 days later.

The Nova Scotia Deal

There were four major elements to the 1982 Nova Scotia agreement. The central purpose of the agreement was to provide for the management and revenue-sharing of Nova Scotia's offshore resources. Federal ownership of these resources was not questioned. Following is a summary of the key elements of the accord.

MANAGEMENT   A Canada-Nova Scotia Offshore Oil and Gas Board for managing petroleum activity in the offshore Nova Scotia area will be created. Three of the five members on the board, including the chairman, will be federal employees and two will be provincial representatives. Both the federal and the Nova Scotia Ministers of Energy will delegate extensive powers to the Board. Retained powers will be allocated geographically between the two ministers.

REVENUE SHARING   The province will receive all revenue from offshore activity (with the exception of the federal corporate income tax) until its per capita fiscal capacity reaches 110 per cent of the national average.

'BACK-IN PROVISION'   One of the elements of the federal National Energy Program was a 'carried interest' or 'back-in' provision, whereby the Crown could claim 25 per cent of an oil or natural gas field where production has already begun. The agreement gave Nova Scotia the right to purchase up to 50 per cent of any Crown share in a natural gas field and 25 per cent in an oil field.

EQUALIZATION OFFSET PAYMENTS   There is a provision to protect the province for up to ten years from the full effects of reductions in equalization payments as it gains revenue from the offshore resources. The 1982 agreement did not specify any formula, but when the legislation giving it effect was tabled in 1984, a complex formula provided for equalization payments not to be reduced by more than 10 per cent in any year from the payment of the previous year.

It has been suggested that one reason why Nova Scotia quickly reached a political settlement with the federal government is that it wished to be the 'centre' of the offshore activity in the Atlantic region. Nova Scotia was eager to be the first off the mark in attracting investment capital related to industries which would prosper as a result of offshore development. Furthermore, the Newfoundland government suspected that the federal government, in signing the Nova Scotia accord, was putting pressure on Newfoundland to sign a similar accord. This suspicion was substantiated in that the federal-Nova Scotia accord included a 'most favoured province' clause, so that, in the event of a better agreement being reached with another province, Nova Scotia could receive the same terms as in that agreement.

In the fall of 1982, Marc Lalonde was replaced by Jean Chrétien as federal minister of energy. A new effort was made to reach a negotiated settlement with the Government of Newfoundland. In renewed talks with William Marshall, Mr. Chrétien insisted that discussions include nothing in writing. An agreement-in-principle seemed imminent in January 1983. However, Newfoundland claimed that the written proposal which the federal government drafted was significantly different from what had been agreed upon during the negotiations. Talks broke off. Until the Supreme Court decision came down over a year later, the offshore issue was, for the most part, fought in the judicial arena.

The case was argued in the Newfoundland Supreme Court in 1982, and a decision was handed down in favour of the federal government in 1983. That was appealed and the case subsequently put before the Supreme Court. The Court heard the appeal in February 1983.

The Supreme Court of Canada Case

Although the case in question dealt specifically with the Hibernia oil field, it was not suggested that the legal issues were any different with respect to Hibernia than with respect to any other portion of the continental shelf off Newfoundland. The Court was asked to decide two questions:

- ☐ Does Canada or Newfoundland have the right to explore and exploit off-shore mineral and other natural resources; and
- ☐ Does Canada or Newfoundland have the legislative jurisdiction to make laws in relation to the exploration and exploitation of the said minerals and other natural resources?

In the *Reference Re Offshore Mineral Rights of British Columbia, 1967* case, the Supreme Court had been asked questions almost identical to those in the Newfoundland reference. In the British Columbia case, the Court unanimously answered in favour of Canada. Newfoundland's principal argument in the present case was that its historical and constitutional position distinguished its situation from that of British Columbia.

The Newfoundland government attempted to show that it entered confederation upon a different footing than did other provinces and this allowed it to maintain rights it had at the time but that other provinces never possessed. Paradoxically, Newfoundland was arguing that it was different from the other provinces – and specifically from British Columbia – and that this difference justified its obtaining resource ownership rights comparable to those held by provinces with on-land resources.

In order to distinguish itself from the *1967 Offshore Reference*, Newfoundland had to succeed on three points:

- ☐ International law must have recognized the right to explore and exploit in the continental shelf prior to Newfoundland's entry into confederation on 31 March 1949.
- ☐ The Crown in right of Newfoundland must have been in a position to acquire these rights.
- ☐ The Crown in right of Newfoundland must not have lost those rights under the Terms of Union with Canada.

In its decision handed down on 8 March 1984, the Supreme Court of Canada reached the following conclusions:

- ☐ Continental shelf rights are a manifestation of external sovereignty.

☐ Canada has the right to explore and exploit in the continental shelf off Newfoundland because:
a) any continental shelf rights available at international law in 1949 would have been acquired by the Crown in right of the United Kingdom, not the Crown in right of Newfoundland;
b) even if Newfoundland had held continental shelf rights prior to Union, they would have passed to Canada by virtue of the Terms of Union.
c) in any event, international law did not recognize continental shelf rights by 1949.

Canada has legislative jurisdiction in relation to the right to explore and exploit resources in the continental shelf off Newfoundland by virtue of the 'Peace Order and Good Government' power in its residual capacity.

While the Newfoundland Supreme Court and the Supreme Court of Canada reached the same conclusion concerning ownership, their reasons were markedly different. This is important because it affects how Newfoundland's preconfederation status is perceived. Moreover, it may reinforce Newfoundlanders' belief that they are neither understood nor respected as a distinct culture by other Canadians. The ruling of the Newfoundland Supreme Court acknowledged that prior to 1949, Newfoundland was a full Dominion and had the right to ownership of the offshore resources. The Court said it was the failure of the government during that period to act so as to exercise such proprietary rights which led to Newfoundland not having ownership prior to entering confederation. (Such rights did not accrue automatically to a nation.) Nevertheless, Newfoundland's argument that it was a Dominion, and recognized as such in international law, was upheld.

In contrast, the Supreme Court of Canada decision did not accept this 'independent' status of Newfoundland prior to 1949. In fact, according to the highest court in Canada, had action been taken with respect to the offshore resources by Newfoundland before it joined Canada, the proprietary rights would have accrued to Great Britain, not Newfoundland. Although the end result of the two court decisions was the same, the Supreme Court decision weakened Newfoundland's pre-confederation status.

Following the decision from the Supreme Court of Canada, the issue shifted back to the political arena. Now, however, the federal government had the unequivocal support of a Supreme Court ruling granting it ownership over the resources. As a result, ownership was no longer an issue to be negotiated.

The Federal Liberal Offer

The federal Liberal government's position was reiterated in a statement issued by Energy Minister Jean Chrétien on 5 April 1984. The proposal was essentially unchanged from what had been offered to Newfoundland in January 1983 when talks had broken off amid acrimony and accusations of bargaining in bad faith.

The federal offer was similar to the deal that had been reached with the Nova Scotia government. Following is a summary of its essential components.

MANAGEMENT   An offshore management board with the federal government appointing the majority of members, including the chairman would be created. Jean Chrétien, in April 1984, noted that 'there would be rules that ensure that, if necessary, and because of his larger responsibilities for national energy concerns, the federal Minister could normally resolve a controversy.'[13]

REVENUE SHARING   The principles underlying revenue-sharing seem to be identical to those contained in the Nova Scotia agreement. The provincial government would receive all provincial-type taxes and the largest federal tax, the Petroleum and Gas Revenue Tax. The provincial government would not be expected to share these revenues with other Canadians until its fiscal capacity reached 110 per cent of the national average (or even slightly higher if the province's rate of unemployment remained well above the national average). The province would receive more oil revenues in the early years of development than it would if it owned the resource.

EQUALIZATION OFFSET PAYMENTS   A provision under the current formula guarantees that equalization payments will not decline more than 15 per cent in one year. (This provision exists in the federal Fiscal Arrangements Act.) This would be in force once the offshore resources began to be produced. Jean Chrétien, in his April statement, also noted that in the Nova Scotia Agreement there was a provision that guaranteed the province will receive payments to offset the reduction in their equalization payments. It was implied that similar arrangements would be available to Newfoundland.

INCENTIVE PAYMENTS   2.5 billion dollars would be paid by the federal government in Petroleum Incentive Payment (PIP) grants by 1986, and even more in federal tax incentives to oil companies working in the offshore area.

The Government of Newfoundland was unable to accept the federal proposals concerning management and revenue-sharing. The provincial representatives would hold a minority position on the board, and the province would only be able to delay, not determine, decisions on important matters.

The province also rejected the federal proposal concerning revenue sharing because it put a ceiling on how much revenue the province would receive over the long run. After attaining a certain fiscal capacity in any year, no royalities would flow to the provincial treasury. This was a key component which distinguished this proposal from treating the resources 'as if they were on land'.

Newfoundland's Response

Following the Supreme Court of Canada decision on the ownership of the offshore, there was substantial pressure on Premier Peckford to sign an agreement similar to that reached with Nova Scotia. Newfoundland's reaction to

Bruce G. Pollard

the Nova Scotia agreement (and by implication, to the federal government's offer to Newfoundland) was captured in Mr. Peckford's statement during CTV's Question Period:

We will not be any better off as a province financially if we sign the Nova Scotia deal, and we will have no say over management, and because our resource is much, much larger, both potentially and actually now, than Nova Scotia's, the impact on Newfoundland society is going to be that much larger and, therefore, we should have some say along the road in its development.[14]

Under the terms of the federal offer to Newfoundland, as well as those provided within the Nova Scotia deal, the provincial government would get virtually all of the resource revenues initially until the province's per capita fiscal capacity reached 110 per cent of the national average. A province's per capita fiscal capacity is defined as its capacity to raise revenues from taxation and from revenue-sharing agreements with the federal government. Even though Newfoundland has a per capita fiscal capacity well below the national average, the government has been able to offer a level of services which approaches that provided by other provincial governments, (although it remains below the national average). This is largely because of equalization payments, and because Newfoundland has levied higher tax rates than have other provinces.

The federal government has claimed that, under its proposal, Newfoundland would become the second richest province in the country. However, it is obvious that it will take more than simply an increase in fiscal capacity to overcome the real deficiencies in the Newfoundland economy: the nation's highest public debt, highest unemployment, weakest productivity, and poorest infrastructure.[15]

The Newfoundland government acknowledges that it has shifted its negotiating position over the years. In an effort to find a reasonable management-sharing and revenue-sharing agreement, it has moved from claiming outright provincial ownership to appealing for joint ownership to a position that completely puts ownership aside.[16] This shift is largely in response to the decisions of both the Newfoundland Supreme Court and the Supreme Court of Canada, which granted ownership to the federal government.

After the Supreme Court rendered its decision, Premier Peckford undertook a national 'tour of understanding', during which he outlined the basic principles guiding his government's position. These were as follows:

- Offshore oil is recognized as a 'national' resource.
- A management board with equal provincial and federal representation is essential in order to alleviate the economic plight of Newfoundland as well as to protect its culture and environment.
- National goals of self-sufficiency and security of supply override provincial management priorities.

☐ Available government resources should be shared from the first day the oil starts to flow, although Newfoundland would get the larger share until it dropped its 'have not' status.[17]

Newfoundland has put forward various reasons explaining why it believes it must have a real say in the management of the offshore. Foremost, the social and environmental impact of offshore development will be felt in Newfoundland.[18] Furthermore, it is Newfoundland that will feel any adverse effect on the fishing industry or other traditional industries. The cost of providing most services, such as education, health, and transportation, which result from the development of the offshore will rest with the provincial government.

Newfoundland has asserted that it needs a real say in management if decisions reached are to be sensitive to local needs and the provincial economy. This is especially important in the initial years since, at this phase, any benefits to the province will mostly be in terms of economic development rather than in terms of revenues. Management decisions will have a tremendous impact on the social fabric of the province. These are the decisions which will determine the pace and rate of development, as well as the location of economic activity.

The Other Provinces

Underlying the position of the Newfoundland government with respect to the offshore resources has been the belief that it was seeking no more than that which other provinces have historically been granted. Despite the British Columbia offshore resources decision of 1967, Newfoundland has pointed out that a precedent does exist for granting ownership of the offshore resources to the province. Oil drilled from the bed of Lake Erie, deemed to be international waters, is the property of the Province of Ontario.[19] More importantly, the provincial government has cited, as an example of the principle of provincial resource control, the 1930 constitutional amendment which transferred to the Provinces of Manitoba, Saskatchewan and Alberta, the same mineral rights enjoyed by the other provinces. As well, the political boundaries of these provinces were extended to enable them to take advantage of the natural resources contained therein. Newfoundland argues that this same principle has not been extended to Newfoundland since it joined confederation in 1949.

The position of Newfoundland on the offshore has been supported on various occasions by other provinces. In 1980, all the premiers agreed that offshore resources should be treated as if they were on land.[20] At the 1983 Supreme Court hearings on the Hibernia offshore ownership issue, the Attorneys-General from the Provinces of British Columbia, Nova Scotia, New Brunswick, Prince Edward Island, Manitoba, and Alberta intervened on behalf of the Newfoundland government.

Bruce G. Pollard

The Atlantic Accord

The Atlantic Accord, signed in February 1985, was based on a letter sent on 14 June 1984, from then Opposition Leader Brian Mulroney to Premier Peckford. According to the 18-point letter, the federal Conservative party, if it won the subsequent election, would offer to reach an agreement with Newfoundland, whereby the offshore resources would be treated essentially as if they were on land.

The federal Conservative offer was based on three principles:

- The recognition of the right of Newfoundland and Labrador to be the principal beneficiary of the wealth of oil and gas off its shores.
- The equality of both governments in the management of the resources.
- The implementation of the agreement, through mutual and parallel legislation, with amendments requiring the agreement of both governments. The federal Liberal offer had provided for the agreement to be put into legislation, but it would have been subject to change without Newfoundland's consent.[21]

While these conditions were much more acceptable to the Government of Newfoundland than those contained in the April statement of Energy Minister Jean Chrétien, they were less than that which the federal Progressive Conservative government of Joe Clark had been prepared to offer during its brief tenure in office in 1979 and 1980. Mr. Clark had acknowledged four principles which would have served as the basis for negotiations:

- The Province of Newfoundland should own the mineral resources of the continental margin off its coast. Ownership should be, to the extent possible, of the same nature as if these resources were located within the boundaries of the province.
- Such ownership of the legislative jurisdiction over offshore resources by Newfoundland would be consistent with and subject to the division of legislative competence as between Parliament and the provincial legislatures under the constitution of Canada.
- The legislative jurisdiction and responsibility of the Government of Canada in areas such as the protection of environment, national defence, customs, management of international trade and pipelines would continue.
- The above principles were to be confirmed and implemented by the signing of an agreement between Canada and Newfoundland.[22]

The question of ownership was not part of the Mulroney offer. Equal participation in management was a key principle, however, and it underlay the subsequent Atlantic Accord. However, if offshore resources were being treated exactly as if they were on land, then ownership would clearly reside with the provincial government, and joint federal-provincial management would be very unlikely.

The details of the Mulroney letter were unveiled in June 1984 on the eve of the Liberal leadership convention in Ottawa. The deal was immediately downplayed as a partisan ploy to upstage the Liberals. However, the significance of this offer, while perhaps not immediately appreciated, cannot be understated. If and when the Conservative party was elected at the federal level, the Peckford government was virtually guaranteed the major concessions for which it had been holding out with respect to the most important resource for Newfoundland.

The deal with the leader of the opposition, Brian Mulroney, was a gamble for Premier Peckford. In one sense, though, he had nothing to lose. In light of the negative court decisions, the odds of getting an agreement with the federal Liberal government which gave Newfoundland an equal partnership in management of the offshore must have been low indeed. The Mulroney offer was his best (and perhaps only) chance to snatch victory from the jaws of defeat. A Conservative party victory in the election of 4 September was all that was needed.

Brian Peckford worked hard for the federal Conservative party in the election campaign. During the two weeks before the election, he undertook a 'prosperity tour' of the province on behalf of the federal leader. Mulroney had earned the support of his Newfoundland counterpart. Peckford's political life may have been contingent on the Progressive Conservative party winning the federal election, but the gamble was probably worth taking because Brian Mulroney had demonstrated a willingness to work with the Newfoundland premier. When the results came in, the Province of Newfoundland had sent four Conservative members to the House of Commons, two more than in the previous election.

During the months following the election of the Progressive Conservative party in Ottawa, the new federal energy minister, Pat Carney, and her Newfoundland counterpart, Bill Marshall, met on several occasions to implement the elements contained in the letter of 14 June. Goodwill abounded and, on 11 February 1985, a memorandum of agreement entitled 'The Atlantic Accord' was signed by Brian Mulroney and Brian Peckford. The Accord will be implemented through mutual and parallel legislation to be introduced by both governments into the Parliament of Canada and the Legislature of Newfoundland and Labrador.

The Atlantic Accord has 68 provisions and gives effect to Brian Mulroney's letter of 14 June 1984. Following are the key elements contained in the Accord.

MANAGEMENT   The Accord provides for the creation of an Offshore Petroleum Board, composed of three representatives of each of the federal and Newfoundland governments and a mutually acceptable independent chairman. The Board will make all decisions relating to the regulation and management of petroleum-related activities in the offshore region, apart from certain specified areas of concern which will remain the exclusive purview of either

Bruce G. Pollard

of the two governments. Such items include, in the federal power, decisions pertaining to 'Canadianization policy' and the application of federal taxes, and in the provincial power, provincial-type revenues and decisions relating to the province's general legislation having effect in the offshore region, such as certain pieces of social legislation.

Certain areas of concern within the purview of the Board have been deemed areas where 'fundamental decisions' are required and, as such, are subject to the approval of the appropriate Minister. A complicated formula has been devised to determine whether the federal or the provincial Minister of Energy is responsible for approving a fundamental decision taken by the Board. In general terms, the federal minister has this responsibility until a period when national self-sufficiency and security of supply are reached, with the corollary that the provincial minister has the responsibility for approving decisions affecting the mode of development, so long as the attainment of self-sufficiency is not unreasonably delayed.

REVENUE SHARING   Principles are to be the same as those which exist between the federal government and other oil and gas producing provinces. General federal and provincial taxes will apply. Royalties will flow to the province, regardless of how much oil is produced.

EQUALIZATION OFFSET PAYMENTS   A complex formula has the effect of ensuring that once oil production has commenced, Newfoundland will receive 90 per cent of the equalization payment it received the previous year. (This is similar to the arrangements granted by the Liberal government to Nova Scotia.)

CROWN SHARE   If the 'back-in' provision were retained by the federal government, a provision in the Accord ensured that the province would receive half of any benefits which accrued.

OFFSHORE DEVELOPMENT FUND   A fund is to be established for the purpose of defraying social and economic infrastructure costs related to the development of the offshore area prior to the commencement of production. The fund will total 300 million dollars, cost-shared 75/25 between the federal and Newfoundland governments.

The Accord contains some elements which give preference to Newfoundland workers and companies. For example, one section states that the offshore area should be managed in a manner which will promote economic growth and development in order to optimize benefits accruing to Newfoundland in particular and to Canada as a whole.[23] Residents of Newfoundland are to be given first consideration for training and employment opportunities, and services and goods from Newfoundland are to be given first consideration on any work program for exploration or field development.

In a related development, the new federal government demonstrated its willingness to consult with Newfoundland on energy policy affecting the province. In the incident at hand, Mobil Oil presented in the autumn of 1984 to the Federal Environmental Assessment Review Office (FEARO), a federal agency, a feasibility and environmental impact study which had been commissioned by the previous Liberal government. FEARO has the authority to ignore or to accept the impact study, and to decide when to make it public, if at all.

On 7 November 1984, federal Energy Minister Pat Carney agreed to a request from the Newfoundland government to delay presentation of the statement. She announced that a joint federal-provincial panel would be set up to review the environmental, social, and economic impact of the Hibernia development.[24] The panel would have two co-chairmen, one from each government. The effect of this was that the province was given the formal right to be involved in Mobil's study and to have a say in what to do with the environmental impact report and with respect to the timing and location of public hearings which are required by federal law. Because the issues and recommendations of the study related to the pace and methods of developing the offshore and, as such, would have a major impact on the economic development of the province, fallout from the public release of the document could be substantial.

Hydro Electricity

Hydro-electric power is the third major resource upon which Newfoundland is relying to improve its economic position. Like the other two – offshore oil and fish – control of this resource has been, to a large extent, out of the hands of the Newfoundland government. The situation regarding hydro electricity is one of the most peculiar on the intergovernmental agenda. It arises from a contract signed in 1969, whereby a Quebec crown corporation purchases most of Newfoundland's hydro electric power at a price well below current market value, a price which is guaranteed for the full term of the contract, 65 years.

The main source of Newfoundland's hydro energy is located in Labrador. There, Churchill Falls is the only major hydro-electric project which has been developed, although the potential exists for other developments. The output from Churchill Falls is substantial. The utility has a rated capacity of 5,225 megawatts (MW) and an average annual energy capability of 34.5 billion kilowatt hours (KWH). It is the largest single utility in the western hemisphere.

In 1961, the Churchill Falls Labrador Corporation (CFLCo), was granted a 99-year lease by the government authorizing development of the Upper Churchill watershed. (Shares of CFLCo are now owned 65.8 per cent by Newfoundland and Labrador Hydro and 34.2 per cent by Hydro-Québec, but at the time, CFLCo was a wholly-owned subsidiary of Brinco Limited.) The lease was made pursuant to The Churchill Falls (Labrador) Corporation Ltd (Lease) Act, 1961. It provided the basis upon which CFLCo was authorized to develop the Churchill Falls generation site and sell the power output.[25]

CFLCo signed a power contract with Hydro-Québec in 1969, giving Hydro-Québec virtually all of the electrical power which flowed from Churchill Falls for a period of 65 years at an established price of just under 3.0 mills per KWH.[26] (In 1979, the average revenue from all sales of Hydro-Québec was 20 mills per KWH.)[27] In exchange, Hydro-Québec assumed the cost and responsibility of developing the falls. This latter point cannot be ignored because without this commitment by Hydro-Québec, Churchill Falls may not have been developed at all and neither Quebec nor Newfoundland would enjoy any of the benefits of Churchill Falls.

Nevertheless, because of the sharp rise in the cost of energy since 1969, the Newfoundland government is receiving for its power only a fraction of its actual value on the world market. According to Premier Peckford in 1984, an assessment by the Economic Council of Canada indicated that Quebec receives benefits from the contract totalling about 790 million dollars per year. In turn, Newfoundland receives approximately seven to eight million dollars annually.[28] Moreover, Newfoundland is locked into this arrangement until the year 2034.

In the 1970s when it became apparent that the 1969 contract was a bad deal, Newfoundland tried to either get out of it or to minimize the damage. The battle with Quebec over Churchill Falls electricity, like the offshore oil dispute with Ottawa, has alternated between the legal and the political arenas. Attempts at reaching a negotiated settlement have been intermingled with a series of court challenges. The following summary focuses first on the legal developments and, second, on negotiations, especially those of the past two years. Chronologically, however, the two routes run parallel.

The Judicial Arena

Two legal approaches have been attempted. First, Newfoundland requested an annual allotment of 800 MWH of power from Hydro-Québec. The request was based on a clause in the lease which specifically provided that the consumers of electricity in Newfoundland be given priority to the output of the plant. Part I, Clause 2(e) of the Lease grants to CFLCo:

the right to transmit throughout the Province [of Newfoundland] any electric power generated as the result of the harnessing of the whole or any part of the Upper Churchill and to export from the Province such power. Provided that upon the request of the Government consumers of electricity in the Province shall be given priority where it is feasible and economic to do so.

When Hydro-Québec refused to grant power in accordance with Newfoundland's request, the provincial government took the case to court. Although court action was initiated in 1976, several legal delays kept the case from being heard by the Newfoundland Supreme Court until 1982. That court's decision was delivered on 13 June 1983. The ruling went against Newfoundland: the Court asserted that the province can only receive power that is surplus to CFLCo's sales commitment with Hydro-Québec. (There is very little that is surplus.) The province appealed to the Newfoundland Court of

Appeal, where the case was heard in October 1984. No ruling has yet been handed down.

Supplementing this legal action, the Newfoundland government has intervened on several occasions before the National Energy Board (NEB) in hearings to review Hydro-Québec's export requests. Newfoundland has opposed export licenses in the absence of any attempts by Hydro-Québec to satisfy Canadian (especially Newfoundland) demand for its electricity. Energy Minister Marshall has argued that there exists:

a critical need in Newfoundland for additional power and energy to supply requirements in Labrador and to support an electrical interconnection to the Island to displace oil-fired facilities and meet a growing electrical load.[29]

During 1984, Newfoundland made three interventions before the NEB. In all cases, Hydro-Québec won approval for the right to export its hydro power (from Churchill Falls) to the northern United States. One reason consistently given by the NEB for ignoring Newfoundland's request is that Newfoundland does not have any means of transporting the hydro from Labrador to the island. Newfoundland's response has been that because of the prohibitive cost of such an undertaking, it could not be financed unless a supply of energy were assured. As such, Newfoundland is caught in a 'catch 22' situation. Interestingly, the lack of a transmission line between Quebec and New York did not prohibit the NEB on 8 March 1984 from allowing Hydro-Québec to export 24 billion KWH of interruptible power annually until 1995 to the New York Power Authority.[30]

Following the March 1984 decision by the NEB, the Newfoundland government appealed both to the Court of Appeal and to the federal cabinet, where the final decision was made. Neither appeal was successful.

An alternative legal approach adopted by the Newfoundland government was an attempt to revoke the legislation which authorized the 1961 lease. In doing this, the power contract would become void. In 1980, the Newfoundland legislature passed The Upper Churchill Water Rights Reversion Act (hereafter referred to as the Reversion Act), returning to the province the right to the use of the waters and to the hydro-electric power as described in the lease. The Act also provided for the repeal of The Churchill Falls (Labrador) Corporation Limited (Lease) Act, 1961, 'thus voiding CFLCo's lease with Hydro-Québec', and for the expropriation of the company's fixed assets used in the generation of electric power. The Act limited the amount of compensation payable to creditors and shareholders. However, rather than proclaiming the legislation immediately, it was referred by the Newfoundland government to the Court of Appeal.

In its decision, delivered on 5 March 1982, the Court of Appeal asserted that the Act did more than merely repeal provincial legislation in that it expropriated the assets of CFCLo, thus raising a constitutional issue. The Court noted the need to:

decide ... whether the legislation is in respect of any of the classes of subjects enumerated in Sec. 92, and assigned exclusively to the provinces and, if so, whether the subject of the Act also falls within one of the classes of subjects in Sec. 91, as a result of which the legislative authority of the Province is thereby overborne.

The Newfoundland Court of Appeal expressed the view that a provincial legislature was fully competent to expropriate property within its territorial limits. It held that the Reversion Act in pith and substance concerned civil rights within the Province of Newfoundland and any extra-provincial effects were incidental. The Court held that the mere fact that the Reversion Act would have an effect on interprovincial trade did not infringe federal power to regulate trade and commerce, since such an effect was incidental to the main purpose of the Act. As well, the Court of Appeal noted that the expropriated works and undertakings are situated wholly within territorial limits of the Province of Newfoundland. The Newfoundland Court held the Act to be *intra vires*.

This decision was appealed by Hydro-Québec and the case was heard by the Supreme Court of Canada during the final week of September 1982. The constitutional validity of this statute was challenged on several grounds. The following four arguments were made:

□ The Act interferes with the status and capacity of a federally-incorporated company.
□ The Act is legislation in relation to property and civil rights outside the Province of Newfoundland.
□ The Act is in relation to the regulation of interprovincial and international trade and commerce.
□ The Act is in relation to an interprovincial work or undertaking.[31]

After two postponements (requested by the governments of Newfoundland and Quebec, while negotiations were underway), the Supreme Court of Canada rendered its decision on 3 May 1984. It noted that the Reversion Act on its face does nothing more than expropriate for all practical purposes all of the assets of CFLCo and make certain provisions regarding compensation to shareholders and creditors. While this would deprive the company of the business it formerly conducted, it cannot be said the corporate being of CFLCo would be affected. The Court concluded that the Newfoundland legislature did not contravene the constitutional strictures against interference with the essential status and powers of a federally-incorporated company.

Concerning civil rights outside the province, the Court recognized the need to make the following distinction:

Where the pith and substance of the provincial enactment is in relation to matters which fall within the field of provincial Legislative competence, incidental or consequential effects on extra-provincial rights will not render the enactment *ultra vires*. Where, however, the pith and substance of the provincial enactment is the derogation from or elimination of extra-provincial rights then, even if it is cloaked in the proper constitutional form, it will be *ultra vires*.[32]

The Court noted that as soon as the Reversion Act came into force, Hydro-Québec's right to receive power according to the terms of the power contract would be effectively destroyed. The Court concluded that the Act was a 'colourable' attempt to interfere with the power contract and thus would derogate from the rights of Hydro-Québec to receive an agreed amount of power at an agreed price. Having found that the pith and substance of the Reversion Act was to interfere with the rights of Hydro-Québec outside the territorial jurisdiction of Newfoundland, the Act as a whole was deemed *ultra vires*. It was not necessary for the Court to address the third and fourth arguments.

Negotiations

Another route which the Newfoundland government has taken in an attempt to rectify the situation has been to negotiate directly with Quebec. Several attempts at reaching a negotiated solution have been made during the past few years between representatives of the two provinces. Most recently, the respective energy ministers sat down together in the fall of 1983. It was because these negotiations were under way that two requests were made to the Supreme Court of Canada to delay delivery of its decision on the Reversion Act case, pending a possible political solution. The Court concurred and optimism that a political settlement would be reached was high.

However, talks broke off in March 1984. Newfoundland decided not to request a third postponement of the Supreme Court decision because it would have given the false impression that progress was being made in the negotiations. Premier Peckford claimed that Quebec had only made its first concrete offer after six months of deliberations, and that the gap between Quebec's offer and what Newfoundland considered to be reasonable was very large.

By not requesting a third postponement from the Supreme Court, Newfoundland forced the high court to hand down its decision. It was delivered on 3 May 1984, and is outlined above. Newfoundland's gamble failed to pay off as the court ruled in Quebec's favour. The government was criticized by some for forcing the court to make its decision. Premier Peckford asserted that he had no choice.

Initially, the Newfoundland premier refused to disclose the details of the Quebec offer, pending a return to the negotiating table. However, after increased criticism, Newfoundland Energy Minister William Marshall finally revealed the details of Hydro-Québec's offer in a statement on 18 May 1984. Quebec's version of its offer to Newfoundland was unveiled nearly a month later on 14 June 1984 by Energy Minister Yves Duhaime at a Chambre de Commerce luncheon in Montreal.[33]

Not surprisingly, the two ministers interpreted the Quebec proposal from rather different perspectives. Mr. Duhaime pointed out that Quebec was willing to give more money, power and guarantees to Newfoundland. In return, it wanted the right to develop projects on the Lower Churchill and to upgrade

Bruce G. Pollard

the existing plant on the Upper Churchill River. According to the Quebec minister, the offer was worth about one billion dollars to Newfoundland.

In his presentation, William Marshall criticized not only the contents of the proposal, but also the bargaining tactics of the Quebec government. He asserted that, prior to negotiations, Newfoundland had secured agreement from Quebec that the Churchill Falls contract elements would be dealt with first, and received assurances that Quebec intended to deal with them in a meaningful manner. September 1983 was the first time that Quebec agreed to address directly the Upper Churchill contract. Prior to that, Quebec would only deal with that contract as part of a package deal.

Quebec, Mr. Marshall said, made its first and only offer to resolve the situation on 23 March 1984. Included was a proposal to index the fixed royalty value of 50 cents per horsepower per year; there was to be no change in the rentals payable under statutory lease. Mr. Marshall noted that the net impact of this would be to increase Newfoundland's revenue from the CFLCo lease by less than 2.5 million dollars in 1984. Quebec, however, pointed out that indexing and doubling of the royalties paid to Newfoundland under the agreement would increase to 100 million dollars over the life of the contract from 50 million dollars.

Concerning access to power, Quebec concluded that the energy capabilities of the plant were greater than that shown in the power contract. Therefore, it was prepared to grant an additional 500MW of its capacity annually to Newfoundland at a 68 percent load factor or 380MW at a 90 per cent load factor level. Access to the full block of power was contingent on seven years written notice. According to Newfoundland, this offer would not enable it to realistically plan an interconnect with the Island. (Earlier studies estimated that Newfoundland needed to receive 800MW to fully utilize one transmission line from Churchill Falls.) The Quebec energy minister claimed that this item was worth about 800 million dollars.

The third element of Quebec's package, according to Mr. Duhaime, was the guaranteed financial stability of CFLCo, the holding company for the power project, at a cost of 130 million dollars to Hydro-Québec.

The fourth and final element involved future development in Labrador. Quebec proposed to develop Gull Island and Muskrat Falls on the Lower Churchill River, with Hydro-Québec getting the right to buy power. These are attractive sources of undeveloped electrical energy, the two sites together having an estimated capacity of 2300 MW, about 45 per cent of the rated capacity of the Upper Churchill.[34] Quebec further proposed to reach an agreement on developing other rivers flowing through Labrador and Quebec.

Newfoundland objected to a 'package deal' because it did not wish future benefits to have to be traded off against readjustments on the Upper Churchill deal. According to Energy Minister Marshall, Hydro-Québec's offer was similar to the Upper Churchill Falls situation. He accused Quebec of wishing to be the broker of all power exported from Labrador and of wanting to deny

Newfoundland the right to transmit and freely sell power generated from the Lower Churchill without first offering it to Quebec. Mr. Marshall stated:

> To suggest that the Lower Churchill and Joint Rivers be developed on the same basis as the Upper Churchill could only be interpreted as a message to us that Quebec is unable to concede there should be any substantive change in our relationships with respect to development of our resources in Labrador.[35]

What does Newfoundland feel is an acceptable solution? First, it has argued that Quebec should never have been permitted to exact more than wheeling costs as the price of transmitting power through its territory. Newfoundland feels that a 60/40 split of benefits in favour of the resource owner would not be unfair. Newfoundland is prepared to entertain a 50/50 split. Second, concerning access to power, Newfoundland is prepared to accept the right to recall not more than 2400MW annually (nearly half of the rated capacity of Churchill Falls), phased in over time.[36]

Third, Newfoundland feels that the 65 year term of the contract should be reduced to 40 years, the term of the original deal. The extension had been added when Quebec had to guarantee extra funds for the project and give other assurances. Newfoundland argues that the 40 year term was sufficient to support the project at its inception. Fourth, with respect to the financial integrity of the CFLCo, Newfoundland believes there should be a rate adjustment to allow a return of 15 per cent to shareholders and to finance extraordinary capital expenditures needed before the end of the 40 year term.

What now? It is generally agreed that a negotiated settlement would be preferred. The possibility of that seems unlikely, though, given the gap between Quebec's offer and what Premier Peckford considers to be a reasonable solution.

Newfoundland's bargaining position is based largely on an appeal to fairness and to the mutual benefit which could accrue to both Quebec and Newfoundland if an equitable solution were reached. There has never been any argument that the contract was not legally binding, only that it was unfair. William Marshall contends that 'if Newfoundland has to accept the reality of that contract, Quebec should accept the other reality of drastically changed circumstances' – resulting primarily from the energy crisis and galloping inflation.[37] The only possibility of a negotiated settlement seems to lie in a 'package deal' in which Newfoundland would have to give Hydro-Québec part of the action in the development of the Lower Churchill River potential in exchange for a reopening of the original Churchill Falls contract.

The Role of the Federal Government

Given the stalemate at the bargaining table, coupled with the various court decisions, Newfoundland's best hope for rectifying its situation may rest with the federal government. In a joint statement issued 3 May 1984, Brian Peckford and William Marshall asserted that in deciding that the provincial government did not have the power to repeal a statute which it had enacted, the Supreme Court of Canada was stating at the same time that it was within the power of the federal government to enact legislation with respect to the lease. Newfoundland called upon the federal government to exercise that power in a fair and equitable way.

The Newfoundland government has stated on several occasions that it is the federal government's responsibility to see that fairness is done – if necessary, by drawing on its trade and commerce power – to revoke the 1969 contract. Alternatively, Newfoundland has asked the federal government to create a power corridor through Quebec so that Newfoundland could export its resources from Labrador. It maintains that the federal government should, under the National Energy Board legislation, provide for wheeling rights through provinces, much as the NEB does for oil and gas pipelines. Premier Peckford is quoted as saying that:

the big problem is that we are not being treated the same in the transmission of our resource which is hydro-electric power as other provinces are treated in the transmission of theirs which are oil and natural gas.[38]

Since 1983, the NEB legislation does provide for such rights in future lines, but does not cover existing transmission lines from Churchill Falls. Moreover, this would be very difficult to enforce if the contiguous province – in this case, Quebec – was opposed.

The Trudeau government chose not to get involved in the dispute. It did, however, intervene on behalf of Quebec in the Supreme Court hearings concerning the Reversion Act, thereby further infuriating the Newfoundland government. Prime Minister Mulroney, however, has expressed a desire to facilitate a solution. In a statement issued in December 1984, he reiterated his intention to use his good offices to help resolve this long standing interprovincial dispute.

The Other Provinces

As far as the other provinces are concerned, an important principle was at stake in this dispute. Hence, some did intervene on Newfoundland's behalf in the Supreme Court hearings. The Attorneys-General for the Provinces of Saskatchewan, Manitoba and British Columbia argued that the lease and the Lease Act were statutory rather than contractual instruments and, therefore, subject to repeal by the legislature of Newfoundland, which had enacted them. The Attorneys-General also argued that the Statute should not be rendered invalid because of any incidental effects it might have on extra-provincial interests. They contended that the Reversion Act was valid legislation and within the purview of a provincial legislature.

A rumour circulated in August 1984 that Premier Peckford was considering an appeal to his colleagues in other provinces to pressure the Quebec government into rectifying the inequitable situation. According to Le Droit, the Newfoundland government was studying 'various ways of persuading the other provinces to put pressure on Quebec to renegotiate the agreement on electricity produced by Churchill Falls in Labrador.'[39] For the most part, however, the eight provincial governments not directly involved have remained outside the dispute.

Regional Development

Regional development policy is not a single policy, but rather a package of various policies, designed to promote development in geographical areas where economic conditions are poorer than in other areas (see Chapter 5). It has been argued by some, including the Government of Newfoundland, that the provincial governments should have the major say in regional development policy. (The basis of this argument is that provincial governments, more than the federal government, are in tune with the needs and capabilities of the particular regions within a province.)

Three general instruments of regional development exist in the Canadian context. The first, and least obvious, is the use of federal policies relating to particular industries or sectors. While there are few sectors in which the impact of policies does not vary from region to region, certain sectors are much more clearly 'regional' in nature than are others. These include energy, transportation and fisheries. Although national policy in these areas has profound effects on regional development, such sectoral policies have not been extensively applied by the federal government to enhance development in lagging regions.

The other two instruments are more explicitly policies of regional development. First are federal government programs of general application to the private sector. The Industrial and Regional Development Program (IRDP) is currently the main mechanism in this category. Although the IRDP was created in July 1983, similar programs had been in place for years. For the IRDP, all areas of the country, as defined by census division, are classified into tiers, based on employment and income levels and the fiscal capacity of the particular province. Depending on the tier to which a region is assigned, differing types and levels of support are available from the federal government.

The IRDP was created by a federal Liberal government eager to deal directly with Canadians, thereby increasing its visibility and, in the process, bypassing provincial governments. The Newfoundland government has been concerned that the application of 'national' criteria has meant that the vast majority of expenditures have been made in Ontario and Quebec.

The third instrument of regional development policy is the cost-shared intergovernmental agreement. The proportion of the costs borne by Ottawa generally depends on the economic condition of the province concerned, and has reached as high as 90 per cent. These agreements are vital to poorer provinces in that they allow them to offer developmental programs which other richer provinces can afford on their own (for example, highway construction, minerals, and agricultural development).

A number of changes in the federal approach to the use of this third instrument occurred in the late 1970s and the 1980s. These were troubling for the Government of Newfoundland. The first development occurred in the federal government's organizational structure, as it related to the administration of regional development policy. In 1982, the Departments of Industry, Trade and Commerce and of Regional Economic Expansion (DREE) were disbanded. In their place was created the Department of Regional and Industrial Expansion (DRIE). As well, the Ministry of State for Economic Development became the Ministry of State for Economic and Regional Development (MSERD). (It was later disbanded in 1984 by Prime Minister John Turner.) The new organizational arrangements had important implications. Regional development policy was no longer represented in a separate department. The federal government argued that regional policy was so important that it should be the responsibility of every department to take into account regional development objectives when making policy decisions. (In 1969, when DREE was created, it was stated that regional development was so important it deserved a distinct department.) The provinces generally felt that the 1982 reorganization meant that the federal government was shifting priorities away from this area.

This suspicion was supported by the second development, a decline in federal funds available for regional development programs. In 1971-2, 1.8 per cent of the total federal budget was spent on regional economic development. During the first years of the 1980s, this figure was about 0.6 per cent. Table 3.3 lists federal DREE expenditures in Newfoundland since 1971-72.

Table 3.3
Dree (GDA) Expenditures in Newfoundland

	($ million)		($ million)
1971-72	31.2	1977-78	56.5
1972-73	29.4	1978-79	56.0
1973-74	30.3	1979-80	76.2
1974-75	56.0	1980-81	46.5
1975-76	60.0	1981-82	36.8
1976-77	52.0	1982-83	34.9

Source: *Submission of the Government of Newfoundland and Labrador to the Royal Commission on Economic Union and Development Prospects for Canada*, September 1983, p. 83.

Because of its poor economic position relative to other provinces, Newfoundland greatly benefitted from a federal government dedicated to removing regional disparities. Alternatively, it was hurt when regional policy was given a low priority by the federal government.

Third, in the early 1980s, the federal Liberal government refused to sign several new agreements with the Government of Newfoundland to replace subsidiary agreements signed during the 1970s (under the rubric of 10-year umbrella General Development Agreements (GDAs)) which had expired. While Newfoundland was eager to have these extended, the federal government was not. As such, between 1980 and 1983, very few agreements were signed between the two governments.

The fourth development was the establishment of 10-year umbrella agreements to replace the GDAs that expired on 31 March 1984. The new agreements, known as Economic and Regional Development Agreements (ERDAs), were introduced in 1983 by the federal Liberal government. Since late 1983, ERDAs have been signed between the federal government and all of the provincial governments. These are enabling documents, under which specific cost-shared subsidiary agreements are signed.

Unlike the agreements signed during the GDA era, which tended to emphasize joint delivery and administration of programs, the new agreements were to:

allow economic development programs and projects to be cooperatively planned, but separately delivered, where appropriate. This new approach will respect the jurisdiction of each level of government and, at the same time, clarify in the public mind which level of government is responsible for a program or policy.[40]

This philosophy was an important element in the Trudeau government's 'new federalism', which emphasized federal visibility and direct delivery of services. Provincial governments preferred joint delivery of services, fearing that federally-delivered programs might not be sensitive to provincial objectives. There are indications that the Mulroney government will soon return to a pattern where the provincial governments will have primary responsibility for the administration of all subsidiary agreements.

The intransigent stance by the federal government changed remarkably in the spring of 1984, and a flurry of agreements was signed with the Newfoundland government in what turned out to be the last days of the Liberal regime. It began on 4 May, about six weeks prior to the federal Liberal leadership convention, when an ERDA was signed between the two governments. In the ensuing four months, seven subsidiary agreements were signed. These are listed in Table 3.4. Included in this batch was a rural development agreement reached on 19 July. The previous five-year agreement had expired on 31 March 1983 and the provincial government had been lobbying since then for a replacement.

Table 3.4
Subsidiary Agreements Signed Between the Governments of Canada and
Newfoundland (May – September 1984)

	Total funding 5 years ($ million)	Cost sharing Ratio (Fed/Prov)
Planning	4.0	50:50
Minerals	22.0	70:30
Burin Peninsula Development Fund	28.0	70:30
Rural Development	18.2	50:50
Pulp and Paper (amendment)	8.0	50:50
Tourism	21.0	70:30
Ocean Industries	28.0	60:40 (41)

Source: Government of Newfoundland and Labrador. *Discussion Paper on Major Bilateral Issues. Canada-Newfoundland,* September 1984, p. 24.

The agreements signed under the GDA umbrella had all been cost-shared by the federal and Newfoundland governments in a ratio of 90:10. The cost-sharing ratio of subsidiary agreements signed under the ERDA rubric has averaged about 70:30. As such, the federal government has cut back its contribution to these programs.

Since the federal election of September 1984, the Mulroney government has showed a willingness to work with the Newfoundland government in reaching agreements in a variety of sectors. Negotiations began almost immediately on several fronts. It was announced on 14 November 1984, that a Canada/Newfoundland Forestry Subsidiary Agreement, due to expire in March 1985, would be extended until 30 September 1985. Moreover, negotiations were proceeding between ministers in both governments to complete a new forestry agreement.[41]

Subsequently, two more subsidiary agreements have been signed. The first, on 20 December 1984, was in the area of Pulp and Paper. It was worth 46.3 million dollars, of which over 80 per cent was to come from the federal government. The other was an agreement to cover highway construction and repair; this was signed in March 1985 during the provincial election campaign. This agreement involved, by far, the largest commitment of funds on the part of both the federal and the provincial governments: 180 million dollars, of which 62.5 per cent was to come from the federal government.[42]

Regional development policy is of concern to all provincial governments. Specifically, all provinces argue for a major role in determining the allocation of funds and in generally making regional development policy. The cooperative nature of the GDAs has generally been applauded by the provincial governments. There is an increasing tendency, since the change in government at the federal level, for ERDA projects to be jointly delivered. However, of greater concern to Newfoundland, as well as to the other Atlantic provinces and to Quebec, has been the reduction in federal funds allocated to regional development. While all provinces are, to some extent, concerned about the limiting of their role in regional development, it is these provinces which are most in need of federal funds for regional development projects.

Conclusion

In conclusion, it is necessary to first evaluate the claim of the Newfoundland government that it has been treated by the federal government differently than have other provinces, that Ottawa has been unfair to the province of Newfoundland. The first of Newfoundland's two central points of contention relates to a 1930 constitutional amendment which transferred ownership of mineral resources from the federal government to the Provinces of Manitoba, Saskatchewan and Alberta. Newfoundland has argued that since these provinces have had their boundaries extended, its area of jurisdiction should be extended as well, so that the offshore resources would fall within its purview.

Because the resources are offshore, though, Newfoundland's situation is quite different from that of the three prairie provinces. Examples from international law, in addition to the 1967 British Columbia offshore decision by the Supreme Court of Canada, weighed against Newfoundland's claim to ownership. Moreover, natural resources are regarded very differently in the 1980s than they were in the 1930s. The significance of provincial ownership of resources has dramatically increased with the greater importance of oil. The federal government is more likely to protect jealously its ownership rights over energy resources now than it was a half-century ago.

Newfoundland's second major complaint has been that the federal government has not taken action to enable it to transmit its hydro-electric power from Labrador through Quebec to export markets. Premier Peckford has pointed out that power corridors have been created by the federal government so that western provinces could export their natural gas and oil resources through adjacent provinces. Again, Newfoundland's situation is quite different. There exists a contract between public corporations of the provinces of Quebec and Newfoundland. Whether judged to be fair or not, that contract not only makes the federal government wary of legislating over Quebec objections, it also sets this situation apart from the Western Canadian examples.

In summary, the legitimacy of Newfoundland's claims that it is being discriminated against by the federal government are difficult to uphold. This is not to suggest, however, that the policy objectives of the Newfoundland government are unreasonable or that they have not been supported by other of the provinces.

All of Newfoundland's major goals have received support from some or most of the other provincial governments. Nearly all provinces have, at one time or another, supported Newfoundland's position with respect to fisheries, including support for a constitutional amendment making fisheries a subject of concurrent federal and provincial jurisdiction. There has also been strong provincial endorsement for the treatment of offshore resources as if they were on land. Several provinces intervened on behalf of Newfoundland in its Supreme Court battle with the federal government over ownership of these resources. Concerning the dispute with Quebec over Churchill Falls, other provincial governments have been hesitant to take sides, although three did intervene in the Supreme Court hearings concerning Newfoundland's Reversion Act. These provinces argued for Newfoundland's right to revoke its own legislation, affirming that what Newfoundland was trying to do was within the power of a provincial government.

While there has existed substantial sympathy for Newfoundland's case, the examples from the other provinces do not support Newfoundland's claim that it has been treated unfairly with respect to the offshore and the hydro issues. This view has been affirmed by the courts. In fact, the two major Supreme Court decisions of 1984 (both going against Newfoundland) undoubtedly played a role in Newfoundland's change in approach toward the federal government. With the constitutional battles lost, the province has had to rely on appeals to fairness. As well, there has been a change in the public mood toward federal-provincial relations. A desire for cooperation has become prevalent in all parts of the country. As such, the older, more aggressive approach to intergovernmental relations was no longer appropriate. In part, the change in government at the federal level provided an opportune time for Newfoundland to change its approach without losing political face. However, the approach of the Mulroney government, and especially its position on the offshore resources, cannot be dismissed as unimportant. It remains a key factor in Newfoundland's change in attitude towards federal-provincial relations.

Although the provincial government's approach to intergovernmental relations is no longer based on a claim of unfair treatment, its objectives are in no way any less legitimate. Newfoundland argues that it deserves joint management of offshore resources and that it needs more say in the management of the provincial fishery and the achievement of self-sufficiency of fairly-priced hydro-electrical power. Only then can there be 'a rate of development which would accelerate Newfoundland's economic growth such that disparities between this Province and the rest of Canada can be narrowed significantly by the end of this century.'43

Acceptance of these objectives must now be based on arguments of fairness and justice, and recognition that the situation in each province is unique. The Mulroney government has brought a new approach to federal-provincial relations; the Atlantic Accord is a showcase example. This approach is rooted in a spirit of cooperation. Negotiations are in good faith. There is a recognition that to not reach agreement hurts both the province and the nation. There is compromise rather than unilateral action. The approach is pragmatic. Constitutional issues and jurisdictional questions tend to be put aside and questions of economic management are at the centre. Finally, there is a tendency towards bilateral, as opposed to multilateral, relations; the need to consider the uniqueness of each province's situation is primary.

What are the implications for Canadian federalism? Some have argued that because of its special equalization offset payments and 'Newfoundland first' policies, the Atlantic Accord grants a 'special status' to Newfoundland. As such, it is said to contravene the spirit of confederation and enhance the balkanization of the economic union. However, special treatment for specific regions in Canada is not new. The Crow rate for western grain farmers, subsidized maritime freight rates, and national oil pricing policies which primarily benefitted, first the West, and then central Canada, are all examples of special treatment for certain regions. Such policies have not hurt the Canadian union. In fact, these may have been essential to the maintenance of the federation. They demonstrate the need for flexibility in Canadian federalism, a need which has been made apparent time and time again in the 118 years since confederation.

Notes

1. Premier Brian Peckford, News Conference, announcing election of 2 April. (11 March 1985.)
2. *Submission of the Government of Newfoundland and Labrador to the Royal Commission on the Economic Union and Development Prospects for Canada,* St. John's, Newfoundland, September 1983, p. 23.
3. CTV Television Network, *Question Period,* 13 May 1984, p. 1.
4. Statement by Minister of Energy William Marshall, 6 April 1984.
5. *Submission of the Government of Newfoundland and Labrador to the Royal Commission on the Economic Union and Development Prospects for Canada,* St. John's, Newfoundland, September 1983, p. 34.
6. *1984 Newfoundland Budget,* presented by Hon. J.F. Collins, Minister of Finance, 20 March 1984, p. 20.
7. Report of the Task Force on Atlantic Fisheries, *Navigating Troubled Waters. A New Policy for the Atlantic Fisheries* (Ottawa: Minister of Supply and Services, 1982), p. 77.
8. Government of Newfoundland, *Discussion Paper on Major Bilateral Issues. Canada – Newfoundland,* September 1984, p. 10.
9. Premier Brian Peckford, Statement, 27 April 1984.
10. Statement to the Press, 26 September 1983.
11. *Submission of the Government of Newfoundland and Labrador to the Royal Commission on the Economic Union and Development Prospects for Canada,* St. John's, Newfoundland, September 1983, p. 54.
12. CTV Television Network, *Question Period,* 13 May 1984, pp. 5-6.
13. Statement by the Hon. Jean Chrétien on Newfoundland and the Offshore, St. John's, 5 April 1984, p. 5.
14. CTV Television Network, *Question Period,* 13 May 1984, p. 5.
15. Jeffrey Simpson, 'How Offshore deal sank in a sea of suspicion', *The Globe and Mail,* 31 May 1984.
16. Government of Newfoundland and Labrador, 'The Offshore: We've been fair', (brochure), 1984.

Bruce G. Pollard

17. 'The Offshore: Sharing from Sea to Sea'. Address to the Canadian Club of Ottawa, 9 May 1984.
18. Premier Brian Peckford and Minister of Energy, William Marshall, *Joint News Conference*, 4 June 1984.
19. Premier Brian Peckford, *Notes for an Address to the Moncton Rotary Club*, 16 April 1984. (Interestingly, the world's first offshore drill was used in Lake Erie in 1914.)
20. Romanow, Whyte and Leeson, *Canada ... Notwithstanding. The Making of the Constitution 1976-1982* (Toronto: Carswell/Methuen, 1984), pp. 74-5.
21. Contained in letter from Prime Minister Brian Mulroney to Premier Peckford, 14 June, 1984.
22. Listed in Brian Peckford, *The Past in the Present. A Personal Perspective on Newfoundland's Future* (St. John's: Henry Cuff Publications Ltd., 1983).
23. Section 50 of *The Atlantic Accord.*
24. Energy, Mines and Resources Canada, *Communique*, 'Hibernia Environmental Impact Statement Postponed', 7 November 1984.
25. *The Energy Priority of Newfoundland and Labrador, Fairness and Equity in the Utilization of the Churchill Falls Hydro Resource*, 21 November 1980, p. 8.
26. The terms of the contract provided for the price of the power to actually *drop* over time: from a high of 3.0 mills/KWH in 1977 to just under 2.5 mills/KWH in 2001, to 2.0 mills/KWH for the final 25 years.
27. Economic Council of Canada, *Newfoundland: From Dependency to Self-Reliance* (Ottawa: Minister of Supply and Services, 1980), p. 122.
28. Premier Brian Peckford and Minister of Energy William Marshall, Joint Statement, 3 May 1984.
29. Letter from Hon. William Marshall to Hon. Jean Chrétien, 13 March 1984.
30. *The Globe and Mail*, 10 March 1984.
31. From Supreme Court of Canada decision concerning *The Upper Churchill Water Rights Reversion Act*, 3 May 1984, p. 19.
32. *Ibid.*, p. 49.
33. Reported in *The Globe and Mail*, 15 June 1984.
34. Government of Newfoundland and Labrador, *The Energy Priority of Newfoundland and Labrador. Fairness and Equity in the Utilization of the Churchill Falls Hydro Resource*, 21 November 1980, p. 11.
35. William Marshall, Statement on the Negotiations between Quebec and Newfoundland on the Upper Churchill, St. John's, 18 May 1984, p. 18.
36. *Ibid.*, p. 19.
37. *Ibid.*, p. 18.
38. Quoted in *The Gazette*, Montreal, 24 May 1984.
39. (Translation) *Le Droit*, 21 August 1984.
40. *Annual Report of the Ministry of State for Economic Development 1982-83*, pp. 8-9.
41. Government of Newfoundland, News Release, 14 November 1984.
42. 'Economic and Regional Development Agreements. Agreements and Memoranda of Understanding Signed as of 14 May 1985', compiled by the federal government.
43. *Submission of the Government of Newfoundland and Labrador to the Royal Commission on the Economic Union and Development Prospects for Canada*, St. John's, Newfoundland, September 1983, p. 57.

III
Issues

4 Alberta: Looking Back Looking Forward

Roger Gibbins

There is little question that 1984 will come to be seen as a pivotal year in Alberta's political history, even though there was no provincial election and no political crisis of major proportions. Indeed, the political front within the province was unusually quiet. The dramatic change came with the federal election on 4 September 1984, although even here little changed *within* the province as voters once again elected a solid slate of Progressive Conservative candidates as they had done in 1972, 1974, 1979, and 1980. This time, however, Albertans found themselves on the winning side, part of a national Tory landslide completely unlike the precarious and short-lived Conservative victory in 1979.

One might have expected a sense of near-euphoria to have gripped the province after 4 September. Finally, Alberta was onside with 21 MPs on the government side of the House and three ministers in the federal cabinet – Joe Clark, Harvie André and Don Mazankowski. Alberta MPs could be expected to play an important role in a new national government that could hardly fail to be more sensitive to provincial and regional concerns than the Liberal governments of the past two decades. Prior to the election the new prime minister to be, Brian Mulroney, had displayed a lively concern for western interests, and his party was pledged to undo the damage inflicted upon the Alberta economy by the National Energy Program. In short, it would seem, happy days were here again.

In fact, however, the provincial reaction to the September election was more subdued. Albertans looked to the future with a noticeable degree of wariness and, in some cases, even unease. To explain this reaction, it is necessary to place Alberta within the context of the 'new West', and to explain the ways in which the 'new West' has been transformed, and transformed again, during the last decade. The picture that emerges is not one of a provincial electorate that is impossible to please, but rather of a province unable to free itself from a dependency on external forces that impact with such dramatic and, at times, such injurious effect.

Before proceeding it must be recognized that Alberta cannot be equated with western Canada. In both an historical and contemporary sense, the Alberta experience has departed significantly from that of Saskatchewan and Manitoba to the east, and British Columbia to the west.[1] Nonetheless, during the heyday of the 'new West' in the 1970s and early 1980s, Alberta was generally seen by Albertans and non-Albertans alike as the regional kingpin. This was not because Alberta was typical of the other provinces, for its oil and natural gas wealth, not to mention its nearly monolithic conservatism, set Alberta apart. Rather, it was because Alberta seemed to embody, in exaggerated form, those features most characteristic of the 'new West'. These included not only wealth and a faith in the future that bordered on unbridled boosterism, but also an intense sense of discontent with the national government and, in more general terms, with the character of the Canadian federal state. Alberta, in other words, was *the region writ small*, a model of what the West could become.

A close examination of the Alberta experience can thus shed useful light on the broader character of the 'new West'. At the same time, the changes that Alberta has gone through in the past few years may enable us to see the rough outline of the West that is yet to come, a West that may bear little resemblance to the 'new West' of old.

Alberta and the 'New West'

To begin, it is useful to sketch in, using very broad strokes indeed, the evolution of the Canadian West. In the first three decades of this century, the prairie West in particular was at the centre of economic and demographic growth in Canada. Settlers poured into the prairies from eastern Canada, the United States, Europe and around the world. The prairies' share of the national population jumped from 7.8 per cent in 1901 to 22.7 per cent in 1931, and Saskatchewan became Canada's third largest province. In an important sense, the prairie West was at the cutting edge of the Canadian society, the land of new ideas, social innovation, and economic growth. There was almost a palpable sense of optimism, a belief that Canada was being recast in line with a western vision of the world.

This sense of optimism, of confidence in both the region and the country, was crushed by the Great Depression of the 1930s. The Depression, of course, affected all parts of Canada and indeed all parts of the western industrialized world. On the prairies, however, its impact was magnified by drought and by the collapse of the world grain market upon which the entire agricultural enterprise in the West was based. From 1929, which marked the onset of the Depression, to 1933 which marked its worst year, per capita income fell by 49 per cent in Manitoba, 61 per cent in Alberta, and 71 per cent in Saskatchewan, figures which compare to more modest drops of 47 per cent in British Columbia,

45 per cent in Prince Edward Island, 44 per cent in Quebec and Ontario, and 39 per cent in Nova Scotia and New Brunswick.[2]

Here it is not the details of the Depression which are to be stressed,[3] but rather the way in which the Depression redefined the place of the prairie West in Canada. The West was no longer the land of the future. The former optimism and self-confidence had blown away in the dust-clouds of the Depression; they departed with the hundreds of thousands of people who packed up and left the region and its economic devastation. From 1931 to 1941 the region experienced a net out-migration of 248,000 people, and between 1941 and 1951 another 268,000 people left. Saskatchewan alone had a net out-migration of 158,000 between 1931 and 1941, and 199,000 between 1941 and 1951.[4]

The Depression signalled the retreat of the prairie West to the margins of Canadian life. When immigration to Canada resumed after the end of the Second World War, few people settled on the prairies where employment opportunities were insufficient to fill the needs of a young farm population coming of age at a time when mechanization sharply reduced the labour requirements of prairie agriculture. While agricultural production on the prairies expanded steadily, agriculture employed fewer and fewer people, and the proportionate contribution of prairie agriculture to the Canadian economy steadily declined. In the depths of the Depression, despite drought and stagnant world markets, prairie agriculture contributed 19 per cent of the total net value of production in Canada, a proportion that fell to less than nine per cent by the early 1970s.[5] The face of modern Canada was no longer defined by rows of harvesting combines silhouetted against the prairie sky, but rather by the new skylines and vibrant urban pulse of Toronto and Montreal. In short, the old agrarian West was in a process of irrevocable decline.

However, even as the old West declined, the seeds of the 'new West' were beginning to germinate in the oil fields of Alberta. The LeDuc discovery in 1947 and the start of commercial oil production in the early 1950s marked the beginning of a more diversified natural resource base for the western economy, one in which the resources lying beneath the soil were to surpass the agricultural resources which could be harvested from the soil itself. (Agriculture's contribution to the net value of production in Alberta fell from 52 per cent in 1931 to 18.7 per cent in 1961 and 16.3 per cent in 1971.)[6] While agriculture would continue to be important, oil, natural gas, coal, potash and uranium came increasingly to the fore to provide the foundations for a new era of economic prosperity for the West, an era that came into full flower with the OPEC-inspired escalation of world oil prices in 1973. With the surge in world oil prices, the 'new West' had arrived.

What, then, were the characteristics of the 'new West'?[7] There was, of course, renewed and previously unmatched prosperity coupled with a surge of in-migration as Canadians from across the country moved to the West in order to share in the resource-drive prosperity. Economic growth occurred across the region, but was particularly evident in Alberta where Calgary and Edmonton experienced an unprecedented boom. Like the agrarian West of the early twentieth century, the West formed the growth pole of the Canadian economy. Unlike the agrarian West, the 'new West' was urban and technocratic. Capital poured into the region, and virtually every day the press carried stories of yet another head office that had moved into the West, of another financial institution that was expanding its western operations, of another highrise that was being constructed or planned.

The West had regained its sense of optimism. There was a cocky, at times even abrasive belief that the West was the Canada of the future, that the years ahead would see a continued growth in the West's economy and in its share of the national population. In the political arena, this belief grated against the hard facts that the incumbent Liberal governments were all but devoid of elected representation from western Canada, and that the region appeared to lack the political muscle to match its economic power. Thus we witnessed an assertive drive for increased political power, a drive led by provincial governments which sought to shore up their existing constitutional powers, to expand their legislative domain and roll back intrusions into that domain by the federal government, to strengthen both their control over natural resources and their input into national decision-making.

We find, then, in the western alienation of the times, a profound discontent with the political status quo – be it partisan, institutional or constitutional – and the insistent demand that political power in the country be realigned in accordance with the shift in economic power to the West. Behind this demand lay a recollection of the Depression years, and a realization that one could not assume that the good times would last, that some day the oil would run out. Thus there was a sense of urgency in the western approach to political change, a desire to reshape the political world while the region still had the economic clout to do so.

1980 – 1984: The 'New West' Transformed

In February 1980, the short-lived Conservative government of Joe Clark, in which the West had enjoyed strong representation, went down to defeat. The re-election of the Trudeau Liberals in that month marked the beginning of four trying years which were to transform the face of the 'new West'. Western Canadians confronted, and confronted is the appropriate word, a national government which had the support of only two western Canadian MPs, both from Manitoba. In the fall of 1980 Ottawa introduced the National Energy Program which was greeted with outrage in Alberta. A bitter and protracted dispute between the Alberta and national governments over the price of oil was to drag on through most of 1981 before an agreement was reached, an agreement that assumed rapidly escalating oil prices and thus rapidly escalating federal and provincial revenues. Instead, the world oil market slumped. Rather than climbing towards the predicted $90 a barrel level, oil prices fell as demand

Roger Gibbins

was cut back in the face of conservation and a prolonged economic recession, and as new oil fields came on stream around the world. Whereas the agreement foresaw the price of Canadian oil climbing to catch an escalating world price, or at least 85 per cent of the world price, the world price dropped towards the Canadian level.

The decline in world oil prices was only part of a more general economic reversal that affected Canada at large but which struck the West with particular force. Sales of natural gas plummetted in the face of excess Canadian supplies and deregulation in the United States which severely undercut Canadian exports. The American market for British Columbia lumber all but collapsed, with devastating impact on the British Columbia economy. Indeed, resource markets across the board were in decline in the face of growing world surpluses, and it was those markets which had fuelled the spectacular economic growth in the 'new West' during the 1970s. The western Canadian economy slumped, and then slumped further. Real estate prices fell drastically, particularly in Vancouver, Calgary and Edmonton. Almost overnight, a shortage of rental units in western cities turned into a glut. Office space built in anticipation of a continued boom went begging as rents fell. Construction all but ground to a halt, and the expected development of new natural resources, including the oil sands in northern Alberta, receded into an uncertain future.

The magnitude of the economic downturn is revealed in the fact that in 1983, and again in 1984, Alberta's population actually declined, something that had not happened even in the depths of the Depression when natural increase offset out-migration. Foreclosures further crippled an already blighted housing market as people packed up and left. Those who remained found themselves in the new situation of a depressed economy, and one that was expected to remain depressed for the foreseeable future. Gone was the previous sense of optimism, the belief that the West in general and Alberta in particular was the land of the future. Once again, the region was in decline. The shift in population and economic power from central Canada to the West had been brought to an abrupt halt, and then reversed.

This is not to say that one should bemoan the present state of affairs in Alberta. The province still enjoys immense reserves of natural gas, coal, and heavy oil. The economy, while far from buoyant, is still delivering a very reasonable level of prosperity to most provincial residents. Taxes remain relatively low, and there is still no provincial sales tax. In a social sense, Alberta has lost some of the raw materialism of the boom period, and the social problems engendered by the boom have abated somewhat. While Alberta may not be as prosperous today, its communities are not necessarily less pleasant environments in which to live. The future, while clouded, is not without its bright spots. The anticipated dismantling of the National Energy Program, the attempts by the Mulroney government to increase oil and natural gas exports to the United States, and the long-term prospects of agricultural and natural resource exports offer some room for optimism.

Nonetheless, the mood of the province has been dramatically transformed during the early 1980s, and transformed in a way that is analogous to, although not as profound as that experienced during the Great Depression of the 1930s. It is this change in mood that sets the state for an analysis of the likely impact of the 1984 federal election.

September 1984 – The National Impact

There is an interesting irony in the 1984 election results. The election meant that the West in general and Alberta in particular were emphatically onside, that the national government was one in which both the region and the province would have a strong and articulate voice. At the same time, however, the election transformed the Progressive Conservatives. The party was nationalized, enjoying for the first time since 1958 strong electoral support in every region of the country. As a consequence, western Canadian influence within the party has been reduced. The price of national victory has been a diminished role for the West within the party, and it is this consequence which has made many Albertans wary about the future.

In the four federal elections held between 1972 and 1980, western Canadian MPs constituted 44 per cent of the Tory caucus, with Alberta MPs alone constituting 18 per cent. Following the 1980 election, 48 per cent of the Conservative MPs came from western Canada, and 20 per cent from Alberta alone. In the new Tory caucus, with 58 Quebec and 67 Ontario MPs, western Canadian representation has dropped to 27 per cent while the 21 Alberta MPs constitute 10 per cent. This is not to suggest that western representatives will go unheard within the Tory caucus, or that the new Conservative government will be oblivious to western concerns and interests. Nevertheless, the Conservative party has been transformed. In the elections following the 1958 Diefenbaker landslide, the party's centre of gravity shifted westward. The West became the Conservative heartland and, to a degree, the Conservative party became a western Canadian party. Now, the Conservative party is a truly national party, perhaps the most national party ever to grace the Canadian political stage. Joe Clark, the first Canadian prime minister to be born in the West, has been replaced as party leader by Quebec's Brian Mulroney. The West's contingent in the Tory caucus is matched by Quebec's. In short, the national Conservative party is now one in which the western Canadian voice will be *no more than proportionate* to the region's population – which appears to be in decline – and to the region's economic clout – which is also in decline.

As an aside, there is an interesting irony to the 1984 election that is worth noting. In 1980, western Canadian expressed anger and dismay that a majority Liberal government had been elected before the polls even closed in western Canada. The West, they protested, had no impact on the outcome of the election; western Canadian voters had been reduced to the status of spectators at a national political event about which they cared deeply but over which they had no control. In 1984, however, this grievance was not raised even though a majority government had once again been elected before the polls closed in western Canada. In neither case had the West been instrumental, much less decisive. The difference is that in 1984 the West ended up on the winning side, which in turn suggests that the real grievance in 1980 was that the West lost rather than that the West did not count.

The argument advanced here is that the 1984 election has significantly altered Alberta's position within the fabric of Canadian political life. In the past, Alberta stood apart in Canadian politics through its exclusion from the nation's governing coalition, and through the virulent alienation that such exclusion engendered. Now, Alberta no longer stands apart; it has been absorbed into the national mainstream. No longer is the province on the outside looking in. At the same time, its position within the governing coalition is not one that confers any special power or recognition. In a partisan sense, Alberta has become a province like the others; its monolithic contingent of Conservative MPs differs only in degree rather than in kind from the parliamentary contingents of other provinces.

For two decades, Albertans have not looked to the national government for political leadership. Instead, Albertans have viewed Ottawa as they might view the capital of a foreign power. Partly as a consequence, provincial political leaders have enjoyed a virtual monopoly in their ability to shape the political climate and mores of the province. However, within the context of the Mulroney government, Albertans can be expected to look more to the federal government for leadership, to take more of their political cues from the national Conservative party and the Mulroney government. The 'we-they' distinction that has been so central to Alberta politics has been blurred although not totally erased by the election results.

Many of the sources of conflict between Alberta and Ottawa have been removed by the 1984 election. The provincial and national government are now of the same party. The constitutional battles that marked the late 1970s and early 1980s have now abated with the proclamation of the Constitution Act, 1982, although both Senate reform and unsettled constitutional issues in Quebec have the potential to reopen constitutional debate. Intergovernmental conflict has declined for at least the short run as both the Alberta and national governments seem intent on pursuing a new climate of federal-provincial cooperation. Conflict in the energy sector can be expected to ease although not disappear. In short, the dynamics of regional, partisan and intergovernmental conflict which have been so central to political life in Alberta have been weakened by the 1984 election. Given their centrality in the past, this change in the political agenda can be expected to have a marked impact on provincial politics *within* Alberta.

September 1984 – The Provincial Impact

Historically, federal-provincial conflict and regional conflict between Alberta and the national community have both dominated and distorted political life within the province. The primary concern of Alberta politicians has been the province's place within the national community, and as a consequence debate over more narrowly-defined provincial concerns has been curtailed. Alberta governments have tended to wage election campaigns against the federal government rather than against provincial opponents; Ottawa-bashing has been commonplace as governments appeal for a mandate in order to strengthen their hand in intergovernmental conflicts. Detailed debate over social services within the province, over education, highways, the environment or the quality of provincial life has been rare. Time and time again, political debate has centred on 'them' versus 'us'.

This in turn has made life very difficult for opposition parties in Alberta. To endorse the provincial government in its battles with Ottawa would be to declare themselves redundant. To accept the provincial government's political agenda, with its emphasis on intergovernmental and regional conflict, was to deny themselves the opportunity to exploit any openings which might arise from discontent with the government's provision of services within the province. To go against the provincial government and side with the national government in federal-provincial disputes was suicidal. To try and outflank the provincial government by being even more strident in Ottawa-bashing was to push opposition parties to the brink of hysteria, although the Western Canada Concept found some electoral nourishment on this brink.

The 1984 election should transform this political agenda by reducing the prominence of federal-provincial and regional conflict. As a consequence, other more 'domestic' issues should climb up the agenda, issues which in turn should provide more openings for opposition attacks. Given the hard times upon which the province has fallen, we should expect an intensified debate over the disposition of the Alberta Heritage Savings Trust Fund; if the money in the fund was socked away for 'rainy days', might not those days be at hand? We should also expect a more extensive debate over the provision of social services, environmental concerns, and the regional distribution of government benefits within the province. In this respect, the internal political climate in Alberta should come to resemble more closely those in other provinces. Here one might anticipate a similar transformation in Quebec, where debate over the province's place within Canada also appears to be on the decline.

This is not to say that we should expect a dramatic revitalization of opposition parties in Alberta, which remain outnumbered 75 to four in the Legislative Assembly. While changes in the political climate can be expected to work to their advantage, the opposition parties themselves are in a state of disarray. Here the most important development has been the October 1984 death of NDP Leader Grant Notley in a plane crash.

Notley's death was more than a tragic loss for Alberta, for it illustrates the very fragile nature of political opposition within the province. In any political system there will be an inevitable turnover among political elites as individuals

Roger Gibbins

retire, experience electoral defeat, change careers or die. In normal circumstances, the departure of any one individual should not be expected to have a major impact on the performance of the political system. However, in a province where there are only four opposition MLAs, and where the two NDP MLAs have only recently attained the position of Official Opposition after years of effort, one man's death can have just such an impact. The subsequent by-election win by the NDP in Notley's Spirit River Fairview riding means that the NDP retains a precarious grip on its status as the official opposition even though the Representative Party also has two seats. (The Representative Party was formed in November 1984 by two independent MLAs, Walter Buck and Ray Speakers, both former Social Creditors.) There is little question, however, that Notley's death has weakened the NDP. It may also shore the Conservatives' position as the party of the moderate centre, poised to hold off a more radical challenge from a resurgent right.

The Conservatives' chief competitor for the centre of the ideological spectrum, if we use the word 'competitor' in its broadest possible sense, has been the Alberta Liberal party. Over the past decade the provincial Liberals have laboured under the very severe handicap imposed by their affiliation, formal or not, with the unpopular federal Liberals and their leader, Pierre Elliott Trudeau. Thus one might expect that the September 1984 election will have a positive impact on the electoral prospects of the provincial Liberals, freeing the provincial wing from its affiliation with an unpopular federal government. Here it is worth noting, however, that while it is correct to see the federal connection as an electoral albatross, the federal Liberals have nonetheless done much better in Alberta than has the provincial party. On average, approximately four to five times as many Albertans have voted for the federal Liberals as have voted for the provincial party. Indeed, if the provincial wing had been able to capture even half of the federal Liberal vote in the province, its electoral performance would have improved immensely. Thus it is not at all certain that the continuing collapse of the federal party across the West will work more to the advantage of the provincial party than did the Liberals' prior national success.

The Liberals have remained on the provincial electoral map largely through the personal efforts and high public profile of their leader, Nick Taylor. However, while Taylor has kept the party on the map and in the news, he has amassed a formidable string of personal electoral defeats in so doing. Should unrest with his leadership grow within the party, the Liberals may lose their most important if notably unsuccessful link with the provincial electorate. Thus, with the federal Liberals on the ropes if not going down for the count across the West, there is little ground for optimism on behalf of the provincial Liberals in Alberta.

While opponents falling to the ideological right of the Lougheed government might be seen as the beneficiaries of Notley's death, they are not without problems of their own. In the years preceding the 1984 federal election, right-wing ideological discontent was but one component of a broader political phenomenon, western alienation, which also embraced partisan and regional discontent.[8] In a sense, ideological discontent was a free-rider on the more powerful currents of regional and partisan opposition to the national government. With the election of the Mulroney government, however, both partisan and regional discontent can be expected to subside, at least over the short run. As a consequence, ideological discontent will be more exposed and isolated. Those arguing for a radically restructured economic and social order will no longer be able to hitch their ideological concerns to the larger vehicle of western alienation. Thus one might argue that ideological discontent may be more difficult to mobilize, and may provide less fertile ground for opposition parties, than was the case prior to the 1984 federal election.

It should also be noted that the electoral strength of the ideological right may also be weakened by the sheer multiplicity of right-of-centre political organizations that have emerged in recent years. As Peter McCormick has demonstrated, the pattern of one-party dominance in Alberta has stemmed from an abundance of partisan alternatives to the governing party:

The problem is not that Alberta has too few parties, but that it has too many. The problem is not that not enough Albertans vote against the government, but that not enough of them vote for the official opposition rather than the other opposition parties.[9]

There are now 12 registered political parties in the province, more than there has ever been in the past. If all 12 field candidates in the next provincial election, the likely consequence will be a fragmented and ineffectual opposition vote.

One might posit a number of election scenarios for Alberta. It could be that opposition parties positioning themselves to the right of the incumbent Conservatives may be able to catch a neoconservative tide stemming from the policies of the federal governments in both Canada and the United States. It is by no means clear, however, that such a tide will materialize or, if it does, that the Conservative government will let itself be outflanked on the right. A more likely scenario is that those on the right will find that prior support which was initially interpreted as ideological discontent will turn out to be largely regional and partisan discontent, both of which can be expected to dissipate over the short run. In this case, neo-conservative standard-bearers could find themselves hung out to dry without a significant electoral base.

Here it is interesting to note that during 1984 the Lougheed government did not move in any significant measure towards the right. Although it is often seen as a conservative government relative to the Canadian norm, and indeed frequently cloaks itself in just such terms, the Lougheed government has not followed the precedents set by the Social Credit government in British Columbia. Admittedly, the government has tried to freeze government spending, but this has been justified by fiscal necessity rather than by the more ideological argument that a smaller, leaner government is intrinsically better. There has been a significant move to privatize the delivery of social programs, but this has not been coupled with any substantial reduction in the funds available for such programs. Universities have had their budgets frozen despite growing enrollments, but this has not been coupled with a governmental attack on the worth of universities such as has occurred in British Columbia. If there is a neo-conservative tide sweeping or about to sweep the country, the Alberta government is by no means in the vanguard.

Perhaps the explanation for this is that Albertans have come to recognize that a strong provincial state is essential if some leverage is to be gained on the external forces which impinge upon the province. As University of Alberta economist Kenneth Norrie has argued, there is little reason for the Alberta economy to prosper in a laissez-faire continental environment.[10] The province is too far from markets and too population-poor to do so. Thus state intervention, be it in the form of tax relief, investment capital, market development, infrastructure support or reduced prices on petrochemical feedstocks may be essential if the Alberta economy is to have hope of diversification and any hope of competing with other jurisdictions which are favoured by their proximity to markets. This conclusion appears to be implicit in the Alberta government's 1984 white paper on economic development which called for more active state intervention.[11]

An interesting illustration of the emerging debate on government intervention is provided in an article by Roy Farran, a Calgary Herald columnist who is noted for his vigilance for any signs of centralization or socialism, creeping or otherwise. In this case, however, Farran takes on a new right-wing group, Albertans for Less Government, who have attacked the provincial government's white paper:

> Their argument is simple enough. Since the least government is best, Edmonton should not dare to address itself to diversification of the economy. Leave that to the market, they say.
> My retort would be that if Alberta does not address itself to the problem, it will not only continue in perpetual subservience to Central Canada after the oil is gone, it will also wither on the vine even more than in the '30s when agriculture was the sole prop. It would not even have a petrochemical industry if the government had not enticed Dow to invest and even today it has a struggle against more favored competitors down East.
> Neither Nova (Alberta Gas Trunk Line) nor Atco would have got into orbit without government help. Nor would Syncrude. It was the government that persuaded Northern Telecom, our great bright hope, to come and there are hundreds of others ...
> The ranchers [behind Albertans for Less Government] are dreaming of a perfect world where the game is played according to a laissez-faire Hoyle. It doesn't exist.[12]

Farran's column nicely captures the arguments that the ideological right will confront as well as the sense of pessimism and suspicion that can still be found in the province in the wake of the 1984 election.

The current government is by no means a government under seige. With a provincial election expected in the fall of 1985 or the spring of 1986, there is of yet no indication of a significant electoral challenge from the left, right or Liberal middle. Nor is there evidence that opposition parties have been able to generate an alternative vision of the province and its future that deviates in any substantial way from that which has guided the Conservative government over the past fourteen years. Nonetheless, the government is troubled in many respects. The provincial economy has been badly hurt, and recovery is unlikely to be either swift or total. Certainly the boom of the 1970s will be difficult if not impossible to re-ignite as external investors, once burned, will react with a greater degree of caution to any predictions of economic recovery. The government's quest for a more diversified provincial economy, one that would be more sheltered from the booms and busts that have afflicted first the grain economy and then the oil economy, has not been successful. Ironically, the quest for diversification fell victim to the energy boom itself – economic players outside the energy sector were unable to compete with the wages and investment returns generated by that sector. Thus the boom increased the province's reliance on oil and natural gas, and set the province up for the economic fall that came in the 1980s.

On the political front there is room for somewhat more satisfaction. Sections of the Canadian constitution, including the amending formula and the new Section 92A on nonrenewable natural resources, appear to have been crafted with western interests in mind. While the constitutional settlement was by no means ideal from a western Canadian perspective,[13] it was not antithetical to western interests. Perhaps of greatest importance, the federal Liberals have been vanquished and the national government now rests in Conservative hands. With Premier Lougheed's announcement in June 1985 of his intention to resign in the fall, an important era in Alberta politics will be brought to a close.

Lougheed's retirement highlights an unfortunate feature of Canadian political life. Under a different set of institutional arrangements, provincial leaders like Peter Lougheed might be expected to move on to national office, to bring their provincial experience and sensitivities to the national government or Parliament. In the Canadian case, however, there are few national opportunities for provincial premiers. There is no appointed post that Brian Mulroney can offer Premier Lougheed that would even come close to having the power and prestige of the premiership. There is no elected office at the national level that would compare to the premiership, no office analogous to that of a U.S. Senator. Leadership of the national Conservative party is not an option, as early retirement by the present incumbent is not to be anticipated. Thus Premier Lougheed is unlikely to move from the provincial to the national stage. His only option appears to be a complete retirement from political life.

Roger Gibbins

Looking Back, Looking Forward

1984 has been described as a pivotal year in the political evolution of Alberta. The nature of the pivot will be a turn *towards* the national community or, alternatively, a turn *away from* the intense regional alienation that has character ized political life in the province over most of the past decade. Given the change in the composition of the national government that resulted from the September 1984 election, Albertans now look forward to a more cooperative and tranquil relationship with the national government. As a consequence, one can expect political debate on issues internal to the province to sharpen as both Albertans and their political leaders become less preoccupied with the place of Alberta within the national community and the Canadian federal state.

At the same time, however, it must be stressed that the face which Alberta will turn towards the national community will be quite different in character from the one Canadians grew accustomed to during the heyday of the 'new West'. There will be less confidence in the future, and an abiding resentment that the fates snatched away the glittering future that seemed to lie before Albertans only a few short years before. We can expect, then, a more sombre stance towards the national community. While the intensity of alienation will be reduced, and while Albertans will be much more comfortable with the Mulroney government than they were with the Trudeau government even at the best of times, a wariness will persist that reflects the traumatic times that the province has been through since 1980. Particularly on the energy front, Albertans can be expected to watch the Mulroney government closely for any sign that Alberta interests are not being served, that the central Canadian political axis has changed its partisan face but not its fundamental character and dominance of national life.

Notes

1. See Gibbins, *Prairie Politics and Society: Regionalism in Decline* (Toronto: Butterworths, 1980).
2. Walter D. Young, *Democracy and Discontent*, Second Edition (Toronto: McGraw-Hill Ryerson, 1978), p. 46.
3. For an account of the Depression years, see James Gray, *The Winter Years: The Depression on the Prairies* (Toronto: Macmillan, 1966) and Michael Horn, *The Dirty Thirties* (Toronto: Copp Clark, 1972).
4. Warren E. Kalbach and Wayne W. McVey, *The Demographic Bases of Canadian Society* (Toronto: McGraw-Hill, 1971), p. 86.
5. R. Daviault, *Selected Agricultural Statistics for Canada* (Ottawa: Economics Branch, Agriculture Canada, 1976), p. 112.
6. Alberta Bureau of Statistics, *Alberta Industry and Resources,* Edmonton, 1973.
7. For a detailed discussion, see John Richards and Larry Pratt, *Prairie Capitalism: Power and Influence in the New West* (Toronto: McClelland and Stewart, 1979).

8. For a conceptual discussion of western alienation, see Gibbins, *Prairie Politics and Society*, Chapter Four.

9. Peter McCormick, 'Voting Behavior in Alberta: The Quasi-Party System Revisited', *Journal of Canadian Studies*, Vol. 15, No. 3 (Fall 1980), p. 91.

10. Kenneth H. Norrie, 'Some Comments on Prairie Economic Alienation', in J. Peter Meekison (ed.), *Canadian Federalism: Myth or Reality*, Third Edition (Toronto: Methuen, 1977).

11. Government of Alberta, *Proposals for an Industrial and Science Strategy for Albertans, 1985 to 1990*, July 1984. The paper called for a more interventionalist approach to the provincial economy including government subsidies for specific sectors of the economy, the more aggressive use of tax incentives to encourage economic activity and growth, the use of the Alberta government as a catalyst to initiate export consortia, and the development of an Alberta procurement policy to give advantage and preference to Alberta based suppliers and contractors (pp. 57-58).

12. Roy Farran, 'Far right would allow Alberta to wither on vine', *The Calgary Herald*, 1 February 1985, p. A8.

13. See Gibbins, 'Constitutional Politics and the West', in Keith Banting and Richard Simeon (eds.), *And No One Cheered: Federalism, Democracy and the Constitution Act* (Toronto: Methuen, 1983), pp. 119-132.

5 The Continuing Struggle for a Regional Development Policy

Donald J. Savoie

In a major policy statement during the 1984 federal election campaign, Brian Mulroney argued that 'despite repeated promises to end regional disparity, the actions of successive Liberal governments have prevented the provinces of Atlantic Canada from achieving their full economic potential.'[1] The problem of regional development is, of course, not new to the country's political agenda: for well over 20 years, Ottawa has made several attempts to define – and redefine – a regional development policy. The issue remains deeply rooted in Canada's political and economic forces.

The centre-periphery nature of Canada's economic structure has given rise to important differences in living standards and to different regional economic specializations. While the Toronto region has been able to develop a highly sophisticated urban structure and a strong industrial base, most of the Atlantic region – some 1,200 miles east – suffers from chronic unemployment, a weak urban structure, and a heavy reliance on natural resources. This situation, repeated in variations across the country, has led people in different regions to perceive their economic interests differently. Southern Ontario, for example, will tend to favour tariff protection while the peripheral regions, particularly the western provinces, are much more likely to espouse free trade.

Our political system itself has also served to promote these differences. Canadian federalism has 'institutionalized regionalism' with provincial governments becoming the channel through which regional interests have been articulated.[2] In *Public Money in the Private Sector*, Allan Tupper remarked that: 'The Premiers have obviously mastered the rhetoric of regional alienation', and went on to suggest that debates about a Canadian industrial strategy are shaped at least in part by the 'often conflicting goals of eleven interventionist governments.'[3]

Provincial governments reject out of hand any notion that their respective economic circumstances are shaped by market forces, and deny that federal policies are geographically neutral. In fact, the provincial governments of the four Atlantic provinces, the four western provinces, and now Quebec, firmly believe that federal economic policies actually retard regional development and favour growth in southern Ontario.[4]

Certainly, the four Atlantic provinces regard regional development and a role for the federal government in ensuring balanced economic growth between the various regions as fundamental tenets of Canadian federalism. Premier Peckford of Newfoundland, for one, recently warned that 'Canada could not survive as a nation unless some tangible progress is made in alleviating regional disparities.'[5] The importance of regional equity in economic policy-making in Canada is such that it is now a part of our constitution. Indeed, in 1982, governments committed themselves through the Constitution Act to 'reducing disparities in opportunity'.[6]

It is thus against the backdrop of these considerations that Mulroney made his pledge to give added priority to regional development. It is also against the backdrop of some 25 years of federal government efforts in this area through a host of different measures. The purpose of this paper is to review these efforts, to consider the various forces which have shaped Canadian regional development policies, and to look at the possibilities the new federal government could pursue.

The Trudeau Legacy

Some 16 years before Mulroney gave his pledge to strengthen the federal government's regional development policy, Pierre Trudeau had done the same. In the 1968 election campaign, Trudeau had stressed time and again the importance of regional development to national unity. He went so far as to suggest that the problem of regional development was as threatening to national unity as the language issue and English-French relations. In fact, he saw the two as somewhat interwoven, in that regions which were predominantly francophone were also economically underdeveloped.

Once elected, he moved quickly to establish a new department with specific responsibilities for regional development. He then appointed his trusted Quebec lieutenant, Jean Marchand, as minister of the new Department of Regional Economic Expansion (DREE).

The new department was able to build upon several programs first introduced by the Diefenbaker government and then continued or expanded in the Pearson era. The two most important programs were ARDA (Agricultural and Rural Development Act) and FRED (Fund for Rural Economic Development). Both these programs were federal-provincial efforts aimed at promoting growth in agriculture and in rural areas. FRED sought to bring forward comprehensive regional development planning in several economically-depressed areas. These were complemented by a number of other initiatives,

Donald J. Savoie

including the Atlantic Development Board which provided funding for the development of infrastructure services in Atlantic Canada, and by incentive schemes to attract the private sector to especially designated regions of the country.[7]

It was clear early on that the Trudeau government had ambitious intentions for regional development. It would attempt to accomplish more, considerably more, than had been done to date. Politically, the Trudeau government had made regional development and language policies central to its goal of giving Canadians a 'Just Society'. Economically, it was possible to stress regional development because in the late 'sixties, the national economy was buoyant, the federal treasury was, relatively speaking, burgeoning, and the trend in policy development gave priority to redistribution. Marchand summed up the situation by pointing out that 'because things are boiling over in central Canada, monetary conditions have to be tightened in order to head off inflation. The restraint may be felt here in Atlantic Canada even though, far from the economy boiling over, there is persistent and severe unemployment.'[8]

Because of these economic circumstances and because of its high priority status, funding for regional development initiatives 'was never a problem in DREE's early years.' DREE integrated the various regional development programs administered by several departments and agencies and introduced two new major ones.

Underpinning the very purpose of these two new programs was the 'growth pole' concept. Inspired by the works of French economist François Perroux, the growth pole concept was one that would see growth concentrated around certain focal points.[9] Perroux suggested that if efforts were made to strengthen these focal points, a process of self-sustaining economic growth would be set in motion.

Marchand and senior DREE officials embraced this concept and came forward with a 'special areas' program and one for 'regional industrial incentives'. The two programs shared the same objective – to encourage manufacturing and processing industries in selected communities from slow-growth regions having growth potential.

Specifically, the following would take place. Industrial centres with the potential for attracting manufacturing and processing firms would be identified. A special area agreement with the relevant provincial government would then be signed. This would provide for the construction of the required infrastructure, such as roads, water and sewer systems, and schools, thus laying the framework within which industrial growth could occur. The thinking here was that the institutional framework and the physical infrastructure in slow-growth regions were as unresponsive and stagnant as the state of industrial activity.

With the required infrastructure in place, the regional industrial incentives program, through cash grants, would then be able to attract new manufacturing industry to the selected centres. The cash grants would lower the cost of setting up production. The intent was to compensate the investor for locating in economically weak regions through a grant sufficiently large that the new production facility would generate the same return on investment that it would have, had the firm located in southern Ontario without the grant.

The special areas program, as noted above, was delivered through federal-provincial agreements.[10] A great variety of projects were sponsored, including highways, water systems, industrial parks, tourist attractions, servicing of industrial land, sewer systems, and schools. Funding arrangements were also varied, ranging from federal financing of 50 per cent of the cost of certain projects, plus a loan for part or all of the remainder. In the case of highway construction, Ottawa paid up to 100 per cent of the cost, excluding land purchases.

The second Marchand program, one that remained important throughout the life of DREE, was the regional incentives scheme. This provided grants to companies calculated on the basis of new jobs created in a designated region and on capital cost of the new or expanded plant. Later, a loan guarantee program was added to the regional incentives scheme.

For both programs, Marchand staked out a policy position from which he never deviated. The first was that DREE's existence was tied to the notion of regional equity in national economic development. He singled out eastern Quebec and the four Atlantic provinces as the regions requiring special recognition. He repeatedly suggested that if DREE were to spend less than 80 per cent of its budget east of Trois-Rivières, then the department would be failing in its purpose.[11]

Only a few years after the two programs were introduced, however, DREE came under persistent attack on at least one program – the special areas program. Provincial governments in particular argued that the program was highly discriminatory in that it favoured certain communities over others. More important, the provinces were highly critical of DREE's approach to federal-provincial relations. Ottawa, provincial governments insisted, had adopted a 'take it or leave it' approach to federal-provincial relations in the area of regional development which made close federal-provincial cooperation impossible.[12] There was, for example, no opting out provision so that provincial governments refusing to go along with federal initiatives were in fact foregoing federal funds.

There was also no convincing evidence that the two programs had contributed in any significant fashion to the reduction of regional disparities after three or four years of operation. If anything, standard indicators of economic wellbeing, such as unemployment and per capita income, had widened among the different regions. With the aid of hindsight, we now know that too high expectations had been pinned on the growth pole concept, a concept which still remains to this day incomplete. Ben Higgins, in *Growth and Change*, put it succinctly when he stated: 'Perhaps never in the history of economic thought has so much government activity taken place and so much money been invested on the foundation of so confused a concept as the growth pole became in the late 1960s and early 1970s.'[13]

Donald J. Savoie

A major policy review of regional development programming was launched inside DREE in 1972. It will be recalled that in the federal election of that year, the Trudeau government had barely clung to power, was in a weak minority position in the House, and had suffered particularly heavy losses in western Canada.

Trudeau immediately launched a series of measures to recapture public support. In the area of regional development, he moved Marchand out of DREE and replaced him with another powerful minister, Don Jamieson of Newfoundland. Trudeau also requested that DREE be involved in the preparation of the Western Opportunities Conference which had been called shortly after the 1972 election.

Jamieson pressed on with DREE's major policy review. Its conclusions were twofold: first, that the special areas program had too narrow a focus and did not lend itself to new and imaginative ways of pursuing development opportunities; and second, that federal regional development programming had to be pursued in close harmony with provincial governments.

It was this policy review that gave rise to the General Development Agreements (GDAs) and to the decentralization of DREE.[14] As has been explained elsewhere, GDAs were broad enabling documents which permitted the federal government and individual provincial governments to sponsor a variety of projects under individually negotiated subsidiary agreements. These subsidiary agreements could be province-wide in scope, or could concentrate solely on a specific sub-provincial area, an economic sector, or even a single industry.

The scope and type of activities sponsored by the subsidiary agreements is mind-boggling. DREE signed well over 100 subsidiary agreements with nine provinces, covering practically every economic sector, including fisheries, agriculture, tourism, industrial development, community development, forestry, transportation, port development, energy, ocean industry, and urban development. All in all, well over $6 billion of public funds were committed under the nine GDAs. None was signed with Prince Edward Island because a 15 year comprehensive plan had been signed in 1969. Like the GDAs, however, the plan was 'multidimensional' in scope and it too sponsored a host of initiatives in a number of economic sectors.

Provincial governments applauded the GDAs and the kind of federal-provincial cooperation that they entailed. From a provincial perspective, the GDAs had numerous attractive features. It meant new discretionary spending in a high profile field – economic development. It had the provincial governments actually delivering the project, so that they were viewed as the benefactors. By and large, the provinces came forward with proposals and the federal government responded.

The GDA approach was not without its problems and critics, however. In Ottawa, the GDAs were criticized for being little other than enabling documents. Senior officials in economic departments, including Finance and

Treasury Board, were puzzled by the hodge-podge approach of the GDAs. They had hoped that the GDAs would 'harden' over time and evolve into strategic documents or at the very least into guides to preferences or priorities for sponsoring initiatives. Thus viewed from Ottawa, the GDAs represented little more than a new source of funding for provincial governments to tap for whatever development initiative they desired, whether or not it corresponded to a coherent strategy.

It is also important to bear in mind that by the late 1980s, economic circumstances had changed considerably from when DREE was first established. In fact, by then there were a number of factors at work which were having a profound impact on the future direction of regional policy. 'Stagflation' had crept into our economic vocabulary, describing the difficult position of having at the same time both inflationary pressure and slow or no growth. An international recession had struck. Canada's industrial structure was found wanting, with some of its major components no longer capable of competing internationally. There was increasing talk about the need for government intervention to assist in the industrial restructuring of Canada's industrial heartland of southern Ontario and southern Quebec. The country's textile industry was in some difficulty, as were the automotive industry and heavy appliance sector. Thus, in some ways the regional problem had spread from eastern Quebec and the four Atlantic provinces into regions which had traditionally led the nation in economic performance. Partly as a result of this, but also because of the country-wide application of the GDA approach, DREE's budget was no longer concentrated in eastern Quebec and the Atlantic region. Montreal became a designated region under DREE's regional incentives program and the department's total expenditure budget was now allocated as follows: Atlantic region, 45 per cent; Quebec, 30 per cent; Ontario, six per cent; and the West, 20 per cent. No doubt Mulroney's criticism that past federal regional development policies have prevented Atlantic Canada from achieving its full potential stems at least in part from this shift in allocation of DREE expenditures.

At the political level in Ottawa, it was fast becoming obvious that cabinet ministers and government members of Parliament were less than enthusiastic about the GDA approach. Essentially, they regarded the GDA approach as an instrument substantially financed with federal funds but clearly favouring the political profile of provincial governments. Even Pierre De Bané, the new Minister of DREE appointed in 1980, suggested publicly that: ' he would be surprised if 10 per cent of Canadians are aware that DREE grants to business account for only 20 per cent of the department's budget, the rest going to the provinces.'[15]

The above forces led the federal government to launch a second major review of its regional development policy. This review revealed that the regional balance in the national economy was changing and that now both problems and opportunities existed in all regions. The opportunities were

Donald J. Savoie

thought to lie in the anticipated economic benefits stemming from 'mega projects' which were primarily energy-related.[16] The Atlantic provinces, for instance, were expected to benefit from a number of mega projects associated with offshore resources. To deal with this development, the review recommended that regional economic development concerns should be central to public policy planning at the federal level. A key element of the review was federal-provincial relations. On this point, the review stressed the importance of close federal cooperation, but stated that 'joint implementation of economic development programming [i.e., DREE's GDA approach] may not always be desirable.'[17] Direct federal delivery of regional development initiatives should be preferred in a number of situations.

Shortly after the policy review was completed in early 1982, the then prime minister, Pierre Trudeau, unveiled a major reorganization of the federal government. DREE would be disbanded, the GDAs would be replaced by a new and simpler set of federal-provincial agreements, a new central agency charged with the responsibility of ensuring that regional development concerns would be central to decision-making in Ottawa would be established, and a regional fund would be set up. DREE, the prime minister explained, had not been able to launch a sustained effort at promoting regional development. As a simple line department, it had been incapable of directing the departments to contribute to Ottawa's overall regional development policy. A new central agency, the Ministry of State for Regional and Economic Development (MSERD), would now be able to ensure a 'government wide' focus on regional development, thus strengthening Ottawa's commitment to regional development. A new line department, the Department of Regional Industrial Expansion, (DRIE), would deliver regional and industrial development programs.[18]

New 'Economic and Regional Development Agreements' (ERDAs) would be different from GDAs in that they would clear the way for the federal government to deliver specific initiatives directly. In practically every other aspect, however, they would resemble the GDAs. In fact, the legal format of the ERDAs and the federal-provincial coordinating mechanism at the officials level are, among other things, virtually identical to the GDAs.

The provincial director general of DREE was replaced by provincial federal economic development coordinators (FEDCs) of MSERD. The FEDC was to ensure that a 'decentralized central agency' would be present in the field and would encourage all federal departments to 'tailor' their policies and programs to correspond to the economic circumstances of the respective provinces.

A regional development fund was also established. The purpose of the fund was to support special regional and economic development efforts and would be funded by 'money freed up as the existing GDAs expire.'[19] In other words, it involved no new funding but was simply a continuation of the funding level established for the various GDAs.

The new Department of Regional Industrial Expansion was essentially an amalgam of the tourism and industry programs of the former Department of Industry, Trade and Commerce, with the addition of DREE's regional industrial incentives program. It was hoped that the new department would 'enhance the administration of regional programs' as well as 'the capacity of [Ottawa] to pursue balanced industrial growth on a national basis.'[20]

Not long after the major government reorganization, a new Liberal government under John Turner was sworn in. He quickly moved to disband MSERD. The federal government, Turner insisted, had become 'too elaborate, too complex, too slow, and too expensive.'[21] The motivation behind Turner's reorganization was thus a desire to streamline government decision-making and was not intended to address regional development policy or programs. Very little was said about regional development during Turner's press conference called to unveil his new organization. The FEDC and the ERDAs were quietly shuffled over to DRIE. Mr. Turner did, however, appoint a junior minister of state responsible for regional development, operating under the aegis of the DRIE portfolio.

The Mulroney Commitment

During the 1984 election campaign, Brian Mulroney outlined a number of specific regional development measures which a Progressive Conservative government would implement. DRIE, he revealed, would be given a 'specific legislative mandate to promote the least developed regions' and 'every department will be required to submit to the Standing Committee of Parliament on Economic and Regional Development annual assessments of the effect of departmental policies on specific regions.'[22] DRIE would also be given a wide range of new policy instruments. For instance, in addition to incentive grants, DRIE would be able to offer tax incentives. In the case of the four Atlantic provinces, efforts would be made to improve other economic infrastructures of the region. Such efforts would include facilities for transportation and communications, as well as training programs, improved market research, and other similar measures. Commitments were also made to put in place measures designed to assist communities suffering from chronic unemployment and very little economic activity.

Though the Progressive Conservative party was highly critical of the Liberals for having 'dismantled' DREE, it did not move to re-establish it when the party came to power. In naming his Cabinet, Mulroney appointed no one responsible uniquely for regional development. He dropped the concept of a minister of state responsible for regional development which Turner had introduced only a few months earlier.

By the time the Mulroney government assumed office, seven ERDA agreements had already been signed. The new government did not attempt to change or to urge the provinces to change the substance of these agreements. In fact, it moved quickly to sign ERDAs with the three remaining provinces, namely Ontario, British Columbia, and Quebec. The three new ER-DAs follow the administrative format and program approach of the seven signed earlier.

Nonetheless, there were some indications that the new government at least had a different approach to federal-provincial negotiations. The Quebec government, for example, made it clear in signing the ERDA that it had consistently refused to sign the agreement with the previous Liberal administration. Pierre Marc Johnson, the province's minister of Justice, explained that 'Negotiations had bogged down with the previous Liberal government, but things changed radically when the Progressive Conservatives came to power ... [they] have a different way of looking at things and [respect] Quebec's jurisdiction.'[23]

The ERDA approach is sufficiently flexible that it will enable Ottawa to present a different posture at the federal-provincial negotiating table. Like the GDAs, the ERDAs are broad enabling documents only, so that new programs and new initiatives can be introduced.

Provincial governments will certainly welcome changes in this area, particularly in how programs and initiatives are actually delivered to client groups. The provinces were unanimous in their support for the GDA approach and also unanimous in their opposition to the ERDA concept when it was first unveiled. Ottawa's direct delivery option under the ERDAs, in particular, incensed provincial governments. The ERDAs provide opportunity for two-track program delivery, permitting both the federal and provincial governments to deal directly with the public. In the past, the provinces had been responsible for delivering all GDA-supported initiatives. A number of provincial governments, notably those from Atlantic Canada, also hurled criticism at the federal government for allocating less funds to the ERDAs than it had to the GDAs.[24]

The new Mulroney government also inherited a fully implemented Industrial and Regional Development Program (IRDP). The program applies throughout Canada and has four levels (or tiers) of assistance, defined according to a region's needs. Need is based on level of employment, personal income, and provincial capacity. Tier one includes the most developed part of Canada, while tier four is designed for the five per cent of the population living in areas of greatest need. Financial assistance for tier four regions is considerably more generous than that for tier one.

In line with its election pledge to promote the least developed regions, the Mulroney government unveiled some adjustments to IRDP on 9 November 1984. DRIE Minister, Sinclair Stevens, pointed out that the adjustments were designed in part to 'ensure that support is provided in areas of the country where it is most needed.'[25] Important restrictions were applied to tier one regions, or the most developed areas of the country. For instance, 'modernization' and 'expansion' projects are no longer eligible for assistance in these regions.

Shortly after assuming power, the press reported that the new Mulroney government was adopting, and would continue to pursue at least during the first months of its mandate, a 'Mother Hubbard' approach.[26] That is, they would maintain that the previous Liberal government had left things much worse than they had anticipated and that very little funding was left to undertake new initiatives.

In the area of regional development policy and programs, the Mother Hubbard analogy is apt: as in the nursery rhyme, the new government found 'the cupboard was bare'.

The Mulroney government inherited no organization, no pool of expertise on regional development issues. DREE's personnel had been dispersed throughout the government when the department was disbanded. Moreover, any hopes that regional development would be awarded added priority with the establishment of MSERD were dashed when former Prime Minister Turner did away with that ministry to streamline government operations. With respect to any established level of funding for regional development purposes, the most that can be said is that it is unclear what levels actually existed when the new government was sworn in. Virtually nothing was said about the regional fund after it was first established. Trudeau had declared that the fund would reach $200 million by 1984-85. It is impossible to determine if in fact it did ever reach that level or, for that matter, even if the fund still exists.

The Mulroney government will thus be defining a new regional development policy with very little to build upon in terms of any central expertise or capacity to assist in the definition process, in terms of government structure, or of existing policies or programs. The government will, however, be able to look at past experiences, at the efforts of DREE, and at a growing body of literature on Canadian regional development policy.

Regional Development: Sorting out the Contradictions

Perhaps the first fact any new government realizes in the regional development field is that it is complex. Possible solutions that at first glance appear to be relatively simple and straightforward can turn out to hold important negative implications for other regional development considerations. Desirable regional objectives are not always mutually compatible. For instance, politicians from the traditional have-not regions may well applaud the substantial progress made in recent years in alleviating regional disparities in family income. They may well overlook, however, the fact that in large part the progress is attributable to federal transfer payments.

Yet, it is now widely accepted that federal transfer payments have also served to blunt economic adjustment in slow-growth regions which have grown dependent on transfer payments to maintain a level of services. In addition, transfer payments could have placed upward pressure on wage rates and thus have had an inhibiting effect on private investment. Similarly, transfer payments to provincial governments in slow-growth regions may have two contradicting effects. On the one hand, they may have allowed the provincial governments to support highly desirable economic and social programs. On the other, they may well have also made it possible for the same governments to avoid difficult adjustments.

To sort out these contradictions, one should start by asking some rather fundamental questions. One such question, which may on the surface appear banal, is simply – what is the central purpose of regional development policy? In the late 1960s, before government restraint set in, its purpose was clear to everyone – to alleviate regional disparities, as measured by per capita income and unemployment rates.

With growing government deficits, regional development planners, particularly those in Ottawa, began in the late 1970s to define regional development essentially as synonymous with economic development, but at the regional level. Thus, the purpose behind a regional development policy was to permit each region of Canada to achieve its full economic development potential, much in the same way that national economic policies are designed to achieve Canada's full economic development potential. Regional economic development policy was now described as constituting a 'no-cost' policy. There could well be some short-run inefficiencies in resource allocation but over time, regions would become economically self-sustaining. DREE, by and large, was responsible for this 'no-cost' myth by producing countless reports pointing to vast untapped economic potential in the lagging regions. Former DREE minister Marcel Lessard explained: '[DREE is not] a welfare agency ... our primary objective ... is to help each region of Canada nurture ... those areas and prospects with the best potential for development.'[27]

Unfortunately, regional disparities, as traditionally defined, persist. There are still numerous pockets of surplus labour, and elected officials representing these areas retain a strong sense of responsibility for doing something about it. There is also unfortunately no solid evidence to suggest that these regions contain vast untapped economic potential.

It was relatively easy for DREE to produce rather optimistic background papers describing the economic potential of a given region. What was considerably more difficult to do, and what was not done very often, if at all, were evaluations describing the full impact of a given DREE-supported project, showing the economic benefits measured against the cost to the public purse.

Thus we now know that solutions to regional disparities are not as easily found and applied as we imagined in the late 1960s. We also know that governments are currently operating under very difficult financial circumstances. What this suggests is that rather than putting forward unrealistic goals such as 'alleviating regional disparities' governments should prepare realistic assessments of what can be achieved in the different regions of the country. They should also establish parameters within which proposals can be compared on the basis of the impact of net economic development and within which they would be prepared to intervene to support initiatives. In attempting to define such parameters, a number of considerations will invariably come into play, considerations which could well prove difficult to manage.

An overriding consideration is federal-provincial relations. Responsibilities and powers for regional development are not explicitly assigned in the constitution to a particular level of government. As well, students of regional development also argue that viable measures to promote regional development must be multi-dimensional and, by their very nature, cut across jurisdictional lines.[28] Thus, close federal-provincial cooperation is essential if every possible lever to promote regional development is to be employed and every opportunity pursued.

Certainly from a provincial government point of view, the most successful era in federal-provincial relations in this field was the mid and late 1970s as represented by the GDA process. However, while there are obvious advantages in having close, harmonious federal-provincial relations, there may also be a price to pay. Provincial governments will quite naturally promote measures designed to strengthen their provincial economies, paying little heed to what these measures may hold for other provinces. And they may well also be tempted to assess the quality of federal-provincial relations in terms of the federal government's willingness to support their proposed measures.

Everyone recognizes that the GDAs gave rise to harmonious federal-provincial relations. From a regional development perspective, however, GDA-supported measures had negative spillover effects on the economies of neighbouring provinces.[29] Pump priming a provincial economy with federal funds may have a certain political appeal and short term economic benefits, but make only a limited contribution to self-sustaining growth.

Increasingly, economists and geographers are looking to the interdependence of provincial and urban economies to explain economic growth. It has been suggested, for example, that the growth of Moncton is tied to that of Halifax. It has also been suggested that no appreciable progress can be made in narrowing the economic gap between central Canada and the three Maritime provinces without somehow developing a sophisticated and interrelated urban structure in the region.

What the above issues call for is a willingness on the part of the federal government to encourage a broader look at the means of achieving economic development. That is, a viable economic package for Prince Edward Island can only be formulated in concert with the economic circumstances of New Brunswick, Nova Scotia, and other eastern provinces. This challenge may well call for politically difficult decisions, such as a refusal to support initiatives in a particular sector if they are likely to have a negative impact on existing facilities in a neighbouring province. The federal government is usually in the best position to spot interprovincial spillovers, and is also usually more willing to put in place measures to integrate better regional economies. Such measures, however, are quite often less popular with provincial governments than are federal funds in support of provincially-prepared initiatives.

The above also leads us to ask another fundamental question. In defining its regional development policy, should the federal government attempt to influence regional balance within a province, as well as among provinces? Federal policy to date has included a strong sub-provincial planning and programming focus: DREE's RDIA boundaries in some instances only covered parts of a province; DRIE's IRDP program currently criss-crosses provinces with different funding levels, and a number of federal-provincial subsidiary agreements were especially designed for selected sub-provincial areas, such as northeastern New Brunswick, the western northlands, Labrador, and so on.[30]

A case can now be made that the federal government should focus exclusively on the provincial level. For one thing, it could be argued that Canada can no longer afford to spread its economic development efforts too widely. For another, with the growing importance of integrating regional economies to promote self-sustaining development, and of encouraging provincial governments to view growth outside their own boundaries as positive, it could be argued that the federal government should concentrate its efforts exclusively on these two points. After all, effective integration implies a nation-wide focus.

In addition, when designating areas for regional development, a trade-off has to be made at some point between concentrating on the most needy regions of the country and those areas large enough to provide real opportunities for development. The federal government could decide to concentrate its efforts on the neediest regions, and limit its programming to, say, only five per cent of the population. However, such a concentration on the poorest regions would carry a cost. The most isolated and thinly populated regions, which invariably are also the poorest, offer very limited opportunities for development. Thus, Ottawa may be tempted to widen geographical coverage, so that a greater number of choices among developmental opportunities are available.

Regardless of what decision is made in this respect, the federal government will have to deal with the real world of politics. If, for example, a decision is made that total integration should take place and thus no regional program should be supported, it would no doubt have a difficult time convincing MPs representing slow-growth regions that the decision should be supported. It is hard to imagine an MP explaining that in the interest of the national economy or even in the long term interest of the region he represents, he does not support any special regional economic assistance for his own riding.

Regardless of its decision on the geographical focus of its regional programs, the federal government has several broad approaches to regional development from which to choose. Here again questions have to be asked as to whether or not governments want to play a highly interventionist role, and what program instruments they wish to employ.

There are several routes open to governments. They can opt for a highly interventionist role and thus put together a comprehensive program package.

Such a package would include a mechanism to provide for federal-provincial consultation and program delivery. The ERDAs, given their flexibility, could be adopted for this purpose. The package could also include a variety of regional incentives schemes, including cash grants, loan guarantees, tax incentives, transportation subsidies, special labour subsidies, infrastructure facilities, such as incubator industrial malls, and so on. In addition, special initiatives at the community-level could be supported through federal-provincial programming or through special 'one-shot' initiatives such as the establishment of a development agency for a given community. This approach would imply a government involvement in the private sector and strong legislative authority to influence the location of business activities. The approach assumes that the nature of regional problems is known and that appropriate instruments and initiative can be brought to bear on them.

Another avenue Ottawa and the provinces could explore is policy and program coordination. Such an approach does not necessarily entail the establishment of new programs or even the continuation of existing ones. Rather, it calls for all federal and provincial departments and agencies to contribute to regional development. It could, for example, require departments to display in their budgets their programs and expenditure levels, by regions. It assumes that further 'regionalization' of existing government programs is possible. The approach thus requires a high level of information and data on regional economic circumstances and government programs and also an administrative structure to ensure that this information is made available. The Mulroney government was pointing in this direction when it made an election pledge to 'require every department to submit ... annual assessments of the effect of departmental policies on specific regions.'[31]

A third possible approach involves the design and promotion of conditions conducive to private sector enterprises. The approach is based on the premise that general framework policies of the federal and provincial governments, such as fiscal and tariff policies, are key determinants of national and regional growth. It is also based on fewer regional development programs and stresses a greater role for the private sector. Its focus is on the need to increase the rate of growth of the national economy rather than on redistributing the gains from growth. Development of slow-growth regions is thus directly linked to strong national growth. This approach also implies fewer and possibly different regional development program instruments. Tax incentives, for example, are preferred over cash grants, in that tax incentives are only of benefit to those able to turn a profit. Firms are encouraged to reach maximum profitability and efficiency and thus bring added benefit to the region in which they are located and to the national economy as well. Cash grants, on the other hand, favour all that apply and are awarded to companies whether they are efficient or not.[32]

Whatever approach or combination of approaches the Mulroney government opts for, the search for a new regional development strategy should be

Donald J. Savoie

guided by more realistic expectations of what can be accomplished than was done previously. One keen observer of regional development policy described past expectations in the following fashion: 'There has been throughout a search for panaceas, and one after another has been presented to the Court of Developers, a blushing debutante, beautifully gowned, soon to be embraced in marriage and sometimes, not long afterwards, divorced.'[33] The one thing we have learned over the past 30 years surely is that there is no panacea for regional development. The very search for an easy solution was likely inspired by a somewhat naive faith in what government programs could accomplish. By accepting that the problem of regional development is both complex and difficult, governments will be able to set more realistic objectives and define new programs and initiatives accordingly.

Notes

1. Statement by the Hon. Brian Mulroney at Halifax, Nova Scotia, 2 August 1984.
2. Allan Tupper, *Public Money in the Private Sector* (Kingston: Institute of Intergovernmental Relations, Queen's University, 1982), pp. 41, 49.
3. *Ibid.*, p. 41.
4. *Ibid.*, Chapter 4.
5. Government of Newfoundland, *Discussion Paper on Major Bilateral Issues: Canada-Newfoundland*, p. 4.
6. Canada, *The Canadian Constitution 1981 – A Resolution Adopted by the Parliament of Canada, December 1981* (Publications Canada, 1981).
7. See, for example, Frank Walton, 'Canada's Atlantic Region: Recent Policy for Economic Development', *The Canadian Journal of Regional Science*, Vol. 1, No. 2, (Autumn), p. 44.
8. Canada, Department of Regional Economic Expansion, *Atlantic Conference '68 – A New Policy for Regional Development*, 29 October 1968, mimeo, p. 7.
9. François Perroux, *L'Economie du XXe siècle* (Paris: Presses universitaires de Paris, 1959), p. 179.
10. See, among many others, J.P. Françis and M.G. Pillai, 'Regional "Economic Disparities" Regional development Policies in Canada' in *Regional Poverty and Change* (Ottawa: Canadian Council on Rural Development, 1973), pp. 136-37.
11. 'The more you extend it,' he insisted, 'the more you weaken it [special areas programs] ... We have to stick to our guns.' See Canada, House of Commons, Standing Committee on Regional Development, *Minutes of Proceedings*, 1969-70, 15 April 1970, p. 3:62.
12. Anthony Careless, *Initiative and Response: The Adaptation of Canadian Federalism to Regional Economic Development* (Montreal: McGill-Queen's University Press, 1977).
13. Benjamin Higgins, 'From Growth Poles to Systems of Interactions in Space', *Growth and Change*, Vol. 14, No. 4, p. 5.
14. See Donald J. Savoie, *Federal-Provincial Collaboration: The Canada-New Brunswick General Development Agreement* (Montreal: McGill-Queen's University Press, 1981).
15. 'Provinces Must Fit Programmes to Ottawa's – DeBané says', *The Globe and Mail* (Toronto), 13 August 1981, p. 1.

16. See Canada, Department of Finance, *Economic Development for Canada in the 1980s* (Ottawa: Department of Finance, 1981).
17. *Ibid.*, p. 11.
18. Canada, Office of the Prime Minister, *Release – Reorganization for Economic Development*, 12 January 1982.
19. *Ibid.*
20. *Ibid.*
21. 'Trudeau – Pitfield bureaucracy first item on Turner's overhaul', *The Globe and Mail* (Toronto), 2 July 1984, p. 5.
22. Statement by Hon. Brian Mulroney at Halifax, Nova Scotia, 2 August 1984.
23. 'Quebec Signs New Economic Development Agreement', *The Gazette* (Montreal), 15 December 1984, p. 2.
24. See, among many others, 'Federal Aid is $100 Million in Arrears, Peckford claims', *The Globe and Mail* (Toronto), 10 February 1974, p. 4.
25. Ottawa, Department of Regional Industrial Expansion, *Adjustments to Industrial and Regional Development Program – News Release*, 9 November 1984.
26. See, for example, 'When do we blame PCs for the deficit?' *The Gazette* (Montreal), 18 October 1984, p. C-4.
27. Canada, *Proceedings of the Standing Senate Committee on National Finance* (21 February 1981), issue no. 3, p. 3A:7 and 3A:8.
28. Donald J. Savoie, 'Co-operative Federalism with Democracy', *Policy Options* (Montreal), Vol. 3, No. 6, pp. 54-58.
29. See Savoie, *Federal-Provincial Collaboration*, Chapter 7.
30. Canada, Department of Regional Economic Expansion, *Summaries of Federal-Provincial General Development Agreements and currently active subsidiary agreements*, (various dates).
31. Statement by Hon. Brian Mulroney at Halifax, Nova Scotia, 2 August 1984.
32. See Donald J. Savoie, *Cash Incentives Versus Tax Incentives for Regional Development: Issues and Considerations* (forthcoming). See also Ken Woodside, 'Tax Incentives Versus Subsidies: Political Considerations in Government Choice', *Canadian Public Policy*, Vol. 5, No. 2, p. 253.
33. Benjamin Higgins, 'The Task Ahead: The Search for a new Local and Regional Development Strategy in the 1980s', United Nations Centre for Regional Development – Nagoya Japan, 11-16 November 1981, p. 1.

Donald J. Savoie

6 Negotiating Aboriginal Self-Government

David C. Hawkes

Introduction

Each spring for the past three years, the Canadian public has witnessed two full days of televised discussion and debate as the Prime Minister, the provincial Premiers, leaders of the Territorial governments, and representatives of national aboriginal organizations met in Ottawa to discuss constitutional reform. These discussions were mandated by the proclamation of the Constitution Act, 1982, and its subsequent amendment in 1983. Although initial discussions addressed a wide range of issues, such as aboriginal rights in the areas of land, resources, self-determination, fiscal relations, language, culture, education, law, economic development, health and social services, recent deliberations have focused on one agenda item – 'aboriginal self-government'. Not only does this term include many of the issues noted above, it also encapsulates the aspirations of Canada's aboriginal peoples. For them, these negotiations represent an opportunity to at least partially reverse hundreds of years of oppressive government policies and neglect, and to improve their intolerable socio-economic condition. Only through greater self-determination do they believe that this can come about.

This Chapter examines recent negotiations on aboriginal self-government, concentrating analysis on developments which have occurred since the election of the Progressive Conservative federal government in September 1984. Throughout the analysis, the positions of the various parties to the negotiations are tracked, proposals and counter-proposals are explained, a sense of the debate and the negotiating strategies is imparted, and the outcomes of the negotiations are examined.

The period under examination, from September 1984 to June 1985, was critical to aboriginal self-government negotiations (and more generally to constitutional reform as it relates to aboriginal peoples) for several reasons. It was the first test of the new federal government whose views on these issues were largely unknown. The opportunity existed, had the new government wished to take advantage of it, to radically alter federal policy in this field. Secondly, this period represented, in retrospect, the end of an era or phase in negotiations on aboriginal peoples and constitutional reform. This phase which began in the late 1970s was marked by discussions regarding the entrenchment of aboriginal rights in the constitution, and by numerous multilateral ministerial meetings and First Ministers' Conferences focusing on constitutional reform. With respect to aboriginal self-government, it represented a 'top-down' approach to the issue – first, recognition of the right to aboriginal self-government in the constitution, and then negotiation of its form and substance.

The approach adopted at the June 1985 meeting of government ministers and aboriginal leaders, perhaps by default, was quite different. It began a new phase, which will be marked by bilateral (federal *or* provincial government and aboriginal people) and trilateral (federal *and* provincial governments and aboriginal people) negotiations on the form and substance of aboriginal self-government at the local, regional and provincial levels. Discussions of constitutional reform will not loom large. Rather, they will focus on more mundane matters such as how aboriginal peoples can effectively deliver services to their people in the fields of education, economic development, and the like, and how aboriginal self-government is to be financed. This represents a shift to a 'bottom-up' approach to the issue – negotiation of the form and substance of aboriginal self-government, and then consideration of its entrenchment or protection in the constitution.

The developments of this period also illustrate a more general phenomenon in intergovernmental relations, one particularly evident in the negotiations on aboriginal self-government. This might be termed the 'ratchetting up' of the lowest common denominator. Intergovernmental negotiations, by their very nature, tend to be slow and incremental. In part, this is a function of the number of parties to the negotiations. In the case of the negotiations on aboriginal constitutional matters, 17 parties have been involved (the federal government, 10 provincial governments, two territorial governments, and four aboriginal peoples' organizations). While progress has been less than dramatic, the lowest common denominator, or the least which all governments are prepared to accept with respect to this issue, has risen significantly since negotiations began in 1983.

Throughout the negotiations, there has been an implicit trade-off between reaching federal-provincial agreement and protecting aboriginal rights, between the cost of reaching agreement at the expense of diluting the protection and recognition of rights. In terms of the intergovernmental negotiations, we will examine the costs incurred in ratchetting up the lowest common denominator, and whether these costs are inherent in such negotiations.

David C. Hawkes

The Chapter begins with a brief review of the background to the current negotiations. This is followed by an exploration of the preparatory Ministerial meetings and the 1985 First Ministers' Conference (FMC) on Aboriginal Constitutional Matters. The follow-up Ministerial meeting to the FMC is then analyzed, and the Chapter concludes with some observations on the outcomes of the negotiations and on what lies ahead.

Background

Section 35(2) of the Constitution Act, 1982, identifies Indian, Inuit and Métis as the 'aboriginal peoples of Canada'. Representing Indian peoples in the negotiations is the Assembly of First Nations, while the Inuit are represented by the Inuit Committee on National Issues. The Métis are represented by two organizations: the Métis National Council (which defines 'Métis' as the descendants of persons of mixed Indian and European parentage, who formed an historic Métis nation in western Canada), and the Native Council of Canada (which defines 'Métis' more broadly: those persons of partial Indian ancestry, regardless of place of residence within Canada).

The proposals of aboriginal peoples for self-government cover a wide variety of possibilities. Most are based on the assumption that self-government exists on a land base, although others have advocated proposals which do not make this assumption, such as guaranteed representation for aboriginal peoples in the federal Parliament and in provincial and territorial legislatures. The issue of land for those aboriginal peoples without a land base may prove difficult to resolve. There appear to be three critical elements to those proposals which do assume a land base:

- [ ] whether the government is public (based on territory) or ethnic (based on ethnicity);
- [ ] whether the government is regional or local/community in scope; and
- [ ] the amount of power exercised by the government, be it autonomous (with legislative powers), semi-autonomous (with mixed powers), or dependent (with administrative powers).

These elements give some indication of the issues to be resolved, and why their resolution will not be an easy task. Especially difficult is the question of which powers and resources are to be assumed by aboriginal governments, perhaps at the expense of federal and provincial governments.

Although the resolution of such issues will be difficult, there is some impetus upon governments, aside from the pressure of public opinion and ethical considerations, to negotiate a political settlement. Should they fail to do so, the aboriginal peoples might take the matter to the courts. If self-government was determined by the courts to be an existing aboriginal right, the costs (both in terms of power and finances) of the court remedy to federal and provincial governments could be greater than that negotiated in the political arena.

Consultations have not always been directed towards such issues. Although the 1984 and 1985 First Ministers' Conferences on Aboriginal Constitutional Matters focused attention on aboriginal self-government, negotiations on aboriginal peoples and constitutional reform began some time earlier.

By the mid and late 1970s, aboriginal peoples' organizations were advocating the constitutional protection of their rights as indigenous people. The first concrete recognition of the issue was contained in the federal government White Paper on the Constitution, entitled *A Time for Action*, and its legislative companion, Bill C-60, which were tabled in 1978. Bill C-60 contained a provision which attempted to shield certain aboriginal rights from the general application of the Charter of Rights, to which all Canadians would be subject. By December 1979, the three national aboriginal organizations at that time – the National Indian Brotherhood, the Native Council of Canada (the sole national organization then representing Métis), and the Inuit Tapirisat of Canada – were meeting with the federal-provincial Continuing Committee of Ministers on the Constitution (CCMC) to discuss the participation of aboriginal peoples in the constitutional reform process.

When the First Ministers' Conference in 1980 failed to reach unanimous agreement on amending the constitution, the federal government decided to proceed with patriation unilaterally. The federal constitutional resolution of October 1980 barely touched on the concerns of aboriginal peoples, much less offered any protection of their rights. National aboriginal peoples' organizations joined in the efforts of eight provincial governments to lobby, both in Ottawa and in London, England, against unilateral patriation.

Unilateral patriation was stopped in its tracks in September 1981 with the Supreme Court decision concerning the federal constitutional resolution (Reference Re: The Amendment of the Constitution of Canada). The Supreme Court ruled that, by constitutional convention, a substantial measure of provincial consent was required on matters affecting federal-provincial relations before such a constitutional amendment could be forwarded to Westminster. It was back to the bargaining table.

At the ensuing First Ministers' Conference in November 1981, a constitutional accord was finally reached. The accord was partial, and remains so, since Quebec did not sign the agreement. During the negotiations, a section of the federal constitutional package which 'recognized and affirmed' the 'aboriginal and treaty rights of the aboriginal peoples of Canada' was deleted, at the request of several provinces. Intense lobbying on the part of aboriginal peoples and several governments led to its restoration in January 1982, but with one important addition. The word 'existing' was placed before 'aboriginal and treaty rights', leaving open the question of what rights then existed.

Patriation was completed with the proclamation of the Constitution Act, 1982 on 17 April. Three sections of the Act relate directly to aboriginal peoples. Section 25 guarantees that The Canadian Charter of Rights and Freedoms will

David C. Hawkes

not 'abrogate or derogate from any aboriginal treaty or other rights or freedoms that pertain to the aboriginal peoples of Canada, including:

(a) any rights or freedoms that have been recognized by the Royal Proclamation of October 7, 1763; and
(b) any rights or freedoms that may be acquired by the aboriginal peoples of Canada by way of land claims settlement.

Section 35 states that:

(1) The existing aboriginal and treaty rights of the aboriginal peoples of Canada are hereby recognized and affirmed.
(2) In this Act, 'aboriginal peoples of Canada' includes the Indian, Inuit and Métis peoples of Canada.

Section 37 provided for the convening of a First Ministers' Conference on Aboriginal Constitutional Matters by 17 April 1983, and for the participation of aboriginal peoples' representatives and delegates from the Northwest Territories and the Yukon in those discussions.

That conference was held in March 1983, and in retrospect, it was a great success. The parties to the negotiations signed an accord covering four topics: a process for negotiating the definition of aboriginal rights; sexual equality of aboriginal peoples; consultation on constitutional amendments affecting aboriginal peoples; and the protection of future and existing land claims settlements. The result was the first amendment to the new constitution. Section 25(b) was amended to read '(b) any rights or freedoms that now exist by way of land claims agreements or may be so acquired'. Two new sub-sections were added to section 35: the first included existing and future land claims agreements in the definition of 'treaty rights'; the second guaranteed aboriginal and treaty rights equally to male and female persons. Section 35 was amended to provide for a First Ministers' Conference to be convened, including representatives of the aboriginal peoples of Canada, before any amendment can be made to the constitution which directly affects aboriginal peoples. And a new part was added to section 37, dealing with constitutional conferences. At least three more First Ministers' Conferences on Aboriginal Constitutional Matters would be held: in 1984, 1985 and 1987.

In a separate but very much related initiative, a House of Commons Special Committee on Indian Self-Government had been struck in December, 1982. Its report, entitled *Indian Self-Government in Canada*, and popularly known as the Penner Report after Committee Chairman Keith Penner, had a dramatic effect on aboriginal constitutional negotiations when it was tabled in November 1983. Although national aboriginal peoples' organizations were increasingly looking towards self-government as a means of both protecting and exercising aboriginal rights, the Penner Report brought aboriginal self-government to the forefront of constitutional negotiations. It also focused public attention on the status Indian peoples of Canada, some would argue at the expense of other aboriginal peoples.

The Penner Report recommended the recognition of Indian First Nations governments with substantial legislative powers through an Act of Parliament, in addition to entrenching the right of Indian people to self-government in the constitution. The result would be that Indian people would determine their own form of government, establish criteria for the self-identification of membership in Indian communities, and exercise jurisdiction in such fields as resources, social services, taxation and education. Block funding would be provided by the federal government.[1]

The federal government's response to the Penner Report was made public on 5 March 1984, a mere three days before the 1984 First Ministers' Conference on Aboriginal Constitutional Matters. The federal response, as later articulated in Bill C-52, an Act relating to self-government for Indian Nations, did not capture the spirit of the Committee's recommendations. For example, sections of the proposed legislation dealt with the 'Breakdown of Indian Nations Governments', and enabled the federal Minister to appoint an administrator to carry out the essential functions of an Indian Nation government if, in his opinion, it was unable to do so. Indian opposition to the bill was swift and strong. Bill C-52 died on the Order Paper with the dissolution of Parliament in 1984, and no amended version of it has since been introduced.[2]

The effect of the Penner Report and the federal response was to further focus the attention of the 1984 Conference on one agenda item – aboriginal self-government. On the first day of the Conference, the federal government tabled, to everyone's surprise, a draft constitutional amendment on aboriginal self-government. It is not surprising, given the lack of preparatory work, that the federal proposal met with stiff opposition. Some even suspected that the motives of the federal government were directed more towards good public relations than achieving constitutional reform.

The 1984 First Ministers' Conference on Aboriginal Constitutional Matters was a failure of colossal proportions. No agreement was reached on either a constitutional amendment respecting aboriginal self-government, or on a work plan for achieving agreement. The Conference ended in suspicion and innuendo, with many First Ministers asking what aboriginal self-government 'meant', and many aboriginal leaders demanding its constitutional entrenchment. The process of constitutional reform as it relates to aboriginal peoples was in serious trouble.

The New Federal Government

The election of a national Progressive Conservative government in September 1984 caused further disquiet. Would aboriginal peoples and constitutional reform remain a priority for the federal government? Would the new federal government take a less progressive position vis-à-vis aboriginal self-government?

The first test came at a Ministers' meeting on Aboriginal Constitutional Matters, held in Ottawa on 17 and 18 December. To the obvious surprise of some

David C. Hawkes

provincial government ministers, the new government was even stronger and more supportive of aboriginal self-government than was the former administration. Justice Minister John Crosbie, the lead federal minister on aboriginal peoples and constitutional reform, tabled a document outlining five general constitutional options regarding aboriginal self-government. The approach he advocated was to recognize the general rights of aboriginal peoples in the constitution, and to give content to these rights through subsequent negotiation. This was the 'top-down' approach.

The approach would work as follows. At the 1985 First Ministers' Conference on Aboriginal Constitutional Matters, agreement would be reached to:

(a)   entrench in the constitution; or
(b)   sign a political accord

for a process of recognizing the right(s) of aboriginal peoples (to self-government), the identification and elaboration of these rights being subject to the negotiating process outlined below. A negotiating process would be instituted at the regional or community level, of a trilateral (federal-provincial-aboriginal) or bilateral (federal-aboriginal) nature, to reach agreements on specific rights to be identified and elaborated, such as the form, structure and powers of aboriginal self-government. These agreements would then be brought to the multilateral level (First Ministers' Conference) for ratification, after which they would be protected under section 35 of the Constitution Act, 1982, as are treaties and modern land claims agreements.

Some of the provincial governments, notably Ontario, were pressing for a political agreement or accord at the 1985 Conference outside of the constitutional framework. Ontario saw an accord encompassing three elements:

☐   a statement of principles to guide the process;
☐   a statement of objectives which would focus discussions in terms of expected results on specific issues; and
☐   a workplan which recognizes the desirability of regional, tripartite discussions focusing on the issue of institutions of aboriginal self-government as they relate to each of the aboriginal peoples of Canada.

The objectives for the 1985 Conference, as Ontario saw them, were to strengthen the political process and to clarify federal-provincial legislative and financial responsibilities for aboriginal peoples.

Another preparatory meeting of government ministers and aboriginal leaders was held in Toronto on 11 and 12 March 1985, less than a month before the 1985 First Ministers Conference on Aboriginal Constitutional Matters. The federal government tabled a 'Comprehensive Draft Accord' for consideration at the First Ministers' Conference. The proposed accord contained two options with respect to aboriginal self-government: 'Option A' was an elaboration of the federal proposal made in December for constitutional amendments relating to self-government institutions for aboriginal peoples. It also contained the text of a draft amendment to clarify the sexual equality clause as it applies to aboriginal peoples.

'Option B' was not a federal proposal at all, but an attempt to consolidate the views of various provincial governments on a non-constitutional (i.e., political) approach, as was put forward by Ontario in December. It described a possible political accord covering such matters as the negotiating process for achieving agreement on aboriginal self-government, the objectives and subject matter of the discussions, the consultation process, the reporting relationship (back to the First Ministers), and constitutional and legislative measures to be taken should agreement be reached. Other elements of the 'Comprehensive Draft Accord' dealt with federal-provincial cooperation on non-constitutional matters affecting aboriginal peoples (e.g. social and economic programs and services), statistical data respecting aboriginal peoples, and preparations for the 1987 First Ministers' Conference. On the last item, two optional workplans and timetables were proposed.

A small explosion of counter-proposals followed the presentation of the federal 'Comprehensive Draft Accord'. Premier Hatfield of New Brunswick tabled a proposed constitutional amendment on aboriginal self-government, similar in some ways to the federal proposal. Ontario altered its position somewhat from the December meeting, much to the delight of aboriginal leaders present. Ontario advocated entrenchment of the right to aboriginal self-government within the framework of the Canadian federation in 1985, agreed in principle to the proposed federal constitutional amendment, but also argued that the amendment should be accompanied by a political accord, which would provide the framework necessary for specific negotiations. Ontario also took the opportunity to admonish its sister provinces for their fears about what the wording of any constitutional amendment may mean, suggesting that responsible governments would not use this as a reason for inaction.

Saskatchewan proposed a 'Statement of Commitments and Objectives' which it advocated be adopted at the 1985 Conference. The statement would guide ongoing discussions leading to the 1987 Conference, but the commitments were for discussions only.

Nova Scotia proposed a rather broad accord which included, among other objectives: government of their own (aboriginal peoples') affairs; preservation and enhancement of aboriginal cultures, languages and traditions; and the provision of public services for aboriginal peoples comparable to those available to other Canadians, in addition to special economic and social initiatives for aboriginal peoples.[3] Appended to the proposed Nova Scotia accord were draft amendments to the constitution under section 35. The first provided for the constitutional protection of aboriginal self-government agreements; the second for the guarantee of equality of aboriginal peoples; and the third for affirmative action measures for aboriginal peoples.

For the information of other governments, Quebec tabled a Motion for the recognition of aboriginal rights in Quebec,[4] which was to be debated in the National Assembly during the following week. (It was subsequently passed.) Not having signed the 1981 accord which led to the Constitution Act, 1982, Quebec has been unable to accept any proposals requiring its amendment. Quebec's participation at these constitutional meetings has been for the stated purpose of representing the interests of aboriginal peoples in Quebec. The Motion, first introduced in December 1984, would commit the Government of Quebec to a wide range of measures vis-à-vis aboriginal peoples. The Motion recognized the existence of Indian and Inuit nations in Quebec, and existing aboriginal rights and those set forth in The James Bay and Northern Quebec Agreement and the Northeastern Quebec Agreement. It also deemed these agreements and all future agreements and accords of the same nature to have the effect of treaties. The Motion urged the Government to pursue negotiations and to conclude, with willing aboriginal nations, agreements guaranteeing them:

☐ the right to self-government within Quebec;
☐ the right to their own language, culture and traditions;
☐ the right to own and control their land;
☐ the right to hunt, fish, trap, harvest and participate in wildlife management; and
☐ the right to participate in, and benefit from, the economic development of Quebec.

It also declared that aboriginal rights apply equally to men and women, and proposed that a permanent parliamentary forum be established to enable the aboriginal peoples to express their rights, needs and aspirations.

When the Ministers' meeting ended on the afternoon of 12 March, the stage was set for the 1985 First Ministers' Conference. The federal government, supported by Ontario, New Brunswick, Manitoba and the Northwest Territories, were advocating the constitutional entrenchment of the right to self-government for aboriginal peoples within the Canadian federation, with that right to be given effect through a series of negotiated agreements at the local and regional levels. Quebec, it appeared, might be willing to consider endorsing this approach as well, should there be sufficient agreement to do so around the conference table. It was recognized that Quebec was in a difficult situation. It had to demonstrate its commitment to a workable Canadian federalism, while at the same time retain its bargaining position for the negotiation of Quebec's entry into the partial accord, a very much larger constitutional issue for the Quebec government.

The Governments of Saskatchewan and Nova Scotia had altered their positions on aboriginal self-government somewhat at the March meeting. Although they preferred a political accord, both went on record as not being opposed, in principle, to entrenching the right of aboriginal self-government in the constitution. Increasingly isolated were the two governments most vocally opposed to entrenchment – Alberta and British Columbia. Other governments at the table, Newfoundland, Prince Edward Island and the Yukon, remained silent.

The federal government was preoccupied with various methods of 'counting up to seven', a reference to the constitutional amending formula, whereby a constitutional amendment requires the support of seven provinces with 50 per cent of the population. Various constitutional texts were circulated during the following three weeks with a view to gaining the support of the requisite seven provinces. Turnkey provinces in the negotiations were Saskatchewan and Nova Scotia. Pressure was placed on them to 'come on side', with a view to levering the support of Alberta and Prince Edward Island respectively.

The 1985 First Ministers' Conference on Aboriginal Constitutional Matters

In the months leading up to the 1985 conference, there was a widespread feeling that the Conference must not be a failure, or be seen to be a failure. This was prompted, in part, by unpleasant memories of the 1984 Conference, which was widely criticized by the media and aboriginal peoples as a failure, and which raised questions about the true motives of governments at the table. Also at stake was the reputation of the new federal government as a conciliator of federal-provincial tensions. A new 'window of opportunity' had been created in intergovernmental relations with the election of the Mulroney government. The new era of federal-provincial cooperation, embodying a fresh spirit of goodwill, must not be allowed to crash on the shoals of constitutional reform as it relates to aboriginal peoples.

Prime Minister Mulroney opened the Conference on the morning of 2 April with a plea for national reconciliation. Building on the goodwill demonstrated at the First Ministers' Conference on the Economy, held in Regina on St. Valentine's Day, and at the National Economic Conference, involving labour and business leaders held in Ottawa in March, the Prime Minister implored parties to the negotiations to search for consensus. He noted the contributions which provincial and territorial governments and aboriginal peoples had made to moving discussions forward. He promised no surprises, and no pressure tactics. He proposed that this Conference be a turning point, an historic step. The key to success, the Prime Minister said, is self-government for aboriginal peoples within the Canadian federation. But it is only a vehicle, he added, through which aboriginal people can realize their aspirations, and gain greater control over their lives.

The objective of the Conference, in the view of the Prime Minister, was the protection of the principle of aboriginal self-government in the constitution.[5] Self-government would be given definition, or form and substance, through subsequent negotiations,[6] at the community or local level.

'Self-Government for the Aboriginal Peoples' was only the first of four agenda items for the Conference. The others were: sexual equality rights, a mandate for continuing discussions, and the nature of an accord. However, it was clear from the outset that self-government would dominate the agenda.

At the close of his opening remarks, the Prime Minister tabled a 'Proposed 1985 Accord Relating to the Aboriginal Peoples of Canada'. It was a further refinement of the 'Comprehensive Draft Accord' introduced by the federal government at the Ministers' meeting in March. With respect to aboriginal self-government, it proposed that the constitution be amended to recognize and affirm the rights of the aboriginal peoples of Canada to self-government within the Canadian federation, *where those rights are set out in negotiated agreements*, and to commit governments to participate in negotiations directed toward concluding agreements with aboriginal people relating to self-government.[7] These agreements would receive constitutional protection under section 35(2) of the Constitution Act, 1982, as do treaties and land claims agreements. The relevant portions of the proposed amendment were:

35.01
(1) The rights of the aboriginal peoples of Canada to self-government, within the context of the Canadian federation, that are set out in agreements in accordance with section 35.02 are hereby recognized and affirmed.
(2) The government of Canada and the provincial governments are committed, to the extent that each has authority, to
(a) participating in negotiations directed toward concluding, with representatives of aboriginal peoples living in particular communities or regions, agreements relating to self-government that are appropriate to the particular circumstances of those people; and
(b) discussing with representatives of aboriginal people from each province and from the Yukon Territory and Northwest Territories the timing, nature and scope of the negotiations referred to in paragraph (a).

35.02
The rights of the aboriginal peoples of Canada to self-government may, for the purposes of subsection 35.01(1), be set out in agreements concluded pursuant to paragraph 35.01(2)(a) with representatives of aboriginal people that
(a) include a declaration to the effect that subsection 35.01(1) applies to these rights; and
(b) are approved by an Act of Parliament and Acts of the legislatures of any provinces in which those aboriginal people live.

The negotiations referred to would include consideration of the type of government (e.g., ethnic, public), the issue of a land base, determination of membership, the nature and powers of the institutions of self-government, fiscal arrangements, and so forth.

The 'Proposed 1985 Accord' tabled by the Prime Minister also addressed other matters. It proposed that the constitution be further amended to clarify the provisions relating to equality rights for aboriginal men and women. It also proposed provisions relating to preparations for the next constitutional conference, and to statistical data on aboriginal peoples. With regard to preparation for the next conference, it proposed that Ministerial meetings (including representatives of aboriginal peoples) be convened at least twice a year for up to two years, so that at least four Ministerial meetings would be held before the next conference.

When the Conference adjourned for lunch on the first day, all parties to the negotiations had publicly stated their positions. In support of the federal proposal were the Governments of Ontario, New Brunswick, Manitoba, Prince Edward Island, Newfoundland and the Northwest Territories. Quebec chose to abstain. Nova Scotia and Saskatchewan were mild in their opposition and indicated that, with some revisions, they might be convinced to support the proposal. Opposition from Alberta, British Columbia and the Yukon was stronger.

Of the national aboriginal organizations, the Inuit Committee on National Issues (ICNI) and the Métis National Council (MNC) were generally supportive. The Assembly of First Nations (AFN) and Native Council of Canada (NCC) were opposed, but willing to negotiate.

It was clear that the federal government did not enjoy the support of seven provinces with 50 per cent of the population. Only five provinces had indicated their support. More cajoling and convincing remained to be done. When the Conference reconvened in the afternoon of the first day, the Prime Minister set out to do just that. He pressed hard for the federal proposal, calling for 'simple dignity' for aboriginal peoples, and for self-reliance rather than dependency. Premier Hatfield also pressed hard, calling for equality for aboriginal peoples, and for governments to exercise leadership.

As the afternoon wore on, the debate became more heated. Near the end, MNC spokesman Fred House and British Columbia Premier Bill Bennett were involved in an unpleasant exchange. The spirit of goodwill and co-operation was visibly dissipating. At that time, the Prime Minister suggested that the Conference break for the afternoon. An evening meeting of aboriginal leaders and government Ministers and advisors was charged with attempting to find an accommodation.

Reports filtering out that evening suggested that the Ministers' private meeting with aboriginal leaders was even more acrimonious than those discussions held in public in the late afternoon. No compromise solution was reached, and emotions were running high.

When the Prime Minister reconvened the Conference on the morning of the second day, he began by asking all parties to avoid making inflammatory statements, and instead to search for an honourable compromise. He then asked his Minister of Indian Affairs and Northern Development, David Crombie, who had been somewhat removed from the heat of the debate, to make yet another effort to draft a compromise accord on self-government, taking into consideration the views expressed during the previous evening. He was to report back to the Conference as soon as he had completed his task. In the meantime, discussions would proceed on agenda items two and three, sexual equality and a mandate for continuing negotiations.

In introducing the equality item, the Prime Minister stated that the Conference would address sexual equality only, and not equality among aboriginal peoples (i.e., equal rights for Indian, Inuit and Métis peoples). With a view to clearing up the matter once and for all, the Prime Minister referred to the various proposed amendments under consideration, which he had tabled the previous day.[8] Most parties were in agreement that the matter be clarified.

On the subject of continuing negotiations, the Prime Minister spoke of the need 'to do our homework', and spoke to the federal proposal of two ministerial meetings per year in advance of the 1987 First Ministers' Conference (FMC). On the issue of an FMC in 1986, the Prime Minister proposed that this be determined at a later date. Alberta adopted a similar position. Premier Lougheed also suggested that the Prairie Treaty Nations Alliance (PTNA) be invited to all future conferences. The PTNA had split from the AFN to enable Prairie Treaty Indians to address their distinct concerns, and had tried, unsuccessfully, to obtain separate and official representation at the Conference. The PTNA views self-government as a treaty right, which should be pursued in bilateral discussions with the federal government, and are opposed to provincial involvement in the process as it affects Treaty Indian people. Manitoba had no objection to the PTNA attending future conferences, while other governments offered no response.

A number of parties supported an FMC in '86, including New Brunswick, the Northwest Territories, the ICNI and the NCC. The ICNI noted, however, that the ongoing process depends upon reaching agreement on aboriginal self-government. There must be something to be ongoing about. The NCC also added a caveat: national aboriginal organizations must be involved in negotiations at the local level.

Finally, at three o'clock in the afternoon, David Crombie emerged with the final federal attempt at a proposed accord. The newly-proposed accord incorporated several important changes. Gone was the constitutional commitment of governments to participate in negotiations leading to aboriginal self-government agreements, a crucial element to the aboriginal peoples. Included was a non-derogation clause to protect the rights of the aboriginal peoples of Canada.[9] In other respects, the newly-proposed accord was similar to that tabled a day earlier by the Prime Minister.

Reaction to the federal accord was structured by the Prime Minister so that provincial governments would respond first. During a few, well-timed coffee breaks, the Prime Minister had spoken privately to provincial and aboriginal leaders, in an attempt to lever their support for the latest federal proposal. Aboriginal leaders wanted to hear the reactions of provincial governments before giving their own responses.

In order to demonstrate that momentum was building for the new accord, the Prime Minister first called upon Saskatchewan and Nova Scotia to respond. They had been mildest in their opposition to the initial federal proposal, and had indicated their wilingness to be convinced, should some revisions be made, to support it.

The new accord incorporated changes that were suggested by Saskatchewan during the evening meeting the night before. 'Where agreements between the aboriginal people and the federal and provincial governments are concluded and ratified by [Parliament and] legislatures, the rights to self-government of aboriginal people are recognized and affirmed .... The change that we recommended to the federal proposal', said Premier Devine, 'was to move the commitment to participate in negotiations out of the constitutional amendment and place it into the attached political accord. Governments will participate in negotiations directed toward concluding agreements that could result in the constitutional protection for the agreed upon rights.'[10] This would have the effect of removing the possibility of court challenges on the way in which self-government agreements are negotiated. Based on these changes, Saskatchewan decided to support the new accord.

Premier Buchanan of Nova Scotia echoed this view, voiced his support, and argued that the agreement should be concluded today. Newfoundland also expressed support.

Premier Miller of Ontario, to the obvious surprise of the Prime Minister, said that while he was generally supportive, he would hold his final decision until he had heard the views of the aboriginal leaders. Ontario was not about to support a proposal which the aboriginal peoples could not accept. Manitoba and Prince Edward Island articulated positions allied with Ontario. Premier Hatfield of New Brunswick, in a similar vein, said that while the accord was not 'good enough', it was better than nothing.

British Columbia Premier Bennett expressed concern that the accord could lead to sovereign aboriginal governments. He then tabled a proposal which would further weaken the latest draft accord.[11] He asked his Minister of Intergovernmental Relations, Garde Gardom, to speak to the British Columbia proposal. Mr. Gardom went on at some length quoting from AFN documents concerning sovereignty and aboriginal title. He concluded by stating that the notion of delegated powers is repugnant to aboriginal peoples.

Premier Lougheed said that he would not sign an accord that day, but would get back to the Prime Minister at a later date. Treaty Indians, he observed, were not at the negotiating table. The PTNA had expressed the view that self-government is a treaty right. The Premier wanted to talk to the PTNA before giving his response. He also wanted to obtain legal advice, and restated his view that there are only two sovereign orders of government in Canada.

Neither could the Northwest Territories support the draft accord, but for quite different reasons. The proposal did not go far enough.

It was time to hear the reaction of the aboriginal peoples' organizations. The Assembly of First Nations stated that it could not accept the proposal. What was required was the immediate constitutional recognition of the right to self-

David C. Hawkes

government, with negotiated self-government agreements later entrenched in the constitution. In the latest federal draft, there was no constitutional commitment for governments to negotiate, or to 'constitutionalize' self-government agreements. Moreover, the federal proposal would allow provinces to veto bilateral agreements between Indian Nations and the federal government. In an insightful analysis, AFN Northern Vice-President George Erasmus observed that the federal proposal appeared to be aimed more at achieving federal-provincial consensus, than at entrenching aboriginal self-government in the constitution.

The AFN thought that the federal proposal, if accepted, would erode Indian rights. In its view, self-government is an inherent (albeit undefined) right in section 35(1). The proposed accord was non-binding and non-justiciable. In any case, delegated authority was not enough. The AFN concluded by saying it they would reconsider its participation in the section 37 process, with a view to going back to a bilateral (Indian Nation-federal government) process.

The Prairie Treaty Nations Alliance, in response to Premier Lougheed's earlier statements, said that it would strongly support the accord, if a bilateral (federal government-Treaty Nations) process were added to it.

In private discussion, the Prime Minister had given Métis National Council leader Jim Sinclair an undertaking that he would meet with Métis and non-status Indian people to discuss their particular concerns, including that of a land base. Based on this assurance, the MNC and the Native Council of Canada supported the proposed federal accord.

The Inuit Committee on National Issues equivocated, stating that it could not 'say yes' without consulting Inuit people. The political commitment to negotiate, it suggested, should be in the constitution. There were also concerns that the accord might alter section 91(24), and affect federal responsibility for the Inuit.

As the afternoon drew to a close, it became apparent that consensus had not been achieved. Although the new accord enjoyed the support of seven provinces, this support rested upon the unwritten proviso that the accord also be acceptable to aboriginal peoples. Only the MNC and the NCC supported it. The AFN had rejected it and the ICNI, although critical, needed more time to consider its position. The accord had been 'watered down' in order to secure adequate provincial support, and in doing so, adequate aboriginal support had been lost.

The Prime Minister was in an awkward position. If he pressed hard on the accord in the face of opposition from both the AFN and the ICNI, support from Ontario, Prince Edward Island, Manitoba and New Brunswick would likely be withdrawn. The Prime Minister announced that he would not proceed unilaterally. Instead, decisions would be held in abeyance for some six weeks, until a meeting of Ministers and aboriginal leaders, already schedules for late May, was convened. This would allow the ICNI to consult its constituents, Premier Lougheed to consult the PTNA and seek legal advice, and the AFN and the British Columbia government to reconsider their positions. The Prime Minister then abruptly adjourned the Conference, shocking most participants.

At the reception held immediately following the Conference, delegates from all parties were wondering aloud at what had happened. Nothing concrete had emerged from the meeting, even on the agenda items of sexual equality and a mandate for continuing discussions, on which there appeared to be widespread consensus. The Conference had not succeeded, but neither had it failed. It had simply put off the decisions. The wisdom of the Prime Minister's judgement in this regard was openly debated. Should he have forced the issue, getting the signatures of at least some parties, or would this have forced some provinces to back away from the proposed accord? Was the six week delay a clever negotiating tactic of a seasoned mediator, during which time a consensus could be forged? Or was it a foolish mistake, which would allow time for provinces, out of the glare of television lights, to reconsider their support and draft numerous amendments to the federal proposal, possibly to water it down even further?

Although a 'saleable package' acceptable to all parties had not emerged, the Conference did not end in acrimony, as did the 1984 FMC. Perhaps it was a sign of maturation and understanding, but delegates seemed to understand why their colleagues on 'the other side' of an issue took the position they did. Inuit delegates understood why Métis leaders felt that they had to agree to the proposed accord. Métis delegates understood why the Indian leaders could not agree. And Indian delegates understood the Inuit decision to consult their people.

Moreover, there had been some movement by provincial governments on the issue of aboriginal self-government. The Governments of Newfoundland and Prince Edward Island had supported the initial federal draft accord, while the Governments of Nova Scotia and Saskatchewan had supported the final 'Saskatchewan draft' (which did not 'constitutionalize' the negotiation process). It would be difficult for these governments to 'back down' from their publicly-stated positions. Pressure, in fact, would be felt in exactly the opposite direction, to yield just a little more in the interests of achieving accommodation.

During the next subsequent two months, arms were twisted and the aboriginal body politic consulted. The only obligation on the part of governments beyond the May Ministers' meeting was one further FMC, to be held before 17 April 1987. A great deal was at stake for the aboriginal peoples.

Anticlimax

The follow-up meeting of federal, provincial and territorial government mnisters and aboriginal leaders was not held in late May, as originally proposed, but on 5 and 6 June. The mood prior to the meeting was not optimistic. A Memorandum to Cabinet from Deputy Prime Minister Eric Nielsen, summarizing the Report of the Ministerial Task Force on Native Programs, had been leaked to the public. The Report was part of the larger Ministerial Task Force on Program Review, popularly known as the Nielsen Task Force. Among other changes, the Memorandum recommended significant cuts to native programs. Although the Prime Minister publicly repudiated media reports on the issue, and stated that there would be no cuts to native programs, suspicion remained. Aside from this event, very little had changed during the intervening two months between the end of the First Ministers' Conference and the beginning of the Ministerial meeting. The stark setting of a Toronto airport hotel, and a meeting devoid of any social function such as a reception, somehow seemed appropriate. Expectations were low, and they were to be met fully.

Federal Justice Minister John Crosbie, who chaired the meeting, picked up on the morning of 5 June where the First Ministers' Conference (FMC) had left off. The same four items were on the agenda, he noted, and the same two proposed accords – the initial federal draft, and the 'Saskatchewan draft' (the one under discussion at the close of the FMC) – were on the table. The latter had a new non-derogation clause.

Mr. Crosbie began by asking parties whether they had altered their respective positions on aboriginal self-government during the interregnum. The Inuit Committee on National Issues responded first. The ICNI had used the two-month interval to consult its constituents on the 'Saskatchewan draft'. ICNI Co-Chairperson Zebedee Nungak announced that the ICNI could not support it, and that a political accord was not enough. The commitment to negotiate self-government agreements must be in the constitution. Moreover, the ICNI also felt that there should be a mutual right to ratify aboriginal self-government agreements (approval by aboriginal peoples and federal and/or respective provincial governments). In addition, it had some concerns regarding a multi-lateral ratification process (involving all provinces) for self-government agreements, which it referred to as the 'provincial veto'. Under such conditions, for example, provincial governments could 'veto' federal-aboriginal government agreements in the Northwest Territories, federal-Indian Nation agreements on Indian reserves, or tripartite (federal-provincial-aboriginal) agreements in a particular province.

The political situation of the Yukon government had changed as well, the result of a territorial general election on 13 May. Tony Penikett, Government Leader of the newly-elected NDP minority territorial government, indicated that while his new administration had not yet formed detailed policy positions on these issues, he was willing to discuss aboriginal self-government with both aboriginal and non-aboriginal people in the Yukon. The 'one-government' approach of the former administration would be unlikely to survive a policy review by the new NDP government. Mr. Penikett also used the occasion to announce that his government would deal with aboriginal constitutional issues before addressing province-hood for the Yukon.

The Government of Alberta had also taken the opportunity, during the two month interim, to consult the Prairie Treaty Nations Alliance, and to seek legal advice on the 'Saskatchewan draft'. The PTNA wished to enter into bilateral negotiations with the Government of Canada, flowing from the special relationship between treaty Indians and the federal government, to entrench treaty rights (including the right to self-government) in the constitution. Milt Pahl, the Alberta minister responsible for Native Affairs, indicated that his government would respect the wishes of the PTNA in this regard. On legal grounds which he did not elaborate, however, Alberta could not support the 'Saskatchewan draft'.

On the issue of aboriginal self-government, Alberta was heading in a different direction. The Alberta minister tabled at the meeting, A Resolution Concerning an Amendment to the Alberta Act, which would grant title in fee simple for Métis Settlement lands to Settlement Métis peoples.[12] This would be accomplished through section 43 of the Constitution Act, 1982, which requires the consent of the Alberta Legislature and the Canadian Parliament. The land would be held communally by Métis Settlement Associations or appropriate Métis corporate entities, but would not include ownership of sub-surface minerals. In addition, the land would continue to be subject to the legislative authority of the Province of Alberta. The Métis would determine fair and democratic criteria for membership in settlement associations, and for the allocation of settlement lands to individuals. The Métis would also be responsible for devising democratic governing bodies for managing the land and governing Métis settlements. The resolution was debated and approved in the Alberta Legislature on 3 June 1985.

The Government of Alberta is going to negotiate 'self-government' with Settlement Métis on a bilateral basis, outside the section 37 process and, for the most part, outside the constitutional framework. It was left unsaid how non-Settlement Métis would be affected. It became evident as the meeting progressed that this was the 'shape of things to come' in other jurisdictions as well – bilateral or trilateral negotiations outside the constitutional framework.

During the afternoon discussion on self-government, both Ontario and British Columbia indicated that they would be commencing discussions with Métis and Indians respectively, on matters within the provincial sphere of jurisdiction. In British Columbia, negotiations are about to begin with the Sechelt Indian Band concerning municipal government powers, including taxation. The Government of British Columbia is advocating the negotiation of self-government models to be implemented by federal and/or provincial legislation. In the case of self-government agreements with Indian bands, these could then become treaties, and protected under section 35 of the Constitution Act, 1982.

As the afternoon wore on, it became obvious that no agreement on aboriginal self-government was in the offing. Mr. Crosbie turned to the second agenda item – sexual equality rights for aboriginal people – and to the six alternative amendments which were tabled at the FMC two months earlier. After a short discussion, it was decided to refer the matter to a meeting of officials, to be held immediately following the close of the afternoon session. As expected, no agreement could be reached among the parties at the officials' meeting on a constitutional amendment.

Day two of the Ministers' meeting began on a more ominous note than had day one. Justice Minister Crosbie announced that the evening meeting of officials had failed to reach an agreement with respect to a constitutional amendment regarding sexual equality. Since ministers were unlikely to make much progress on the issue, the Chairman suggested that the meeting address the next agenda item – the next steps in the section 37 process between 1985 and 1987 or, as he put it, 'Where do we go from here?'

Reference was made to the federal proposal on this matter tabled at the FMC, on which there was no disagreement. Two annual Ministerial meetings would be held before the 1987 First Ministers' Conference. The first of these, the Chairman speculated, might take place early in 1986, and would have as one of its agenda items the Assembly of First Nations' Draft Composite Amendments to the constitution.[13] If enough progress were made, a further FMC could be called in 1986, although it was generally acknowledged that this was an unlikely development. In the meantime, self-government negotiations would be led, on the federal side, by Indian and Northern Affairs Minister David Crombie.

In describing these negotiations, Mr. Crombie said that they would be community-led, community-based (i.e., local), tailored to individual circumstances, and that they would take place at a practical level and at a measured pace. Meetings had already been held in Ontario and British Columbia, and others were scheduled.

In addition, meetings were to be held between the Prime Minister and the Métis (MNC and NCC), and between the Prime Minister and the PTNA. These were tentatively scheduled for the fall.

The follow-up meeting, as it adjourned, lived up to its advanced billing. Widely-held expectations that no progress would be made were completely fulfilled. The meeting was an anticlimax to the First Ministers' Conference held some two months earlier. At the same time, however, disappointment was not great. No one had expected a breakthrough. The process would continue over the next two years, but in a venue largely outside the National Conference Centre in Ottawa. Negotiations on aboriginal self-government would be taking place at the local, regional, territorial and provincial levels. The 'bottom-up' approach – that of implementing self-government prior to entrenching it in the constitution – would now be given its acid test.

Conclusion

The outcomes of negotiations to date on aboriginal self-government, pursuant to the section 37 process, are being interpreted in widely different ways. While they have been less than a smashing success, few would consider them a failure. The new 'window of opportunity', as it is called, in intergovernmental relations, imbued with a fresh spirit of federal-provincial cooperation, has not closed. The new federal government has been vigorously tested on the issue of aboriginal self-government and, from the perspective of most observers, has risen to the occasion.

Progress since 1982 has been significant. In that year, the concept of aboriginal self-government was the subject of much ridicule, both within governments and the non-aboriginal population at large. Today, negotiations are underway regarding how to give it form and substance – 'how to do it'. There has occurred a gradual ratchetting up of the lowest common denominator, of the minimal government response to the proposals by aboriginal peoples for self-government. The 'Saskatchewan draft' accord is now the lowest common denominator.[14] Although the proposed accord represented substantial movement on the issue, securing the support of the federal government, seven provincial governments and two national aboriginal peoples' organizations, it was not enough to achieve an accommodation. The cost of reaching agreement among the requisite number of federal and provincial governments – the 'watering down' of the accord, and diluting the protection of aboriginal rights – was too high. While sufficient provincial government support had been won, adequate aboriginal support had been lost.

That there will be costs involved in reaching an accommodation on this issue should be obvious. Such costs are inherent in intergovernmental negotiations, and they will be borne by all sides, by all parties to the negotiations. What is crucial in reaching an accommodation is finding the appropriate balance, so that the participants feel that the costs involved are shared in a reasonably equitable manner. The search for that balance and that accommodation will be an enduring theme between now and the First Ministers' Conference in 1987.

Some of the cost considerations, while significant, have been kept far from the public eye. There is fear in some quarters about a possible 'white backlash', should some proposals concerning aboriginal self-government, such as the prospect of additional lands for aboriginal peoples, go ahead. There is fear on the part of some governments that the courts will intervene to determine the character, the powers, and the costs of aboriginal self-government, rather than having these issues settled in the political arena. Even if a political accommodation on self-government could be reached, governments would remain concerned about the financial costs involved.

Aboriginal political leaders have fears as well. For many of them, their political careers are tied to a 'successful' resolution of the self-government issue. There is a fine line between achieving a 'successful' resolution and 'selling out' their aboriginal birthright. In terms of reaching an accommodation, how far can they go before they are repudiated by their own people?

David C. Hawkes

Moreover, for many aboriginal peoples, self-government is a new and untried experiment. Fear of the unknown and fear of failure are also present. At the same time, the social costs of not acting, of the status-quo, are all too well known.

Another outcome of negotiations to date has been the shift in approach noted earlier, from top-down to bottom-up. Bilateral and trilateral negotiations on aboriginal self-government will be taking place outside of the constitutional framework. A number of provincial governments, including British Columbia, Alberta, Saskatchewan, Ontario and Quebec, have already indicated their intentions in this regard. These negotiations will not be viewed without suspicion. The opinion has been expressed that national aboriginal leaders are putting forward unrealistic proposals and making exaggerated claims, and that governments would do better to negotiate more limited agreements for the delivery of services at the local or perhaps regional level. Such a strategy of 'going directly to the people' would be reminiscent of former Prime Minister Trudeau's 'New Federalism', and his 1981 proposal for a referendum as part of a constitutional amending formula. Instead of bypassing provincial governments, it would entail going around the national aboriginal organizations and leaders, and dealing directly with aboriginal people at the local level.

It is too early to know if such suspicion is warranted. For now, the future of aboriginal self-government negotiations is focused at the local level, and outside the constitutional framework. The next year will tell whether the move to a bottom-up approach was a wise one, or whether participants should have 'stayed the course' in terms of searching for a constitutional amendment.

During the coming year, consultations will take place with Métis peoples on the issue of a land base, with the Assembly of First Nations on their draft composite constitutional amendments, with the Prairie Treaty Nations Alliance on self-government through the treaty process, and with a large number of aboriginal people on self-government at the community or local level.

The significance of this agenda to the next (and perhaps final) First Ministers' Conference on Aboriginal Constitutional Matters in 1987 is not clear. Should self-government agreements be successfully negotiated, these could be given constitutional protection in 1987. Should the bottom-up approach fail, however, discussion would likely return to the issue of entrenching the right or principle of aboriginal self-government in the constitution. It is possible, of course, that agreement on this may not be forthcoming either.

The prospect of achieving a constitutional agreement at or before the 1987 FMC is uncertain. Trepidation prevents those from answering the question: 'What if nothing happens?'

Notes

1. David C. Hawkes, *Aboriginal Self-Government: What Does It Mean?* (Kingston: Institute of Intergovernmental Relations, 1985), pp. 54-55.
2. *Ibid.*
3. Nova Scotia, *1985 Accord Respecting Matters Affecting the Aboriginal Peoples of Canada,* Toronto, 11-12 March 1985, CICS Document 830-173/010.
4. Government Motion 49, Quebec National Assembly, Fifth Session, Thirty-Second Legislature, 18 December 1984.
5. *Notes for an Opening Statement by the Right Honourable Brian Mulroney, Prime Minister of Canada,* First Ministers' Conference, The Rights of Aboriginal Peoples, Ottawa, 2-3 April 1985, p. 6.
6. Canada, *Self-Government for the Aboriginal Peoples: Lead Statement,* Ottawa, 2-3 April 1985, CICS Document 800-20/009.
7. The Prime Minister of Canada, *Proposed 1985 Accord Relating to the Aboriginal Peoples of Canada,* First Ministers' Conference, The Rights of Aboriginal Peoples, Ottawa, 2-3 April 1985, pp. 1-2 [emphasis added].
8. Canada, *Proposed Equality Rights Amendments Currently Under Consideration,* First Ministers' Conference on Aboriginal Constitutional Matters, Ottawa, 2-3 April 1985, CICS Document 800-20/008.
9. Canada, *Proposed 1985 Accord Relating to the Aboriginal Peoples of Canada,* First Ministers' Conference on Aboriginal Constitutional Matters, Ottawa, 2-3 April 1985, CICS Document 800-20/041.
   Self-government agreements would not derogate from existing aboriginal rights recognized in section 35 of the *Constitution Act, 1982.*
10. Saskatchewan, *Speaking Notes: The Saskatchewan Proposal,* First Ministers' Conference on Aboriginal Constitutional Matters, Ottawa, 2-3 April 1985, CICS Document 800-20/043, p. 2 [emphasis added].
11. *British Columbia Proposal,* First Ministers' Conference on Aboriginal Constitutional Matters, Ottawa, 2-3 April 1985, CICS Document 800-20/035.
12. Alberta, *A Resolution Concerning an Amendment to the Alberta Act,* Federal-Provincial Conference of Ministers on Aboriginal Constitutional Matters, Toronto, 5-6 June 1985, CICS Document 830-188/009.
    To hold in 'fee simple' means to have as absolute property, and is the most common form of property ownership in Canada (e.g., farmers and homeowners).
    In 1938, the Government of Alberta set aside certain unoccupied Crown lands for Métis people. There are currently eight Métis Settlements, located in northern Alberta, comprising 1.28 million acres of land. It is estimated that 4,000 Métis live on these settlements.
13. Assembly of First Nations, *AFN's Draft Composite Amendments (Revised 13 December 1984),* Federal-Provincial Meeting of Ministers on Aboriginal Constitutional Matters, Ottawa, 17-18 December 1984, CICS Document 830-160/008.
    The AFN Draft Composite Amendments to the constitution are rather far-reaching, compared with discussions to date in First Ministers' Conferences. Included, for example, are the recognition and guarantee of 'sovereign title', 'the ownership of and jurisdiction over all land and resources within the traditional territories of each First Nation', the provision of 'fiscal resources to First Nation Governments', and the commitment of governments to negotiate treaties with those First Nations now without treaties.
14. The Government of Alberta, as indicated earlier, does not support the 'Saskatchewan draft' and hence, is not included in the lowest common denominator.

7 Federal-Provincial Tensions in the Administration of Justice

John D. Whyte

Introduction

There has been remarkably little federal-provincial conflict over responsibility for administering laws throughout much of Canada's history. Authority over the administration of laws by and large flows from the holding of primary legislative authority. Consequently, it is not surprising that, once it has been settled which level of government has responsibility for enacting laws, there have been few misunderstandings over responsibility for their administration. What is surprising is the extent to which stability in this area has been shattered in recent years; long-standing arrangements that had been assumed to be both functionally and constitutionally appropriate have been challenged and 'the administration of justice' has joined the ranks of trade regulation, resource management and criminal sanctioning as one of the active areas of constitutional conflict.

Neither accounting for this conflict, nor describing the constitutional regime on which resolution will be based, is an easy task. One cause of new tensions in the administration of justice has been the increasing tendency to play out divergences in the policy objectives of the two levels of government in the realm of legal administration. This tendency is most clearly evident in the case of the considerable degree of federal-provincial conflict over juvenile justice. Policy conflicts are also seen in the dispute over the proper scope of jurisdiction for the Federal Court--the superior court which was created by Parliament in 1971 to take over judicial supervision of federal public administration.

Another cause of conflict has been the increased interest by both the federal government and the provinces to control the levers of influence: the provinces want a greater role in the appointment of judges and the federal government appears to want, or until recently to have wanted, more authority over criminal prosecutions. Recently, these conflicts, whether produced by policy divergences or sheer competition for power, have lessened under the general policy of the federal government to cooperate with the provinces and to recognize and respect their concerns and interests. A mood of cooperative federalism, under which national objectives are to be modified and adapted to accommodate provincial goals, has been nurtured (at least at a rhetorical level) since the Conservative government came to power in September 1984, and this has helped to reduce competition for authority over the administration of justice. This can be seen in the quietening of the formerly intense debates over the appointment of judges and over which level of government should be responsible for criminal prosecutions. This change, however, may be as much the result of simple failure to pursue debate as it is the result of an active process of reconciling conflicting views and policies. For instance, with respect to an issue which received a great deal of ministerial debate in the early 1980s – the removal of constitutional restrictions on provincial administrative structures in order to give provinces greater flexibility in creating agencies to implement legislative objectives – federal-provincial discussions have simply stopped being conducted.

Complexity and imprecision are dominant features of the legal framework of these disputes. The simple assignment to the provinces of jurisdiction over 'The Administration of Justice in the Provinces', in head 14 of section 92 of the Constitution Act, 1867, is placed, in the constitutional text, in a convoluted context which is created by a number of other allocations of authority which touch on this matter. For instance, the federal level of government gains authority over the administration of justice from a number of sources. First, it has the power to appoint judges of superior, district and county courts. Second, its legislative jurisdiction over criminal law, including procedure in criminal matters, gives it some access to the administration of laws. Finally, administrative powers derive from holding primary jurisdiction over substantive matters such as trade and commerce. Further complications arise from the provincial power over the administration of justice being conditioned by the constraints on administrative arrangements created by Part VII of the Constitution Act, 1867: 'Judicature'. That part of the constitution preserves for courts a class of judicial functions and thereby precludes provinces (and possibly the federal level of government) from having a free hand in creating mechanisms for the administration of provincial laws and regulatory regimes. There is, then, an arrangement of constitutional provisions which lacks certainty about both the meaning of specific provisions and the relationship between the various sections.

The areas of recent conflict within the general field of legal administration are: the appointment of superior court judges; the jurisdictional overlap between provincial courts and the federal court; removal of the limitations placed by Part VII of the Constitution Act, 1867, on the creation of non-judicial administrative arrangements; the question of who has authority over criminal prosecutions; and, finally, policies for dealing with the criminal activity of juveniles.

As has already been noted, the last area is one in which competition between substantive federal and provincial policies accounts for inter-governmental tensions while the first of these topics – judicial appointments – is a matter in which policy conflicts are not as significant. The nature of conflict in the other three areas is more difficult to assess. Clearly there are policy implications to these federal-provincial struggles. For instance, is it appropriate that there be a special federal court which has exclusive supervisory jurisdiction over all aspects of the administration of federal law? Or, must a system of independent judicial administration be maintained at the cost of preventing some regulatory authority being given to specialized tribunals? And, again, is it better that the administration of federal criminal law be conducted through a national agency or by local agents acting under the direction of provincial Attorneys General? Behind these questions there is the larger question, prevalent in all debates over our federal structure. Are these matters ones which require unity and national consistency or are diversity, experimentation and responsiveness to local political authority more appropriate values to pursue? As in many other aspects of Canadian constitutionalism, our basic constitutional text is not free from ambiguity. It sends forth both the message of the need for national standards affecting the conditions of liberty and respecting rights and, on the other hand, the message that provinces must maintain sufficient autonomy to reflect the diverse values that are found in the many regions of Canada. Public and judicial administration, both civil and criminal, shape our political communities and should, perhaps, be shaped by them. Like all other regulatory powers, they should to be seen as instruments through which our diversity is reflected. These are the larger issues of constitutional and social value which are at stake in the conflict over the administration of justice.

The Appointment of Superior Court Judges

Section 96 of the Constitution Act, 1867, gives the Governor General (in effect, the cabinet) the power to appoint the judges of 'the Superior, District, and County courts in each Province'. Superior courts in this provision include provincial Courts of Appeal so that all judges in the provinces except magistrates (now called provincial court judges) are appointed by the federal government. Over the years federal Ministers of Justice have adopted various practices of consultation with their provincial counterparts. There has been strong provincial demand for such consultation (and even for a veto power over appointments) because the courts to which the judges are assigned are the courts of the province and because, since the creation of the Federal Court in 1971, their workload consists almost entirely of the application of provincial laws. Furthermore, there is a constitutional provision requiring that judges be appointed from the bar of the relevant province and it is felt that members of the provincial administration have a better sense of a person's suitability and acceptability than does the federal Minister of Justice.

During the last years of the Liberal government the two Ministers of Justice, Jean Chrétien and Mark MacGuigan, failed to consult with (or, in some cases, even inform as a matter of courtesy) some provincial Attorneys General about judicial appointments. The cause of this breakdown in the pattern of informal consultation may have been the inter-governmental rancour that developed over the federal government's plan in 1980 to proceed unilaterally with constitutional reform. The chief instance of public exposure of this friction occurred in Saskatchewan. Soon after the new Conservative government took office in April 1982 the provincial cabinet acted to prevent the federal cabinet from making any judicial appointments at all in Saskatchewan. It had apparent authority to do this because, though appointment is constitutionally a federal matter, the positions to be filled are created by the province under section 92(14) of the Constitution Act, 1867: 'The Administration of Justice in the Province, including the Constitution, Maintenance, and Organization of Provincial Courts ....' All that was necessary was for the provincial cabinet to pass Orders in Council which reduced the size of the province's Court of Appeal and Court of Queen's Bench – which it regularly did. In all there were five such orders, each one of which reduced the size of the two courts to the number of judges then currently holding office. In this way, from the spring of 1982 until November 1984, when this strategy was stopped, no vacancies arose in either court and the federal cabinet was able to make no judicial appointments in Saskatchewan. By the spring of 1984 the Court of Appeal had been reduced to four members from the 1982 size of seven positions and the Court of Queen's Bench was down to 24 members from a high of 30.

A group of Saskatoon lawyers launched an application in the Court of Queen's Bench for a declaration that the Orders in Council reducing the size of the courts were unconstitutional because they invaded the federal appointment power under section 96, which reads: 'The Governor General shall appoint the Judges of the Superior, District, and County Courts in each Province, ...' The applicants also argued that the orders were invalid on the ground that they exceeded the authority that had been delegated to the cabinet by the two acts which established the courts. In the course of the trial, lawyers for the provincial Attorney General argued that the court was not entitled to investigate the motive for the reduction in the size of the courts. Although Attorney General Gary Lane had made many statements lamenting the federal practice of making judicial appointments without consultation and although it is clear that the purpose of the reductions was to persuade the federal government to change its appointment practices, the Court agreed that it could not consider these facts in assessing the validity of the orders.[1] This decision seriously undercut the constitutional challenge since provincial action to reduce the size of the courts was not *per se* hostile to the appointment

John D. Whyte

power. If the political context of the action is ignored it can easily be surmised that the reductions were motivated by fiscal or efficiency considerations. Of course, if the courts had been more substantially reduced it would have been possible to infer, even without confirming evidence, that the government's motive had been to make the provincial superior court system ineffective. Such a destruction of the role of the federally appointed judiciary would have been contrary to section 96 as being destructive of the appointment power or would have been contrary to the whole of Part VII (of which section 96 is just one provision) in that it would have undermined the constitutionally entrenched judicial function. However, such levels of undercutting had not been reached in the Saskatchewan situation and the court was not able to conclude that the conduct of the provincial executive was invalid as being directed to the federal appointment power.

Notwithstanding the failure of the constitutional challenge, the Orders in Council reducing the size of the Court of Queen's Bench were struck down as being beyond the power of the cabinet under Saskatchewan's Queen's Bench Act.[2] That act requires there to be at least one judge in each judicial centre and this standard could not be met under the reductions.[3] The judge noted the unsatisfactory nature of this result:

I regret the conclusion I have come to because the needs of the Court of Appeal are the greatest. Litigants are now waiting many months and even years to have their appeals heard and disposed of. The situation in the Court of Queen's Bench is not yet so severe.[4]

Both the Attorney General and the group of Saskatoon lawyers appealed from this decision and the latter group again argued that the orders were contrary to section 96. Before the Court of Appeal could issue its decision the new Conservative Minister of Justice, John Crosbie, and the provincial Attorney General came to an agreement on the provincial role in judicial appointments and immediately the cabinet issued new Orders in Council restoring the two courts to their original size. Appointments to both courts began to be made in December 1984. The lawyers for the Attorney General applied to the Court of Appeal to have the case considered moot and urged the Court not to issue a judgement. By the end of June 1985, neither the application to suspend the judgement nor the case itself had been decided. It is thought likely that the Court, having not ruled for such a long period on the application to abandon the case, intends to issue a full judgement on the merits. If so, it will potentially add to our understanding of the border line between the provincial power (under section 92(14) of the Constitution Act, 1867), over the constitution, maintenance and organization of the courts, and the federal power of judicial appointment.

A related matter, although not one bearing directly on federal-provincial tensions, was the storm over patronage in judicial appointments that arose with the Liberal government appointments, mainly to the Federal Court, just prior to the calling of the 1984 federal general election. Both the Canadian Bar Association and the Canadian Association of Law Teachers immediately formed committees to investigate the manner in which judicial appointments are made and to recommend changes. After a year the CBA committee had not reported but the CALT committee reported that the present method of appointment is seriously deficient and that mechanisms are badly needed to replace present considerations of political affiliation with considerations of merit in making appointments. The CALT proposal for achieving this is the establishment of judicial nominating councils – one for each jurisdiction as well as one for the Federal Court. These councils would consist of representatives of the judiciary, the bar and the general public and would establish a list of names of persons suitable for appointment to which the federal cabinet would be restricted in making appointments to the bench.

It is expected that the CBA will make a similar sort of recommendation, although it is likely that it will urge a somewhat more prominent role for the organized bar in the formation of nominating councils. It is not at all self-evident that the interests which are most thoroughly represented in the organized bar are preferable to the interests represented within Canadian political parties. Of course, the virtues which appear to be gained from significant participation of the bar in appointments are legal competence and political neutrality. This may be illusory. Notions of acceptability for judicial appointment are no less deeply political simply because they are hegemonic within the band of society constituted by lawyers.

Jurisdictional Overlap Between the Federal Court and Provincial Superior Courts

It has long been established that judicial supervision of governmental action, whether legislative or executive, is an essential part of our constitutional system. This review power represents the cornerstone of the 'rule of law', the constitutional principle by which those in power are required to act within the limits of power granted to them either by statute or by the constitution. The authority of judicial review, though nowhere explicitly bestowed has been seen to have been constitutionally confirmed in the Constitution Act, 1867.[5] Given its constitutional status it would be surprising if this review role could be removed, or significantly tampered with, by ordinary legislation of either Parliament or the provincial legislatures. Yet federal legislation, in the form of the 1971 Federal Court Act,[6] has affected the pattern of judicial review of public administration. Under the 1971 act Parliament established a new superior court and conferred on it broadly based exclusive jurisdiction to review the administration of federal laws. This grant of jurisdiction clearly narrowed the provincial superior courts' established competence to deal with all matters of federal and provincial law,[7] including review of the constitutionality of federal and provincial legislation.[8] The Federal Court Act, therefore, brought to an end the Canadian practice of an essentially unitary court system based in the provinces. Although the creation of the Federal Court did not produce a completely dual court system, under which provincial courts could handle only provincial laws and federal courts could handle all judicial applications of federal law, the limited bifurcation created a series of procedural problems for litigants. From the points of view of both procedural complexity and judicial politics the most interesting problem has been the question of whether challenges to the constitutionality of federal and provincial laws can be launched only in the respective federal and provincial court systems.

As for the political dimension of these issues, provinces have been concerned that the Federal Court, created and maintained by Parliament, and comprised of federally appointed judges would somehow become captive to federal influences. Certainly, the common constitutional arrangement of countervailing powers (for example, regulatory power vs. spending power, or, over-arching federal general power vs. provincial jurisdiction over 'property and civil rights') has been abridged by the establishment of the Federal Court. Nowhere would this concern be more pronounced than in respect of the always politically sensitive matter of striking down laws as being unconstitutional. (Although final authority over these cases has been, since 1949, with the Supreme Court of Canada, also federally established and appointed, prior to 1971 challenges to federal laws were almost always commenced in provincial courts). However, even those who are most opposed to the creation of the Federal Court, would not argue that there was danger of political control of the court. Rather, questions of the appearance of neutrality, as well as sensitivity of judges to the federal political pulse, were the concerns.

Concern over total bifurcation in the judicial administration of law, including applying the constitution, were reduced in 1982 with the Supreme Court's decision in the *Jabour* case.[9] The Court accepted the argument that the Federal Court Act's grant to the Federal Court of exclusive jurisdiction over suits against the federal government did not have the effect of removing from provincial superior courts their power to hear challenges against federal agencies, when those challenges are based on constitutional invalidity. The Court reasoned that the terms of the Federal Court Act are limited to that which the federal Parliament is empowered under section 101 of the Constitution Act, 1867. This section allows Parliament to establish courts 'for the better administration of the laws of Canada,' and that latter phrase means only laws enacted (or capable of being enacted), by the Parliament of Canada. Therefore, according to the Court, legislation enacted under section 101, as is the Federal Court Act, could not exclude actions which are based not on 'the laws of Canada' but on the constitution of Canada. As a result, the exclusive jurisdiction over federal agencies, which the Federal Court act purports to grant, does not stop provincial courts from declaring federal statutes to be invalid under the constitution.

In 1983, the Court in *Canada Labour Relations Board v. Paul L'Anglais*[10] applied and extended *Jabour*. The Court again had to consider whether the jurisdiction of provincial superior courts to hear challenges to federal laws on constitutional grounds had been undermined by the Federal Court Act. The employees of Paul L'Anglais Inc. had sought certification before the Canada Labour Relations Board. Paul L'Anglais Inc. was a subsidiary of a television broadcasting company and was involved in selling sponsored television air time to advertisers. The Board concluded that the company was a federal undertaking and, therefore, its employees performed work that fell under its jurisdiction. The company moved in the Quebec Superior Court to set aside the decision on the basis that the activity of its employees fell within the authority of the provincial labour board. The first issue for the Court was whether the challenge to the federal Board's jurisdiction was properly raised in the provincial Superior Court. The company argued, in effect, that the Superior Court has jurisdiction where the answer to the challenge 'must be found ... in the principles governing the constitutional division of authority over labour relations'.[11] The Supreme Court agreed. Applying the *Jabour* decision, it held that in such cases the terms of the Federal Court Act cannot supersede the superintending power of the Quebec Superior Court. It had been argued that the *Jabour* case did not apply to this constitutional challenge to the Canada Labour Relations Board; the former case raised the constitutionality of the federal legislation itself, while the *L'Anglais* case was concerned only with interpreting legislation to keep it within the constitutional limits on Parliament. This latter enterprise, it was suggested, was part of the administration of 'the laws of Canada' and could, therefore, be assigned to the exclusive jurisdiction of the Federal Court. However, the Court could 'not see any difference ... between constitutionality and applicability: both relate to constitutional jurisdiction.'[12]

Another 1983 case, the *Northern Telecom* case[13] also dealt with which court could hear constitutional challenges. Again the constitutional question was whether the Canada Labour Relations Board has jurisdiction over workers in firms which are associated with firms clearly under federal jurisdictions. This time, however, the issue was placed before the Federal Court of Appeal and, hence, the secondary issue became whether the Constitution Act, 1867, empowers Parliament to give jurisdiction over constitutional questions to its Federal Court. It might be thought that, since Parliament's only authority in relation to creating courts is to create courts for 'the better Administration of the Laws of Canada', and since the latter phrase does not include constitutional law, the purported grant of jurisdiction to the Federal Court to hear constitutional questions was invalid and that only provincial superior courts could deal with issues of constitutionality. The Supreme Court, however, found otherwise, largely for functional reasons. Since the supervisory power of the Federal Court over the work of the federal boards is undoubted, it makes little sense to exclude this single aspect of court review; its responsibility for

John D. Whyte

the validity of a board's conduct should include validity from a constitutional viewpoint. The Federal Court is in the same position as any statutory court, provincial or federal – able to 'determine the constitutional issue arising as a threshold question in the review of the administrative action in issue'.[14] Otherwise, the Federal Court would be engaged in the administration of the laws of Canada without being able first to determine whether what it is administering is valid.

As for the textual problem posed by the phrase 'the laws of Canada' the Court simply said that 'the laws of Canada' means 'laws enacted by the Dominion Parliament and *within its competence*',[15] thereby confirming that an inextricable part of legal administration is the assessment of the constitutional validity of that which is to be administered.

Although these cases by no means resolve the whole of the range of problems created by Canada's partial creation of a dual court system they establish the important point that litigants wishing to challenge the constitutional validity of federal legislation, or executive acts taken in the administration of that legislation, are free to raise these challenges in either provincial or federal courts. With the vast increase in constitutional challenges (produced mainly by the enactment of the Canadian Charter of Rights and Freedoms) it is no small consolation to know that Canada's partial bifurcation of the court system has not created a complex procedural hurdle for litigants wishing to make these challenges.

Removing the Constitutional Constraints on Non-Judicial Administration

Section 96 of the Constitution Act, 1867, which, as we have seen, confers on the federal cabinet the power of judicial appointment has been developed to serve a far more weighty role in the ordering of Canadian public life. That section's import had been taken to be that provinces cannot assign functions traditionally performed by superior and county court judges to non-court agencies such as rent review boards or labour relations boards.[16] In other words, section 96 (as well as the other provisions of Part VII of the Constitution Act) have constitutionally entrenched the jurisdiction of superior and county courts.[17] The consequence has been that provinces have not been unconstrained in creating provincial agencies to administer provincial laws: if the administrative acts are the same as those performed by courts at the time of Confederation, or are analogous to those performed by superior, district, or county courts, then the administrative structure will be seen as undercutting the constitutionally entrenched judicial function (and, of course, the federal appointment power) and will be struck down.

In 1981, the Supreme Court of Canada gave judgement in the *Residential Tenancies* case,[18] a matter in which six provinces had appeared to urge the court to allow Ontario to create a specialized agency to handle disputes between landlords and tenants of residential premises. Despite the logic of this arrangement in terms of the appropriateness of creating a special agency offering state-assisted dispute resolution in respect of a single vital social relationship, the Court found the Ontario scheme to be unconstitutional. Furthermore, in two cases from Quebec, one decided in 1978[19] and one in 1981,[20] the Court also struck down administrative appeal bodies created by that province. These three cases confirmed the degree to which Part VII could limit the provinces in designing systems for administering their laws. Since most provincial regulatory regimes require some degree of adjudication – the investigation of factual contexts and the interpretation and application of legislation – the line between permissible administrative regulation and an impermissible encroachment on the entrenched judicial power has become difficult to discern.[21] For this reason provinces moved for a constitutional amendment to section 96 which would give them a free hand in assigning the administration of provincial laws to specialist agencies. In January 1983, both federal and provincial ministers responsible for constitutional matters met to discuss constitutional reform issues, other than aboriginal rights, which could be dealt with during the First Ministers' Conference on Aboriginal Rights scheduled for the following March. The ministers, including the federal minister, tentatively agreed to an amendment to section 96 which would have let provincial legislatures confer on provincial tribunals (other than courts) jurisdiction over any matter which is within the legislative authority of provinces. (A further section would have preserved for courts their traditional role of judicial supervision of administrative tribunals to ensure that any decisions or actions taken by the tribunals were within their jurisdiction and to ensure that they followed the standards of procedural fairness, where appropriate.)

The federal government's willingness to accede to provincial desires in this matter may have been partially motivated by the Supreme Court hearing of the *McEvoy* case[22] in the fall of 1982. It was a clear possibility that the Court would hold that Parliament in its creation of bodies to administer federal laws, was also subject to, and limited by, Part VII of the Constitution Act. Since normally there would be no problem with federal appointments when dealing with federal tribunals the restrictions that would apply against the federal level would be those relating to tenure (or removal), qualification and compensation – those matters which establish the autonomy of an independent judiciary. Hence, Parliament, like the provinces, might also have been required to leave the administration of some of its laws to superior courts. The case, when decided in May 1983, confirmed these possibilities.[23] The amendment, which had been agreed upon earlier that year, dealt only with the provincial aspect of the problem and it is only speculation that the federal government saw an arrangement which, by means of a simple two-word amendment, it could tap into in order to avoid the potential implications of *McEvoy*.

When the First Ministers met in March 1983, Prime Minister Trudeau stated that he could not accept the proposed amendment. It is likely that he opposed it because he saw in it an open invitation to the PQ government in Quebec to move virtually the whole of the administration of justice away from the

John D. Whyte

Quebec superior courts and assign it to provincially created and provincially appointed boards. Clearly the wide-scale use of the proposed amendment to section 96 would adversely affect the appearance of independent administration of a province's system of laws. Not only would this weaken political and popular support for the legal process but would undermine one of the country's unifying public institutions. The loss of the greater part of the role of the Quebec Superior Court would underscore Quebec's separateness from the rest of Canada through the creation of a distinctive regime for administering laws.

Nevertheless the proposal did not die. In August 1983, the federal Minister of Justice, Mark MacGuigan, issued a discussion paper[24] which contained the amendment that Trudeau had rejected five months earlier, together with a description of the difficulties which had been created by the section 96 jurisprudence. The background review was fair to provincial concerns and made the case for an amendment which would weaken the section 96 constraints on creating administrative tribunals. The paper ended with an invitation for comment from interested persons. A number of constitutional scholars responded to this invitation, some of them taking the position that the potential loss of judicial independence would not be a tolerable price to pay for added administrative flexibility.[25] Furthermore, many superior court judges have been opposed to the amendment and at a meeting of the Canadian Institute for the Administration of Justice (an organization dominated by superior court judges) plans for presenting a brief to the minister, opposing the amendment, were made. In the nearly two years since the federal discussion paper was issued the bulk of comment on it has been critical. Furthermore, provinces have not sustained their campaign of support for the amendment; the problem of freeing up provincial administrative arrangements has not been placed back on the agenda of federal-provincial meetings of ministers responsible for the administration of justice. It is not clear whether there is any life left in the movement to amend section 96.

The Fight Over Criminal Prosecutions

Is it the provinces that have authority to conduct criminal prosecutions? This issue, which has been in dispute for the last decade, is important because of its bearing on the uniformity of criminal law – as applied and enforced –across the country. The enactment of criminal law is clearly a federal matter but its day-to-day operation in the community was considered, until recently, to be largely a provincial responsibility. One of the exceptions to this pattern was that drug prosecutions – prosecutions under the Narcotic Control Act,[26] were conducted by agents for the federal Attorney General. In the mid-1970s, Hauser, a defendant in a prosecution brought under that act, argued that since the drug legislation was passed under Parliament's jurisdiction to enact criminal law, prosecutions under the law were criminal prosecutions. Since the assignment to provinces in section 92(14) of the Constitution

Act, 1867, of the administration of justice gave provinces exclusive authority over criminal prosecutions, the prosecution brought by the federal Attorney General was unconstitutional. This argument depended on two further claims. The first was that federal jurisdiction over 'The Criminal Law ... including the Procedure in Criminal Matters' did not include prosecutions; although prosecutions are indeed a matter of criminal procedure they are a specific administrative matter which has been subtracted from the general criminal procedure power and assigned to provinces. The second view was that, although administrative power routinely follows legislative power – for example, the federal government administers fisheries laws, the provinces administer education laws – the normal rule simply did not apply in this instance of specific constitutional allocation.

All of the provinces, except Manitoba, supported the argument of the accused, when the case came before the Supreme Court. This was a surprising show of support and represented provincial commitment to maintaining the long-standing arrangement under which provinces have responsibility for conducting prosecutions. The Supreme Court's decision in *Hauser*,[27] in 1979 did not, however, accept the position of the provinces. On the other hand it did not reject it. Instead a majority of the court found, contrary to both expectation and common sense, that the Narcotic Control Act was not criminal legislation but, rather, legislation passed under another federal source – the power to make laws for the peace, order and good government of Canada. Therefore, prosecutions under the act were not 'criminal' prosecutions. Since the federal level has the power to administer its own non-criminal laws, it had authority over the administration of this law, even when that administration took the *form* of criminal prosecutions.

For the three years following this decision the matter of responsibility for criminal prosecutions loomed large on the agenda of every federal-provincial meeting of ministers responsible for the administration of justice. Provincial ministers, especially, wanted both levels of government to come to an agreement as to which Attorney General, federal or provincial, would be responsible for the myriad federal criminal (or quasi-criminal) statutes – relating to taxation, airports, importing, competition policy, drugs, pollution, etc. The years of discussion produced no agreement, possibly because government officials simply had no clear idea of the extent of federal constitutional authority in this matter.[28]

In the meantime, two other accused persons, one charged under the Combines Investigation Act[29] and the other under the Food and Drug Act[30] again challenged federal authority to conduct prosecutions. Since both pieces of legislation had been held, in earlier cases, to have been enacted under the federal criminal law power[31] the Supreme Court could not avoid the issue by denying that the prosecutions were criminal. The decisions of the Court in 1983, in the two new cases – *Canadian National Transportation*[32] and *Wetmore*[33], established that the federal government does indeed have authority to conduct the administration of criminal law, including the prosecution of offences under the Criminal Code.[34] In effect, the Court faced directly the claims that had been advanced on behalf of Hauser and rejected them. Unfortunately, the *CN Transportation* and *Wetmore* decisions created maximum potential disruption to the Canadian pattern of administering criminal justice and neither constitutional language, nor general propositions of constitutional interpretation, led in any compelling way to the result reached. The cases produced a constitutional revolution in a situation in which there was neither sociological nor doctrinal excuse for such a revolution.[35] Chief Justice Laskin claimed that four traditional analytic modes of constitutional law – analysis of specific constitutional provisions, reference to constitutional history, resort to precedent, and structural analysis of the division of powers – supported the Court's conclusion. In none of these cases, however, is the case for federal authority convincingly made out, as was demonstrated by the powerful dissent of Mr. Justice Dickson in the *Wetmore* decision.[36]

As has been indicated the potential implications of these cases are far reaching[37] and flow from provincially conducted criminal prosecutions becoming mere exercises of delegated authority. The cases do not simply extend the federal head of 'criminal procedure' to cover prosecutions, thereby creating an area of concurrent jurisdiction. They are based on the view that criminal prosecutions are expressly excluded from section 92(14), and, therefore, they establish that when provincial Attorneys General, or their agents, conduct criminal prosecutions the only authority they are exercising is that which has been delegated to them by the Parliament of Canada.

The significance of this is that Parliament now clearly possesses the power to reverse the delegation and allow the federal Attorney General to assume responsibility for all criminal prosecutions. Furthermore, it is not clear that the delegate status of provincial prosecutors does not also apply to other sectors of provincial criminal administration, such as policing and corrections. Certainly there has been a strong tendency to see the investigation of crimes and prosecutions to be two halves of a single scheme of criminal administration.[38]

However, in the year and a half since these decisions were handed down, the federal government has not moved to exercise the powers newly recognized by the Supreme Court. It is doubtful whether Mr. Mulroney or his Attorney General, John Crosbie, will wish to do so. In many respects it is Mr. Mulroney's policy to leave to the provinces areas of public administration to which the federal government, under Mr. Trudeau, had been laying claim.

In a federal country, debates over which level of government is capable of doing the better job are seldom conclusive. The provincial claim in this case is that the processes of investigation, prosecution and incarceration, touching so directly on liberties of the subject, are most tolerably exercised when they are subject to the greatest amount of political accountability. That condition would seem to be best met when it is the provinces – or, under delegation from the provinces, municipal police forces – that hold these powers. Provincial and municipal administration may also be defective but, if it is accepted that liberty is better protected in a smaller, more open political environment than in a large, unnoticed, and largely unchecked public administration, then the potentially large size of the federal prosecutorial bureaucracy gives rise to concerns.

Other uncertainties arise from the holding that provincial prosecutions are conducted under a delegation of executive authority from the federal government. Which level of government is responsible for bearing the cost of prosecutions? Are the provinces free to refuse to perform delegated tasks unless they are compensated for the cost of doing them? Apart from the issue of financial burden, may some provinces simply refuse to accept some elements of the delegated authority? On the one hand, if the provinces can refuse to handle prosecutions of some offences – for example, choose not to prosecute under the abortion, or obscenity, sections – this would clearly frustrate federal policy. Such prosecutional decisions would perhaps be unconstitutional as undermining, and thereby, violating, the federal criminal law power. On the other hand the notion of divided sovereignty in the federal state may mean that one level of government cannot impose public duties and expenses on the other level and cannot control functioning of the other level, unless through legislation of general application. If governmental responsibilities and costs in this area can be imposed on the provinces through Parliament's exercise of its criminal procedure power, so likewise could Parliament relieve the federal government of other undesirable, costly or politically troublesome parts of its executive responsibilities. Accordingly, it does not seem to be constitutionally improbable to assert that the provinces could, if they wished, decline to continue with prosecutorial activity. Of course, there is no indication that provinces have any intention of voluntarily getting out of this field.

A further set of problems that arises from the constitutional position, created by these cases – that Parliament has delegated its prosecutorial responsibility to provinces – relates to possible challenges to the exercise of delegated authority. First, since the provinces no longer exercise the inherent powers of Attorneys General but act under statutory delegation, possibly there will be closer scrutiny by the courts of exercises of prosecutorial discretion. This could occur when defendants to criminal charges bring applications before courts to set aside decisions to prosecute on the basis of bad faith, inconsistency, or arbitrariness. Although such applications to a court were possible when prosecutions were thought to be a completely provincial responsibility and technically there had been no narrowing of prosecutorial discretion, it is likely that courts will extend less deference to prosecutorial choices made by those who are acting under an administrative delegation than to decisions made by those acting directly as agents of the Attorney General.

Second, a new possible Charter attack has been opened. Since all prosecutions in Canada now stem from the same authority, it is possible to apply the

John D. Whyte

standards of even-handedness found in the equality provision of the Charter to prosecutions. Although it is not possible to claim denial of equality on the basis that one province's legislative schemes differ from another's, it will be possible to show unequal treatment when a single public authority makes distinctions based on factors not relevant to the scheme being administered. Once it is accepted that there is no independent provincial responsibility for prosecutions, which is the result of *CN Transportation* and *Wetmore,* the province in which the alleged criminal conduct took place should not be germane to the enforcement of the criminal law. Therefore there will be a strong case that if prosecutors in Quebec choose not to proceed against an abortion clinic, while in Ontario or Manitoba prosecutions are launched, accused persons in Ontario or Manitoba can claim that their criminal liability is being determined, in part, on the basis of which province they committed the act in, a factor which should be totally irrelevant to the criminal charge which is brought and to the scope of authority to administer the criminal standard.[39]

The implications of these cases are potentially vast. Since the terms of the constitution cannot be considered to have compelled this result, this judicial development is unfortunate.

Juvenile Justice

Considerable federal-provincial conflict has arisen in recent years over the federal enactment of the Young Offenders Act,[40] an act establishing a new regime for dealing with young persons who commit offences. This act marks a shift away from the welfare oriented philosophy of the Juvenile Delinquents Act,[41] originally enacted in 1908. The principles of the new act are, first, that young persons should bear responsibility for their deviant conduct; second, that young persons who commit offences need special treatment distinct and separate from the sanctions imposed on adult offenders; third, that alternative measures – in other words, diversion from the court process – are appropriate for dealing with some young offenders and; finally, young people charged with an offence are entitled to due process, including the right to counsel.

Implementation of these principles has been resisted by some provinces, both because of a conflict of social values and because provinces were asked to bear many of the costs of implementation.

Policy conflict in this area did not, however, originate with the new act. A prior instance of differences over how to treat young offenders is found in the 1981 Supreme Court decision in *Lechasseur*.[42] In that case the Quebec policy of diverting young people from the criminal justice system to the control of the provincial Director of Youth Protection[43] was challenged by an angry citizen victim as being in conflict with exercise of Parliament's criminal law power represented in the Juvenile Delinquents Act and the Criminal Code.[44] The Court agreed with those attacking the provincial scheme and, given the Court's later acceptance of the primacy of federal prosecutorial authority, the result is not surprising. Nevertheless, the effect of the case was that undoubted provincial jurisdiction over child welfare[45] was reduced in scope.

Federal-provincial conflict over the treatment of juvenile crime grew to far greater proportion with the introduction of the new federal legislation. Quebec, however, was no longer the protagonist in the dispute; the policies of the Young Offenders Act are closer to Quebec's view than to those of other provinces, notably Ontario (though, of course, this could change under the new Liberal, NDP-backed, provincial government).

As for the costs of implementation, provincial opposition has focused on the requirement to provide special custodial facilities for 16 and 17 year olds. The act created a nationally uniform maximum age for young offenders of 17 years. For some provinces this represented a two year raise in age and imposed on them the relatively expensive system of incarceration for persons that were formerly treated as adults. Provinces also objected to establishing a program for diverting young offenders from trials and to providing legal counsel to young persons who are proceeded against. The conflict has somewhat diminished as a result of the making of federal-provincial agreements which provide for the cost-sharing of legal aid and training programs and confer direct grants to help offset the costs of the initial implementation of alternative measures programs. Nevertheless policy disagreements continue.

An example of provincial resentment of the Young Offenders Act leading to the frustration of the new policies is the refusal of some provincial legal aid plans to provide assistance without a direct order from the court compelling them to grant assistance. The act stipulates that all young persons who are 'unable to obtain' counsel shall be provided with counsel by court order; the provincial attorney general has financial responsibility for complying with these orders. The act seems to require judges before whom young persons appear to first direct the young persons to *apply* to the provincial legal aid plan, and only when that fails are they able to order that assistance be given.[46] This has caused many young persons to be deprived of legal assistance simply because the resulting process of multiple appearances before arriving in court *with* counsel is far too daunting. Furthermore, the process extends the period of experiencing distress over being in trouble with the law. As a result some of the rehabilitative and integrating aims of the act are defeated by this delay.

With respect to the vital policy of alternative measures, or diversion away from the trial process, Ontario has failed to establish any program or system of alternative measures. The Young Offenders Act states that alternative measures shall be pursued only if the provincial Attorney General has created a program. In this way Parliament has recognized the political wisdom (and, perhaps, the constitutional necessity) of provincial concurrence in employing non-curial procedures for restoring a young person to a constructive relationship with his or her community. However, such processes represent an important element in the range of appropriate responses to juvenile crime

John D. Whyte

and it is unfortunate that not all provinces are responding to the federal invitation to become involved in this program.

The policy of the act touching on special custodial arrangements for young offenders is also being frustrated. Some provincial correctional or youth protection agencies have adopted the expedient of simply designating existing portions of adult facilities as being separate from adult offenders or as being open custody when in fact, they are neither truly separate nor truly open. In one case the Manitoba government was challenged as acting in violation of the act when it labelled one building in a complex of buildings as being a place of open custody. (The act defines open custody as being a home, a residential centre or a camp.) However, the Manitoba Court of Appeal rejected the challenge.[47]

Thus the federal attempt to reform and make more effective the way we treat young offenders has come face to face with the reality of Canadian federalism – provincial powers and provincial interests are not easily overridden and national 'solutions' must bend to the country's political and social diversity.

Conclusion

The administration of justice is a topic which catches the paradox that justifies federalism – the administration of laws is at one and the same time a central component of national citizenship *and* properly reflective of local social communities. It ought not, therefore, be a matter of regret that federal-provincial complexity has reached the workings of Canada's systems of legal administration. Certainly, forms of reconciliation may be possible and ought to be pursued. However, so long as federalism catches our social and potential reality as accurately as it currently does, the conflict we have experienced in recent years in this area is preferable to the simple ascendancy of one level of government over the other.

Notes

1. *Saskatoon Criminal Defence Lawyers Association and Maltby v. Saskatchewan and Lane* [1984], 3 W.W.R., 707 (Sask.Q.B.) at 713.
2. R.S.S. 1978, c.Q-1.
3. *Supra*, note 1 at 717. The act gives the Executive Council no power to require a judge to change his or her residence. Consequently, a vacancy in a judicial centre cannot be filled by an order transferring a judge.
4. *Ibid.* at 719.
5. See, W.R. Lederman, 'The Independence of the Judiciary' (1956), 34 Canadian Bar Review 769, 1139.
6. R.S.C. 1970, c. 10 (2nd Supp.).
7. See, *Valin v. Langlois* (1879), 3 S.C.R. 1.
8. See, e.g., *Attorney General of Canada v. Canard*, [1976] 1 S.C.R. 170 at 216.
9. *Attorney General of Canada v. Law Society of British Columbia; Jabour v. Law Society of British Columbia*, [1982] 2 S.C.R. 307.,

10. (1983), 146 D.L.R. (3d) 202.
11. *Ibid.* at 208.
12. *Ibid.* at 213.
13. *Northern Telecom Canada Ltd. v. Communication Workers of Canada* (1983), 147, D.L.R. (3d) 1.
14. *Ibid.* at 17.
15. *Ibid.* at 18.
16. See, e.g., *Toronto v. York,* [1938] A.C. 415 (J.C.P.C.) and *Labour Relations Board of Saskatchewan v. John East Iron Works,* [1949] A.C. 134 (J.C.P.C.).
17. The view that Part VII of the *Constitution Act, 1867,* reveals the intention to constitutionalize in Canada a superior court system that matches in independence and jurisdiction the English central royal courts has been mostly cogently developed in W.R. Lederman, 'The Independence of the Judiciary', *supra,* note 5.
18. *Reference re Residential Tenancies Act,* [1981] 1 S.C.R. 714.
19. *Attorney General of Quebec v. Farrah,* [1978] 2 S.C.R. 638.
20. *Crevier v. Attorney General of Quebec,* [1981] S.C.R. 220.
21. For instance, in recent years the British Columbia system of allowing appeals to the B.C. cabinet from the Pollution Control Board and Saskatchewan's protection of farmers from defective agricultural implements through the Agricultural Implements Board have been attacked as violating section 96. See, *Capital Regional District v. Concerned Citizens of B.C.* (1983), 141 D.L.R. (3d) 385 (S.C.C.); *Massey-Ferguson Industries Ltd. v. Government of Saskatchewan* (1981), 127 D.L.R. (3d) 513 (S.C.C.). However, in both cases the Supreme Court of Canada held in favour of the provincial scheme.
22. The case was decided in May 1983. It is reported as *McEvoy v. Attorney General of New Brunswick* (1983), 148 D.L.R. (3d) 25 (S.C.C.).
23. Because of the anomalous fact situation in the *McEvoy* case, it is not exactly clear what constitutional restrictions are created by it. For a commentary on the case see J. Whyte, 'Developments in Constitutional Law: The 1982-83' Term (1984), 6 Supreme Court Law Review 49 at 74-81.
24. The Honourable Mark MacGuigan, *The Constitution of Canada: A Suggested Amendment Relating to Provincial Administrative Tribunals* (Ottawa, 1973).
25. There are many provincial administrative regimes which are not analogous to historic judicial functions (e.g., the administration of social welfare programs), and, therefore, are not subject to the constraints imposed by section 96. Hence, the preference for judicial independence over administrative flexibility is selective in its application, preserving judicial independence for the administration of laws relating to 'old' interests and 'old' property (property and interests which existed in the nineteenth century and were the subject matter of disputes that were resolved by courts). 'New' property (statutory rights and interests created as part of the modern activist state), on the other hand, may be administered by provinces without concern for preserving the judicial role.
26. R.S.C. 1970, c. N-1.
27. *R. v. Hauser* (1979), 98 D.L.R. (3d) 193 (S.C.C.).
28. One view of co-operative federalism is that inter-governmental agreements cannot normally be reached when the parties are unsure about the powers actually held by each level of government. See, W.R. Lederman, 'Some Forms and Limitations of Co-operative Federalism' (1967), 45 Canadian Bar Review 409, reprinted in Leder

John D. Whyte

man, *Continuing Canadian Constitutional Dilemmas* (Toronto, 1981) 314, at 314-15 and 335.

29. R.S.C. 1970, c. C-23 as amended.
30. R.S.C. 1970, c. F-27.
31. See, *Proprietary Articles Trade Association v. Attorney General of Canada* [1931] A.C. 310 (J.C.P.C.) and *Standard Sausage Co. v. Lee* [1934] 1. W.W.R. 81 (British Columbia Court of Appeal) in respect of the Combines Investigation Act and the Food and Drugs Act, respectively.
32. *Attorney General of Canada v. Canadian National Transportation* (1984), 3 D.L.R. (4th) 16 (S.C.C.).
33. *R. v. Wetmore and Attorney General of Canada* (1984), 2 D.L.R. (4th) 577 (S.C.C.).
34. R.S.C. 1970, c. C-34 as amended.
35. For critical analyses of the decisions see, J. Whyte, 'The Administration of Criminal Justice and the Provinces' (1984), 38 Criminal Reports (3d) 184, and A. Petter, 'Note on *Canadian National Transportation and Wetmore*' (1985), 63 Canadian Bar Review 162.
36. *R. v. Wetmore and Attorney General of Canada, supra*, note 33 at 58-296. See, also, the dissent of Mr. Justice Dickson in *R. v. Hauser, supra* note 27 at 210-54, in which a more thorough demonstration of provincial jurisdiction over criminal prosecutions is presented.
37. The following analysis is taken, in part, from J. Whyte, 'The Administration of Criminal Justice and the Provinces' *supra*, note 35.
38. See *Di Iorio v. Montreal Jail Warden*, [1968] 1 S.C.R. 152.
39. An argument akin to this was advanced by defence counsel for Drs. Morgentaler, Smoling and Scott in an application to quash an indictment charging conspiracy to unlawfully procure an abortion. The argument failed. See, *R. v. Morgentaler*, (1984), 47 O.R. (3d) 353 at 371-72.
40. S.C. 1980-81-82-83, c. 110.
41. R.S.C. 1970, c. J-3, repealed by S.C. 1980-81-82-83, c. 110, s. 80.
42. *Attorney General of Quebec v. Lechasseur*, [1981] 2 S.C.R. 253.
43. See, Youth Protection Act, S.Q. 1977, c. 20, s. 61.
44. *Supra*, note 34.
45. See, *Reference re Adoption Act*, [1938] S.C.R. 398.
46. This problem is dealt with in *R. v. Ronald H; R. v. K.M.; R. v. K.Q.* (1984), Young Offenders Service 3305. The court in this case, seemingly stretching the language of the act, concluded that the two stage process of referring young persons to legal aid plans and, then, ordering legal representation is not, in fact, required by the act.
47. *C.F. v. R. and Minister of Community Services and Corrections*, [1985] 2 W.W.R. 379.

8 Minority Language Rights in Four Provinces

Bruce G. Pollard

> Number is going to make us weak, and since under our constitutional system number is power, we are going to find ourselves at the mercy of those who do not love us.
>
> Alexandre-Antonin Taché (1823-94)
> Archbishop of St. Boniface, Manitoba[1]

Introduction

Events in four Canadian provinces since 1983 have once again placed the issues of bilingualism and minority language rights on the public agenda. Although progress falls short of the goal of equality of English and French within the federal public service, as noted in the 1984 report of the Commissioner of Official Languages, D'Iberville Fortier, the conflict aroused by the passage of the Official Languages Act in 1969 has generally subsided. Furthermore, the bitterness surrounding the air traffic contollers' strike of 1976 has seemingly disappeared. Nonetheless, language issues continue to raise tensions at the provincial level in the four provinces with the largest official language minority communities: New Brunswick, Quebec, Ontario and Manitoba. The debate in these provinces has spilled over into federal politics as well.

The federal nature of the Canadian state means that responsibility for government services is divided between two levels of government. Key areas of responsibility involving interaction between citizen and government – such as social services, health, education, and administration of justice – fall within the purview of the provinces. Many of these sectors are important for the maintenance and enhancement of a language. Somewhat ironically, many of these areas were entrusted to the provincial governments so that Quebec would control the instruments to enable it to preserve its French culture and language on an English-speaking continent. While aiding the Francophone community in Quebec, that development has hurt the Francophones outside of Quebec, and has enabled the provincial government, during the past decade, to limit the rights of the Anglophone minority within. Because of federalism, the rights of official language minorities may be less well protected in some respects than they would be in a unitary state.

What is the role of the federal government? The federal government has traditionally been dedicated to the notion of the equality of the two languages and, in the face of certain oppressive provincial policies, has championed the cause of minority language rights. It was the principal force behind the creation of the Canadian Charter of Rights and Freedoms, which guarantees certain minority linguistic rights. It has provided financial support to groups and individuals fighting for the protection and extension of these rights. Beyond that, it has put pressure on various of the provincial governments to offer services and guarantees to their linguistic minority communities. However, the federal government is limited in the extent to which it can protect these minorities.

Canada is a bilingual country with two historically dominant languages. Approximately two-thirds of the nation speaks English and about one-quarter speaks French. Yet, the geographical distribution of the linguistic communities is such that most provinces are dominated by one or other of the two language groups. Nearly one and a half million Canadians reside in provinces where the language they generally speak at home, while one of the official languages of Canada, is a minority language. Over 90 per cent of these citizens live in four provinces: New Brunswick, Quebec, Ontario, and Manitoba. As such, the language policies of the governments in these provinces will have a major impact on the fate of the official language minority communities in Canada. Table 8.1 illustrates the size of these communities, both in absolute terms and as a proportion of provincial populations.

Table 8.1
Official Language Minority Population

	Total Population	Home Language		Non-official	Official Language Minority As % of Total
		English	French		
New Brunswick	689,370	468,550	216,580	4,240	31.4
Quebec	6,369,070	809,145	5,256,830	303,095	12.7
Ontario	8,534,260	7,337,255	332,945	864,065	3.9
Manitoba	1,013,705	872,075	31,040	110,580	3.1

Source: 1981 Census of Canada, *Population. Mother Tongue, official language and home language* (Statistics Canada 92-910), 1983.

Policy towards linguistic minorities may have several dimensions. In particular, five can be noted:

□   language used in courts and legislature;

Bruce G. Pollard

- education (language of instruction);
- provision of services, other than education, in the minority language;
- equality of opportunity in the public service;
- protection of rights in the private sector.

The first of these has little impact on the daily lives of most people. It provides for the use of a minority language in the proceedings of the courts and the legislature within a particular jurisdiction. This often includes the publication of statutes, records and other documents of the legislature in the minority language.

The second, education, may be the single most important form of support for a minority language community. The debate over education has generally focused on the right to instruction in the minority language and the provision of such schooling by the government.

Third, the extension of government services other than education, is generally considered only after a government has been committed to providing the first two categories of minority language guarantees. It is possible for any government service to be provided in the minority language. At a more developed level, a government may guarantee the right to receive any government service in the minority language.

There is a qualitative difference between the first three and the final two categories. The fourth is not simply a further extension of services in the minority language. It comprises policies aimed at meeting equality of opportunity in the civil service. Policies of this sort include: 'affirmative action' programs which give preference in hiring to members of a minority; the establishment of quotas in public service employment; and regulations forcing the use of a minority language in the public sector.

The fifth category involves language policies that apply to the private sector and non-government organizations. This is an omnibus category that can include policies concerning a vast array of aspects in the workplace – such as public signs, correspondence, language of work, and hiring practices.

These categories may be viewed as roughly forming a continuum. Generally, minority language policies have developed in the order in which they have been presented here. The various provincial jurisdictions are at different points along this continuum.

Another issue concerns the means through which language rights are established, or may be claimed and enforced. Is primary reliance to be placed on legislation and administration, or on constitutional guarantees? A declatory statement that a minority language has official status could be constitutionally entrenched. Such a statement, which in itself is more symbolic than substantial, is usually accompanied by specific constitutional guarantees. These may be narrow in scope, applying only to language use in the legislature and courts. Or they may establish the right to virtually any of the types of policy outlined above. Constitutional entrenchment, being especially visible and suggesting irreversibility, contains great potential for conflict. It has been a central element in some of the recent debates over minority language rights.

The struggle over the rights of minority language groups during the past two years has surfaced in provincial legislatures and the House of Commons, in the courts (both the Supreme Court of Canada and lower courts), in public hearings, and in the arena of federal-provincial relations.

This chapter will present a description of the recent events in the four provinces of New Brunswick, Quebec, Ontario and Manitoba. Subsequently, it will seek to determine the current state of minority language rights in Canada. Finally, a brief analysis will explore several factors which bear on the controversies in these four provinces.

New Brunswick

The eruption of controversy over the language rights issue in New Brunswick in 1984 came as a surprise to many. New Brunswick has often been considered a prime example of two linguistic groups living peacefully together. Francophones comprise 31.4 per cent of the population. Only in New Brunswick does the official language minority comprise such a large proportion of the population.

The province has embraced official bilingualism in Canada since 1969, the year of the federal Official Languages Act, when it passed the Official Languages of New Brunswick Act. According to that Act, both French and English are official languages in the province. The statute provides for the use of both French and English with respect to the legislature, provincial statutes, and the courts, essentially as are provided for the federal and Quebec jurisdictions in section 133 of the Constitution Act, 1867.

Beyond that, the 1969 Act grants the right to obtain services from any government department or agency in either official language. It also states that any municipal council is authorized to choose the language or languages it wishes to use in any proceeding.

In 1981, the Legislative Assembly passed Bill 88, An Act Recognizing the Equality of the Two Official Linguistic Communities in New Brunswick. This extended the concept of individual rights which had been asserted in the 1969 statute. Bill 88 compels the Government of New Brunswick to ensure protection of the equality of status and the equal rights and privileges of the two linguistic communities. This includes their right to distinct institutions within which cultural, educational and social activities may be carried on.

Since 1982, the equal status of the two languages in New Brunswick has been constitutionally entrenched. Relevant sections in the Canadian Charter of Rights and Freedoms state:

16(2) English and French are the official languages of New Brunswick and have equality of status and equal rights and privileges as to their use in all institutions of the legislature and government of New Brunswick.
17(2) Everyone has the right to use English or French in any debates and other proceedings of the legislature of New Brunswick.

Bruce G. Pollard

18(2) The statutes, records and journals of the legislature of New Brunswick shall be printed and published in English and French and both language versions are equally authoritative.

20(2) Any member of the public in New Brunswick has the right to communicate with, and to receive available services from, any office of an institution of the legislature or government of New Brunswick in English or French.

In 1980, more than a decade after the passing of its Official Languages of New Brunswick Act, the government launched a review of this statute to determine 'what might be done to ensure that the Act, and the policy, meet changing needs and circumstances.'[2] The review process was to involve four phases: first, study, analysis and proposals by a task force; second, extensive public consultations by a provincial advisory committee; third, report by that committee; fourth, consideration of the report by the government and submission of proposed amendments to the Legislative Assembly.

The first phase began on 23 May 1980, when a task force was established to analyze and evaluate various aspects of the Official Languages of New Brunswick Act and to make recommendations concerning its revision. It was to evaluate the impact of bilingualism on all sectors of activity in the province. On 7 May 1982, the task force report, entitled 'Towards Equality of Official Languages in New Brunswick', was tabled in the legislature.

Generally, the task force found serious inadequacies with the 1969 statute. 'Written in such a way as to establish an obligation to meet the demand for services in both official languages in the Provincial civil service, it [nonetheless] does not establish basic rights in education or justice, ignores municipalities, hospitals, professional corporations and public utility companies and does not have any penalties or mechanism of implementation.'[3] The task force called for complete equality of the two languages. Two potent sections in its proposed 'New Brunswick Language Rights Act' stipulated that:

Every person has the right to demand that the public service, Crown corporations, professional associations, provincial trade unions and public utilities communicate with him in the official language of his choice.

Any public notice, public sign, pamphlet, brochure or other document directed to the general public and produced by the bodies referred to [above] is to be printed and made public at the same time in the two official languages under appropriate conditions with respect to accessibility and quantity.[4]

The recommendations of the report had important implications for most elements of New Brunswick society. With respect to the private sector, it recommended that all standard form contracts be issued in both official languages (Recommendation No. 69). Professional associations would be required to recognize equally the French and English designation of their association and to draft and publish their enabling legislation and regulations in both languages (Nos. 62 and 63). Moreover, it was recommended that in companies with more than 100 employees, collective agreements, working conditions and general regulations be published in the two official languages (No. 72).

The report recommended affirmative action programs be instilled to increase the proportion of Francophones in the civil service, especially in the administrative ranks. In 1983, 30.4 per cent of New Brunswick public servants were Francophones. In the capital city of Fredericton, this figure was only 17.9 per cent.[5] The report recommended that the objective of 'achieving a just representation of both official language communities in the Civil Service be affirmed and a precise timetable be adopted to that end' (No. 8). Moreover, it recommended that 'the decision of the government to make bilingualism an important element with regard to hiring and promotion within the Civil Service be affirmed' (No. 10).

The report recommended a major restructuring of departments. It accepted the general principles of 'duality' and 'regionalization' and rejected the concept of unilingual linguistic regions. Nevertheless, the authors maintained that it was necessary to recognize regional identity and preserve the linguistic homogeneity of the province's Francophone regions.

Concerning the concept of duality, the report stated: 'In general, every administration shall have a French and an English component, the language of work in each being that of the group of civil servants working in each component. Coordination between components and common services of departments and agencies shall be provided by bilingual personnel' (No. 81). In 1974, the Department of Education had adopted administrative structures which put in place almost total duality; this included two deputy ministers, one Anglophone and one Francophone, each responsible for programming and evaluation in his own sector.[6]

Another recommendation which would have a major impact on the provincial bureaucracy concerned administrative regions. It was suggested that all departments and agencies take part in a review of their administrative regions, with the objective of reducing their number, simplifying their organization, and assuring that each region is 'structured in such a way that it takes into account the linguistic characteristics of the population served' (No. 82). The report also recommended the decentralization of various provincial agencies to regions with a Francophone majority.

Various recommendations were made with respect to the provincial justice system. All were designed to better serve the French-speaking members of the province. The general thrust of these proposals favoured the provision of unilingual as opposed to bilingual proceedings to be made available to members of both language groups.

The Task Force report had important implications for the province's municipalities. The authors felt that the Official Languages of New Brunswick Act should obligate municipalities to adopt bilingualism officially in all their services. It recommended that bilingual publications, signs, and services be required for every New Brunswick city where the smallest official language community constitutes 20 per cent of the population or 1500 persons. Moreover, it was recommended that each city establish a hiring policy based on its linguistic requirements.

In tabling the report, Premier Hatfield rejected the concept of duality for government departments and agencies. The report caused little public reaction when it was released.

It was not until two years later, in March 1984, when Premier Hatfield created a seven-member Provincial Advisory Committee on Official Languages, that the report received widespread attention. Established not to make recommendations but rather to sound out and report on the public response to the report of the task force, a series of information sessions and public hearings was planned. Mr. Hatfield stated that, 'the socio-cultural dimension of this historic challenge requires that we send out an appeal for participation from all citizens.'[7]

In three of the 10 information sessions held in the autumn of 1984, rather ugly confrontations occurred between segments of the two linguistic communities. Fuelled by inadequate information about the task force's recommendations and by fears that Anglophone civil servants who were not bilingual would be fired or denied promotion, some English-speaking citizens lashed out against the task force report.

One of the most vocal of the opponents was Len Poore, founder and head of the New Brunswick Association of English-Speaking Canadians. Mr. Poore asserted that the provincial government has already gone too far in extending French-language rights. He objected to the government's decision to cut the civil service by 10 to 20 per cent by 1986, while the task force report recommended that Francophone representation in the civil service be increased.[8]

Quebec

Quebec's Charter of the French Language, better known as Bill 101, is generally considered to be both the most popular of all of the Parti Québécois' legislation among French-speaking Quebecers and the most contested and opposed within the Anglophone community. Introduced in 1977, it was designed to 'make Quebec as French as Ontario is English'.[9] The PQ government felt that even though Francophones comprised 82.5 per cent of the population, the survival of the French language was threatened. For generations, the Anglophone minority has generally enjoyed a high socio-economic status in Quebec, and English has been widely used throughout the province. This phenomenon has been aided by the fact that Quebec is part of a predominantly English-speaking North America.

Bill 101 was very comprehensive; it affected nearly all aspects of Quebec society, including education, the work place, the civil service, public signs and place names. All policies were geared towards the enhancement of the French language in Quebec. Some of the policies infringed guarantees provided in the Constitution Act, 1867, and in the respective Canadian and Quebec

Charters of Rights. As a result, there has been a string of court challenges to various sections of the statute since it was first passed by the National Assembly. Certain sections of Bill 101 have been struck down by the courts. Partly due to judicial decisions and partly due to public pressure, the government itself made revisions to the Act in December 1983. The result is that many of the more adverse elements in the statute have been mollified; however, the essence of Bill 101 remains.

It has been argued that an underlying reason for the tempering of Bill 101 is that the statute is no longer necessary. The French language in Quebec is not fighting a battle for survival nor is it a liability to be unilingually French in that province. Some would argue that the statute was never necessary; the fact that a provincial government could pass such a law in the first place was proof that it was not required. Others maintain, however, that the survival of the French language in Quebec cannot be taken for granted. The Quebec government's Draft Agreement on the Constitution, released in May 1985, pointed out that only two per cent of North Americans were French-speaking. Specific measures were required to protect French as the everyday language.

Judicial Challenges

There have been court challenges to various portions of Bill 101 almost since its inception. Generally, such challenges can be divided into three categories. First, some challenges have been on the grounds that the statute contravened the Constitution Act, 1867. Second, some have said that provisions of the Canadian Charter of Rights and Freedoms have been infringed and, third, some have asserted that Bill 101 contravened Quebec's own Charter of Human Rights and Freedoms.

The first category comprises those challenges to Bill 101 on the grounds that it contravened the Constitution Act, 1867. One of the key constitutional provisions protecting the minority Anglophone community in Quebec is section 133 of the Constitution Act, 1867, which guarantees that:

- either French or English may be used in the debates of the Quebec legislature;
- both languages shall be used in all records and journals of the legislature;
- all of Quebec's statutes shall be printed and published in both languages;
- either language may be used in any court of Quebec.

Section 133 also applies to federal courts and to the House of Commons and Senate. Even the provisions contained in section 133 were initially restricted by Bill 101. A 1979 Supreme Court ruling (the Blaikie decision) declared those sections of the Quebec statute unconstitutional.[10]

In December 1984, another case challenging Bill 101 on the grounds that it contravened section 133 was heard by the Supreme Court of Canada. That case arose in 1981 when Duncan MacDonald was issued a summons for a traffic violation in French only. Mr. MacDonald argued that section 133 of the Constitution Act, 1867 gave him the right to be summonsed in the language of his choice. This position was supported at the Supreme Court hearings by the Société franco-manitobain and Alliance Quebec. The key part of section 133 states that either French or English may be used by any person or in any pleading or process in or issuing from any court in Quebec. The position of the Quebec government is that its courts have the same status as a 'person'; as such, this gives them the right to issue documents, such as summons, in the language of their choice.[11] Although Mr. MacDonald has received funds from the federal Secretary of State to help him fight his case, the federal government intervened in the Supreme Court hearing on behalf of the Quebec government. The Court has not yet rendered a decision in this case.

The most significant development in recent years, from a legal perspective, has been the Canadian Charter of Rights and Freedoms, which came into effect on 17 April 1982. Some of the challenges to Bill 101 have been on the grounds that certain sections contravened the Charter. Ironically, Quebec has never agreed to the passage of the constitutional package which included the Charter. The package was the result of an accord signed in November 1981 by the other nine provincial premiers and Prime Minister Trudeau.

One of the most controversial sections of Bill 101 concerned the right to education in the English language. Sections 72 and 73 (the so-called 'Quebec clause') permitted Quebec residents to send their children to English schools only if one or both parents received their primary education in English in Quebec. However, section 23 (the 'Canada clause') of the Canadian Charter of Rights and Freedoms guarantees all citizens of Canada who have had their primary education in English the right to have their children educated in English.

The 'Quebec clause' was struck down by the Quebec Superior Court in 1982 and by the Quebec Court of Appeal in 1983. The provincial government appealed the latter decision to the Supreme Court of Canada. Two days of hearings were held in February 1984. Lawyers for the Quebec Association of Protestant School Boards, the federal and the New Brunswick governments argued that Bill 101 contravened the Charter.

The Supreme Court of Canada ruled on Bill 101 on 26 July 1984. The seven-member unanimous decision concurred with that of the two Quebec courts. Sections 72 and 73 of Bill 101 were found to be inconsistent with section 23 of the Charter, which had been drafted with the Quebec restrictions very much in mind. This was the first Charter decision by the Supreme Court which resulted in a law being declared unconstitutional. Quebec Justice Minister Pierre Marc Johnson complained that the ruling meant that Quebec no longer had full control over its education system.[12]

In its proposal for a constitutional accord, released in May 1985, the PQ government stated its desire to be exempt from the force of section 23 of the Canadian Charter which, in effect, neutralized measures adopted by the National Assembly to ensure the survival, affirmation and development of the

French identity. Nonetheless, the government did state it was prepared to amend Bill 101 to secure access to the English school system for the children of those who have received their primary instruction in Canada in English.[13]

The third category of cases are those which have challenged sections of Bill 101 on the grounds that they contravened the province's own Charter of Human Rights and Freedoms. Following is a summary of three of the most recent of these cases.

The first concerns Vivian Bromfield, who was fired in 1980 by the Miriam Home for the Retarded. She was dismissed verbally in English and later by letter, also in English. She and her union asked the arbitrator to overturn the dismissal on the grounds that it violated the language law.[14] A Quebec Court of Appeal judgement handed down by Justice Marcel Nichols on 25 March 1984, determined that employees have the freedom of choice in the language they use to communicate with individuals, although workers can request exclusive use of French in documents they receive. The decision implied that although French was the official language in the province, it does not make French the exclusive language of work. The provincial government cannot order employees and employers to communicate with one another strictly in French.

A second case concerns compulsory French testing for professionals. Government regulations empower civil servants at the Office de la langue française to set passing grades for the tests. However, only those people who have not attended a French-language secondary school for three years have been required to take the test.

In September 1984, two of three Quebec Court of Appeal justices ruled that these regulations were invalid because they were discriminatory and violated Quebec's Charter of Human Rights and Freedoms. This ruling overturned an earlier Superior Court ruling. The case at hand concerned Nancy Forget, a former nursing assistant who was able to pass the oral French test, but repeatedly failed the written part.[15]

Justice Minister Johnson announced on 23 September that the Quebec government would ask the Supreme Court of Canada to overturn the Court of Appeal ruling.[16] The government intended to argue against the lower court's interpretation of delegated power.

A third case concerns Bill 101's prohibition of bilingual signs. Judge Pierre Boudreault of the Quebec Superior Court ruled on 4 January 1985 that this prohibition contravened Quebec's Charter. This decision contradicted an earlier ruling on this section made by Quebec Superior Court Judge Jacques Dugas in March 1982. Judge Dugas had ruled in the case of stationer Allan Singer's English-only signs that language is not an essential element of freedom of expression. Because of the confusion surrounding the section of Bill 101 dealing with the language of signs, Deputy Premier Bernard Landry announced that the Quebec government would appeal the 1985 ruling. Quebec's Court of Appeal agreed on 5 March 1985 to review the two lower court decision in the fall of that year.[17]

In a related development, it was expected that a ruling of the Quebec government's own language commission would be challenged in the courts. Six Quebec municipalities, including Aylmer and Buckingham, were denied on 10 August 1984 a request to be recognized as bilingual by the language commission. Under Bill 101, these communities could not provide services in English because that was not the mother tongue of most residents. The municipalities argued that the proportion of people who are bilingual rather than 'mother tongue' should be the measure.[18] Article 113(f) of Bill 101 states:

The Office [de la langue francaise] shall recognize ... the municipal bodies ... that provide services to persons who, in the majority, speak a language other than French.

On 13 August the municipalities announced that they would appeal the commission's decision. In light of the commission's refusal, there was speculation that the municipalities would take their case before the courts.

Changes Through Legislation

Somewhat ironically, many of the language issues on the judicial platter in 1984 had already been addressed by the provincial government in its amendments to Bill 101 passed in the final days of 1983.

The Quebec National Assembly passed Bill 57 in December 1983 just prior to the end of the legislative session. This Act provided for a series of changes to the Charter of the French Language, to be effective on 1 February 1984. Following is a summary of the most important changes:

- The preamble now refers to the institutions of the 'English-speaking community.' This recognizes not only the 'English' institutions, but also the character of the community as based on language rather than ethnic origin. Included in this category are English health and social service institutions, schools, school board and municipalities.
- It is clearly established that for English institutions, it is the institution and not individual employees that must be capable of providing services in French.
- Certain provisions now allow greater use of English within English institutions. For example, two English-speaking employees may now communicate with each other in their own language.
- English institutions may now append English translations to French texts when communicating with one another.
- Municipalities will be able to use bilingual names.
- Language testing will be abolished for professionals who have obtained a Quebec high school certificate (English or French) as of 1986.
- Concerning education, access to English schools is now permitted for those children who have one parent who received his primary education in English in a province which, in the view of the Quebec government, provides educational services to its French-speaking minority which are com-

parable with those provided for English-speaking Quebecers. To date, only New Brunswick's education system has qualified.
- ☐ Bilingual signs for businesses specializing in the sale of ethnic or foreign products are now permitted, although the general prohibition of English on signs and posters is maintained.

New legislation in the field of education has had important implications for the status of the minority language in Quebec. Bill 3, introduced on 1 November 1984 and given assent on 21 December 1984, purported to make education in the province English and French, rather than Protestant and Catholic. This has been vehemently criticized by both Catholic and Protestant school boards. On 25 June 1985, the Act was struck down by the Quebec Superior Court as being in conflict with the Constitution Act, 1867. Although an appeal will be launched by the Quebec government, a court injunction prohibits application of the statute. Should it eventually be found valid, it will create new school boards based on language rather than religion. Within the boards, each school will have to decide whether it is Protestant, Catholic or neutral. Every child will be guaranteed the right to receive Protestant or Catholic religious class, or a religiously neutral morals class, in every school.

Ontario

Two major developments took place on the language rights front in Ontario during 1984. First, there was a resurgence in the debate over whether or not Ontario should adopt official bilingualism. The second development was a decision of the Ontario Court of Appeal concerning minority language education rights in the province.

In comparison to most other provinces, Ontario's record in providing services in the French-language is admirable. That record includes the following:

- ☐ Translation of legislature records and statutes is proceeding. In addition, most government documents are published in both languages.
- ☐ French is recognized as a language of use in the Ontario legislature.
- ☐ French is an official language of the courts of Ontario, according to section 135 of Bill 100, given royal assent on 1 May 1984. Bilingual courts are available in twelve districts and counties where French is widely spoken.
- ☐ The minister of education has accepted the principles of the right of a Francophone student to receive instruction in French and the right of Francophones to administer their own schools.
- ☐ Special services exist for the Francophone community, especially in the twelve districts deemed 'bilingual'.

Official Bilingualism

The issue of making Ontario officially bilingual was first proposed in the report of the federal Royal Commission on Bilingualism and Biculturalism in 1965. It resurfaced, however, several times during the Trudeau years.[19]

Although the Francophone community comprises less than five per cent of the population of Ontario, it is the largest group of French-speaking Canadians outside Quebec. The federal government is concerned that the rights of so many people be constitutionally protected.

Moreover, the constitutional recognition of French in Ontario would correct an imbalance which has existed since 1867. While section 133 of the Constitution Act, 1867 allows the use of both French and English in the legislature and courts of Quebec and requires that all records and journal be written in both official languages, there are no such provisions pertaining to Ontario.

The federal government has felt that this imbalance is unfair and that it fans the flames of separatism in Quebec. Quebecers feel they are being treated unfairly when they are forced to accommodate the Anglophone minority, while across the Ottawa River there is no similar protection afforded the Francophone population there.

In 1984, Prime Minister Trudeau made a final effort before leaving politics to convince Premier Davis of the value – indeed, necessity – of adopting official bilingualism in Ontario. He sent two letters to the Ontario premier in 1984. The first was carefully and logically argued, while the second was much more of an emotional appeal. The first, dated 23 March 1984, asserted that the main reason for entrenchment was the protection of the rights of Franco-Ontarians. Other than in the field of education, this portion of the population has no recourse if its linguistic rights are infringed. (Minority education rights are entrenched in the Canadian Charter of Rights and Freedoms and, as such, can be defended by the courts.)

Prime Minister Trudeau asserted that language policy in Canada has two dimensions. The first concerns the provision of services, facilities and practical opportunities required to do justice to French-speaking Canadians. The second involves the constitutional recognition and protection of the rights of French-speaking Canadians. While acknowledging that Ontario has made some progress towards fulfilling the demands of the first dimension, Mr. Trudeau urged the Ontario government to provide the protection inherent in the second dimension.

Premier Davis defended his government's policy of incrementally providing services for the Francophone community over the past decades. He dismissed the need to entrench the rights of the minority language group, arguing that national pressures to do so must be balanced with a design and a timetable that reflects Ontario's needs. Mr. Davis argued that the Ontario government's approach reflects its deep-seated commitment to the 'political traditions of steady maturation and dynamism.'[20] It is implied that the provincial government has a better idea than does the federal government of what would work in Ontario.

In one of his final acts as prime minister of Canada, Pierre Trudeau wrote to Premier Davis on 29 June 1984, assuring him that he had no doubt the people of Ontario were ready to accept official bilingualism.

French-language Education

The most important development in 1984 affecting the status of the minority French language came in the area of education. The Ontario government had made a reference in August 1983 to the Ontario Court of Appeal, requesting a ruling on the constitutionality of the Education Act in light of the minority language education provisions of the Canadian Charter of Rights and Freedoms. Two basic issues were involved: the right to education in the French language and the role of Francophones in the administration of the schools.

With respect to the former, Ontario's Education Act currently provides for instruction in French where 25 primary or 20 secondary Francophone pupils request it. Education Minister Bette Stephenson had announced on 23 March 1983 that the government would be changing the statute to guarantee instruction in French to any Francophone student who wished instruction in his or her mother tongue. A bill providing for this was introduced in December of that year just prior to the closing of that legislative session. A similar bill has not been re-introduced.

In its ruling which was delivered on 26 June 1984, the Ontario Court of Appeal declared that the provisions of the Education Act violated the Charter. Four reasons were given:

□ The provincial statute provides French classes to a much narrower class of people than does the Charter, which guarantees it for the children of anyone who took primary classes in French, whose first language is French, or who has another child studying in French in Canada.
□ School boards have too much discretion to provide French-language instruction.
□ The arbitrary limits of 20 and 25 students contravene the Charter because instruction must be provided wherever in the province the number of children who have such a right is sufficient.
□ School boards cover too small an area; the Charter's minority language provision transcends the geographic boundaries of school boards.

The Court also ruled that the Charter's minority language education guarantees apply equally to public and separate schools.

With respect to the second issue, the Court of Appeal found sections of the Education Act to be inconsistent with the Charter in that Francophones entitled to have their children receive instruction in the French language were not being accorded the right to manage and control their own French-language classes of instruction and French-language educational facilities.

The Ontario government issued in March 1983 a White Paper on the administration of French-language schools. That report concluded that where there are 500 or more minority language students, or where they make up at least 10 per cent of enrolment, a school board must create a panel of trustees to represent them. The Court of Appeal was asked if it were within the authority of the Legislative Assembly to amend the Education Act to provide for the election of minority-language trustees to Roman Catholic separate school boards to exercise certain exclusive responsibilities. The Court ruled that the proposals were within the legislature's regulatory power to establish an effective method of achieving proper minority language instruction in Ontario.

This decision was applauded by the federal government, which had argued that the Francophone minority should have the equivalent decision-making authority over its schools as does the Anglophone majority.[21] The federal government was also of the opinion that it was up to the provincial government to determine how that authority should be exercised. Although all mechanisms must meet a basic constitutional standard, the Charter does not dictate a specific method.

The Ontario government announced in November 1984 that it will pass a law guaranteeing minority language representation on school boards in time for trustee elections in the fall of 1985.[22] A maximum of seven trustees will be added to each board where Francophone students number more than 500 or 10 per cent of total enrolment.

A second development in the realm of education in 1984 had an incidental effect on Ontario's French-language education. Premier Davis announced in June that the Ontario government would extend the public financing of Roman Catholic separate schools to all grades.

Because of this decision, the campaign for homogeneous French-language high schools in Ontario could be set back. Ontario's public school system currently includes 30 all-French high schools and 30 mixed high schools where students can take courses in either French or English. The Roman Catholic separate school system includes only two all-French high schools (in Sudbury and Ottawa).

The new policy raised the possibility of new French-language schools in the Catholic system for the 23,000 Francophone Catholic students now in the public school system. As a result of the new government policy, several Roman Catholic separate school boards began preparing to offer French-language programs once government financing became available. Members of Ontario's Francophone community were worried that this development would draw students away from the French-language public schools. It was opposed because of the greater likelihood of assimilation in the mixed schools.[23]

Manitoba

On 13 June 1985, the Supreme Court of Canada ruled that most laws passed by the Manitoba legislature since 1890 were invalid because they were enacted only in English. The Court also said that these laws would remain in force indefinitely, pending their translation into the French language.

The fate of Manitoba's unilingual laws came to be heard by the Supreme Court of Canada after the New Democratic government failed to pass through the provincial legislature a proposal providing for the constitutional recognition of French as an official language and for legislative guarantees of services in the French language. When the Manitoba legislature was prorogued on 27 February 1984, after the opposition Progressive Conservative party had refused to allow the legislature to vote on the contentious bill, the rights of the French-speaking minority had been thwarted by what Pierre Trudeau called 'a determined opposition'.[24] It was illustrative of why many viewed constitutional entrenchment of minority language rights as essential.

Background

The legal history of French-language rights in Manitoba dates from 1870, when section 23 of the Manitoba Act – the statute which provided for the entry of the province into confederation – declared that all laws must be printed and published in both English and French and that both languages would be permitted in all provincial courts and the legislature. Twenty years later, in 1890, after a rapid decline in the proportion of the French-speaking population (largely due to a high rate of immigration), the Official Language Act was passed, declaring English to be the only language of legislative records, journals, and statutes, as well as of court proceedings, in Manitoba.

During the next 87 years, the matter lay dormant, except on two occasions when the 1890 statute was challenged in a lower court. In 1892 and again in 1909, two lower Manitoba courts ruled that the 1890 Act which declared English to be the only official language was unconstitutional. The provincial governments of the day chose to ignore these rulings and did not appeal them. As such, the cases were not heard by higher courts.

Perhaps the same fate would have met a 1977 challenge launched by George Forest, had not the appellant himself taken the case to a higher court. That case resulted in a 1979 Supreme Court of Canada decision which found the 1890 Official Language Act to be unconstitutional. In response, the Manitoba government under Premier Sterling Lyon passed legislation formally revoking the 1890 statute and began the arduous job of translating many of Manitoba's statutes into French.

The 1979 decision left an important question unanswered: what was the status of all the acts passed in English only by the Manitoba government since 1890? Roger Bilodeau was the first to take this question beyond the county court level; he fought a speeding ticket in 1980, challenging the validity of Manitoba's Highway Traffic Act and Summary Conviction Act, which governed the issuance of the ticket, on the grounds that they were in English only.

In a split decision, the Manitoba Court of Appeal ruled in 1981 against Mr. Bilodeau. Its decision was appealed and the Supreme Court of Canada agreed the following year to hear the case.

It was this pending court case which prompted the Manitoba government to attempt to reach an 'out of court' settlement. The government was afraid of the possible repercussions of a Supreme Court decision in Bilodeau's favour. The court could have deemed all of Manitoba's English-only laws to be invalid, creating legal chaos for the province. Or it could set strict and costly

Bruce G. Pollard

deadlines for the government to meet in getting its statutes translated. (The government had been lax in this. In fact, since the 1979 Supreme Court decision (the Forest case), only 47 laws have been translated, published, and adopted by the legislature, with another 54 ready to be published.)[25]

A provisional agreement was reached in May 1983 among the Manitoba government, the federal government, and the Société franco-manitobaine (SFM). In exchange for the constitutional recognition of both French and English as official languages, modest guarantees in certain French-language services, and a commitment to translate 450 of the more important current statutes by 1993, and all of the statutes passed after 1984, Mr. Bilodeau agreed to adjourn his challenge.[26] The Manitoba Act would be amended to: include a 'saving provision' ensuring that no Manitoba statute would be without force solely because it was printed and published in only one official language; commit the Manitoba government to the program for the translation of current and future statutes that was part of the 1983 provisional agreement; and guarantee the provision of government services in the French language in areas where there was sufficient demand. The federal government offered rather substantial financial assistance to defray the costs of translation.

There was an overwhelming negative reaction. Much of it was based on two fears: the need to be bilingual in order to work in the civil service and the need for municipalities to offer bilingual services. The government maintained that these fears were unfounded. In amended drafts of the proposal, municipalities and school boards were explicitly excluded from the purview of the legislation. Concerning the civil service, it was estimated that only three per cent of Manitoba government employees would need to be bilingual in order to provide the required French-language services.[27]

Opposition in the provincial legislature was led by the leader of the Progressive Conservative party, Sterling Lyon. His criticism was focused on two factors: the way in which the provisional agreement had been reached (behind the scenes, and involving the federal government and a small interest group, representing less than five per cent of the population); and the possibility that the majority could someday be held hostage by the French-speaking minority if their rights were entrenched beyond the reach of the elected provincial legislature.

Public opposition was widespread and, at times, malicious. In a plebiscite accompanying the elections of 26 October 1983 in several Manitoba municipalities, including Winnipeg, over 75 per cent of the respondents expressed disapproval of the Goverment's plans concerning the French language.

To assuage some of the dissension, the Manitoba government twice modified its proposal. The first set of amendments did little to stem the tide of opposition.[28] The second revisions were unveiled in mid-December 1983 and subsequently introduced in the legislature in January 1984.

The 1984 proposal comprised two parts. The first was an amended version of the 1983 resolution to amend the constitution, guaranteeing the use of both French and English in Manitoba. The major changes to the original resolution included a change in the declaratory statement, section 23.1. The 1983 proposal had asserted that 'English and French are the official languages of Manitoba.' The revised proposal stated:

As English and French are the official languages of Manitoba, the freedom to use either official language enjoyed under the law of Manitoba in force at the time this section comes into force shall not be extinguished or restricted by or pursuant to any Act of the Legislature of Manitoba.

Proposals guaranteeing the right to government services and communications in either official language were not included in the 1984 proposed constitutional amendment. Unchanged, however, were the provisions concerning the translation of provincial statutes.

The second part of the government's plan was introduced in the Manitoba legislature as Bill 115, An Act Respecting the Operation of S. 23 of the Manitoba Act. It proposed to give French-speaking Manitobans the right to deal in French with all government head offices and with government offices serving communities having more than 800 Francophones or where Francophones comprised at least eight per cent of the population. The bill also provided for a language ombudsman and a council to advise government on bilingual services. This commitment was to be contained only in legislation, however, and not entrenched in the constitution.

Although not happy with the diluted proposal, the SFM voted to support it, preferring to reach a political accord to submitting the case to the Supreme Court. The SFM recognized that even the revised proposal would give them an official status and provide for a level of services that a legal victory in the Bilodeau case would not guarantee. Moreover, if Mr. Bilodeau lost his case, even the limited constitutional protection granted in section 23 of the Manitoba Act might be rendered impotent. The SFM may have been wary of taking that risk.

The 1984 version of the French-language proposal failed to placate the Progressive Conservative opposition under newly-elected leader Gary Filmon. After an eight-month recess, the second session of the 32nd Manitoba legislature recommenced in January 1984 with many hours of discussion on the French-language proposals, and several aborted attempts by the government to impose closure. The opposition refused to allow a vote even on Bill 115 which provided for legislative guarantees. It walked out of the legislature (thereby allowing the bells to ring) for 263 hours. On the rather ominous note of ringing bells, the legislative session ended. With it died the Manitoba government's French-language plan.

In response to these events, Roger Bilodeau requested that the Supreme Court of Canada proceed with his case. Since a political accord could not be reached, the Manitoba government would be forced to have the constitutionality of its laws tested by the highest court in the land.

It must be emphasized that the Bilodeau case would only test the validity of two Manitoba statutes. It would not address the central elements of either the May 1983 provisional agreement or Bill 115, that is, French-language services and the declaration of French as an official language. These issues had been removed from the agenda. When Bill 115 died on the order paper in February 1984, it represented a major setback for the minority Francophone community.

The Role of the Federal Government

At the height of the 'Manitoba crisis', the Parliament of Canada passed two unanimous resolutions addressing the situation. In October 1983, a resolution explaining why the federal government had a stake in the issue urged the Manitoba legislature to pass expeditiously the proposed legislation.[29] The resolution emphasized that the need to remedy the injustice in Manitoba was a legitimate and urgent concern for all Canadians.

On 24 February 1984, the House of Commons unanimously passed a second resolution regarding the Manitoba language issue. More anxious in tone, it implored the provincial legislature to consider the proposal in an urgent manner.

When Bill 115 died in February, the federal government evaluated its options. On 22 March, it chose to make its own reference to the Supreme Court of Canada. It could have relied on the Bilodeau case to deal with all the important issues. The Federal government was concerned, however, that a decision on the Bilodeau case might address the constitutionality of only the two statutes in question. The federal government wanted the fate of all unilingual laws in Manitoba to be decided once and for all. In fact, it also wanted the high court to address the fate of unilingual laws which could be conceivably passed by a future National Assembly in Quebec or by a future federal Parliament. The ultimate intent of the federal reference was to ensure that another unilingual law would never again be passed in any of these three jurisdictions.

The Supreme Court was asked in the federal reference to answer four questions:

☐ Is it mandatory for the Governments of Manitoba, Canada and Quebec to enact laws in both French and English?
☐ Are all Manitoba laws not published in English and French invalid?
☐ If these laws are invalid, do they have any legal force at all, and if so, to what extent and under what conditions?
☐ Are any of the provisions of An Act Respecting the Operation of Section 23 of the Manitoba Act in Regard to Statutes, passed by the former Conservative government of Manitoba in 1980 in order to retroactively deal with the language problem, inconsistent with provisions of section 23 of the 1870 statute?

One possible factor underlying the federal government's decision to make its own broad reference was that it had intervened on behalf of the Government of Manitoba in the Bilodeau case when it was heard at the Court of Appeal level in 1981. However, in the Supreme Court hearing, it intervened on behalf of Mr. Bilodeau. Making a separate reference enabled the federal government to make less obvious this apparent flipflop. Justice Minister Mark MacGuigan asserted that this was not a real reversal because the federal government has always wanted some kind of constitutional recognition of French-language rights in Manitoba, and at the same time has wanted to avoid legal chaos.[30]

The issue of the federal government's involvement in this matter was an ongoing source of contention. Much of the public opposition in Manitoba was based on the perception that the extension of minority language rights was a federal government idea that was being foisted upon the province. (The federal government was a party to the 1983 provisional agreement).

The federal Parliament's resolutions endorsing the French-language proposal were not welcomed by the leaders of either the NDP or the Conservative party in Manitoba. Both noted that despite the unanimous support for the federal government's resolution, it was impotent. It should be recognized, however, that according to section 43 of the Constitution Act, 1982, had the Manitoba government been successful in passing its resolution to amend the constitution, the approval of the federal Parliament would have been essential.

Some members of the Manitoba government objected to the federal government making its reference case to the Supreme Court, feeling that Manitoba would have a better chance of winning the Bilodeau case (it had won at a lower court level) than the broader reference.[31] There were some, as well, who wanted the Supreme Court to rule narrowly on only the two specific Manitoba statutes in question.[32] If these were deemed unconstitutional, the entire legal system of the province would not be disrupted. However, it would serve notice that the Supreme Court was treating the requirements of section 23 of the 1870 Manitoba Act seriously. This might have precipitated a political solution, and avoided the need for further litigation.

The Federal Reference Case

The Supreme Court of Canada decided to hear the federal reference before it heard arguments for the Bilodeau case. It announced in June 1985 that judgment in the Bilodeau case will be delivered at the same time as a decision is delivered in the Quebec case of Duncan MacDonald. 11 June 1984 was set as the date for the reference case hearings to begin. Intervenors included the Manitoba and Quebec provincial governments, the federal government, Alliance Quebec, SFM, Roger Bilodeau, and a group of six private citizens, which included Russ Doern, a former member of the NDP government and an outspoken critic of its language proposals. Following is a general summary of the positions of each of the intervenors.[33]

Bruce G. Pollard

QUEBEC   Manitoba's obligation to enact laws in both languages is 'imperative' and, as such, its unilingual laws should be declared void.

MANITOBA   The province's English-only laws should not be found void. The requirement for laws to be in two languages is directory only and not mandatory. The bilingualism requirement is not important enough to render a unilingual law invalid.

THE FEDERAL GOVERNMENT   Manitoba's English-only laws should be found invalid. Because of the chaos which would result, however, the doctrine of necessity could be used to validate them for two years (the time the federal government considered sufficient to translate and re-pass 4500 statutes in both languages). This is a very severe timetable compared to that contained in the provisional agreement.
The principle of necessity allows for laws, either passed illegally or authored by an illegal regime, to be recognized as valid to preserve legal continuity and order in society. If this doctrine were adopted, the court could determine which of Manitoba's statutes were valid.

ALLIANCE QUEBEC   The requirement to enact laws in both languages is mandatory and the doctrine of necessity cannot be used to save the provincial laws. Remedy lay either in an immediate provincial election under a pre-1890 electoral law, which would create a valid legislative assembly capable of passing a constitutional amendment, or a specific court ruling sustaining the current legislature and government solely for the purpose of passing an amendment. However, if the Court chose to accept the doctrine of necessity, the necessity warranted deeming the 1983 provisional agreement to be in force for all purposes.

SOCIETE FRANCO-MANITOBAINE   The requirement to enact laws in both languages is mandatory and the doctrine of necessity cannot be used to save the provincial laws. The Court should render the current legislation valid, and all rights, contracts, penalties and actions flowing from Manitoba laws binding until the day of the Court judgment. Thereafter, the legislature would continue to exist, but all of the unilingual laws would be inoperative until the legislature corrected them, either by adopting the constitutional amendment or by immediately passing all its laws in French.

ROGER BILODEAU   The requirement to enact laws in both languages is mandatory and the doctrine of necessity cannot be used to save the provincial laws.

THE SIX MANITOBA CITIZENS   While the requirement to publish laws in both languages is mandatory, to declare all unilingual laws invalid would create chaos. Since chaos is opposite the intention of a constitution, the court must find the unilingual laws from the past 90 years to be valid.

While the positions of Manitoba, Ottawa, and the six citizens all stressed the preservation of Manitoba's laws, the SFM and Alliance Quebec believed the

Supreme Court's principal task is to uphold the constitution of Canada. This case brought into conflict the country's written constitution and the inherited tradition of evolving British common law.[34] Counsel for Canada, SFM and Alliance Quebec argued that the language rights are mandatory. Counsel for Manitoba, however, argued that the language guarantees must be interpreted through British common law. Common law looks not simply at the written word, but at the consequences as well; the consequence of finding the guarantees to be mandatory would be chaos. The Supreme Court had to wrestle with two mutually incompatible desires: to enforce constitutional rights and to prevent chaos.

The federal reference case created some rather interesting paradoxes and some uneasy alliances. First, opposition to the Manitoba government's proposals, as led by Sterling Lyon, was focused on the notion that control of French-language rights should be in the hands of elected politicians and not entrenched beyond the purview of the legislature, thereby leaving its interpretation up to the courts. Because of the 'success' of that opposition, the constitutional entrenchment did not occur. However, as a result, the politicians sat on the sidelines while the judiciary decided the fate of the bulk of Manitoba's laws.

Another paradox is that the NDP Manitoba government, which had been quite prepared to entrench French-language guarantees and work towards having important statutes translated into French, was arguing that 90 years of unilingual laws were constitutionally acceptable. Although it had signed a provisional agreement with the federal government and the SFM in 1983, it found itself ranged against them one year later.

Moreover, the Manitoba government was aligned with a group of six citizens who had been strongly opposed to its language package. Both the government and the group of citizens were fighting to uphold the validity of the Manitoba laws. They argued on quite different grounds, however, such that the group of six undercut the basis of the provincial government's case. While the Manitoba government argued that section 23 of the Manitoba Act was more declaratory than mandatory, the 'six' accepted that section 23 was mandatory, but argued on the basis of the doctrine of necessity that the Supreme Court could not render chaos on the Province of Manitoba.

This case put Quebec in a peculiar position. The Parti Québécois government was forced to ally itself with the federal government. According to Quebec Justice Minister Pierre Marc Johnson, the reference case was of particular interest to the Quebec government for three reasons.[35] First, Quebec wanted to safeguard those interests which touched upon its own constitutional obligations. Second, Quebec had a direct interest in the general principles that would underlie the Court's ruling on the validity of unilingual Manitoba laws. Third, Quebec wanted to take a position in regard to its solidarity in heart and spirit with Francophones outside Quebec. Some argued that the Quebec government had moved substantially away from its advocacy of separatism and its belief that the French-Canadian nation could survive only in an independent Quebec. Others argued, however, that a strong and thriving French-speaking Quebec is essential if the Francophone minorities in the other provinces are to have any chance of survival.

The Supreme Court ruling, delivered on 13 June 1985, addressed the four questions laid out in the federal reference. First, the requirements of section 133 of the Constitution Act, 1867 and of section 23 of the Manitoba Act were deemed to be mandatory. Therefore, all records, journals and statutes of the Parliament of Canada and of the legislatures of Quebec and Manitoba were to be printed and published in both French and English.

Second, the Court found those statutes and regulations of the Province of Manitoba that were printed and published in only one language to be invalid. In response to the third question, the Court noted that while these English-only laws have no legal force and effect because they are invalid, the current acts of the legislature would have temporary force and effect for the minimum period of time necessary for their translation, re-enactment, printing and publication. The Court did not have adequate information to determine what that minimum period might be; it did offer, however, to make such a ruling if the Attorney-General of either the Government of Manitoba or of the Government of Canada made such a request within 120 days.

The Court noted that to declare the unilingual statutes invalid would create a legal vacuum with consequent legal chaos in the Province of Manitoba. The constitutional principle of the Rule of Law would be violated by this consequence. The Court noted that, 'the Rule of Law requires the creation and maintenance of an actual order of positive laws to govern society .... This Court must recognize both the unconstitutionality of Manitoba's unilingual laws and the Legislature's duty to comply with the supreme law of this country, while avoiding a legal vacuum in Manitoba and ensuring the continuity of the Rule of Law.'[36] The Court did state explicitly that all laws passed by the Manitoba legislature after the date of judgment would need to be enacted, printed and published in both French and English in order to be valid.

The fourth question in the reference concerned the 1980 Act, passed by the Lyon government, dealing with the translation of statutes. The Court concluded that if An Act Respecting the Operation of Section 23 of the Manitoba Act in Regard to Statutes were not enacted in both official languages, then the entire statute was invalid. However, even if it were enacted, printed and published in both English and French, then sections 1 to 5 were inconsistent with section 23 of the Manitoba Act, 1870. These sections, in effect, made the English version of laws prevail over the French version in the event of a conflict in interpretation. As well, the effect of some of these sections was that the two versions did not have to be published and enacted simultaneously. In its ruling, the Court drew heavily from the 1979 Blaikie decision concerning section 133 of the Constitution Act, 1867. That decision determined that for the Quebec legislature, section 133 required simultaneous enactment of legislation in both

English and French, and equal authority and status for both versions. Since section 23 of the Manitoba Act, 1870 is virtually identical to section 133 of the 1867 statute, the Supreme Court ruled that the Manitoba legislature was required to meet the same obligations.

Conclusion

Over 90 per cent of the Canadians who are members of official language minorities reside in the four provinces in this study. As such, the policies of these four governments are critical to the protection of minority language rights in this country. This analysis begins with an evaluation of the minority language policies in these four provinces.

New Brunswick offers the best hope for minority language rights. However, this should not be surprising as, there, the minority Francophone community includes one out of every three citizens. The debate in New Brunswick is clearly of a different order from that which exists in any other province. There, the battle for the provision of basic provincial government services in both official languages appears to have been won. Debate in New Brunswick concerns the equality of opportunity in the public service for members of both linguistic communities and the provision of bilingual services by municipalities and private sector organizations. There has been substantial opposition to a task force report which recommended changes in order to attain these objectives. Public hearings concerning the contentious report began in the spring of 1985.

In Quebec, the only constitutional protection for the Anglophone community, apart from that relating to education, is found in section 133 of the Constitution Act, 1867. The language policies of the Parti Québécois government have sought to replace the 'de facto' bilingualism which has existed in Quebec with a predominently French-speaking society. Perhaps not surprisingly, the Anglophone minority in Quebec has been one of the strongest defenders of minority language rights in recent years. It has seen a shrinking of rights once taken for granted.

The Ontario government continues to advocate a policy of slowly and incrementally increasing its services to the Francophone minority in the province. With respect to the language of the legislature and the courts, the province offers nearly the same services as are required in section 133 for the federal and Quebec jurisdictions. In addition, Ontario offers rather extensive French-language services in designated 'bilingual' regions. As such, it would not be a costly venture for Ontario to 'opt into' section 133 of the Constitution Act, 1867, thereby establishing parity between the minority linguistic communities of Ontario and Quebec.

However, the Ontario government has decided to avoid the constitutional route, fearing a possible backlash if special status were given to a minority language group by entrenching its rights in the constitution. The Ontario government sees in neighbouring Manitoba an example of what it has been able to avoid. The likelihood of the French language receiving any constitutional protection in Ontario in the near future is remote.

As a result of the June 1985 Supreme Court decision, the Manitoba government must proceed to translate all of its English laws into French. While this ruling was a victory for the Franco-Manitoban community, it was a small one indeed. Essentially, the right of the French language to 'section 133-type' protection (that is, guaranteed use in the courts and legislature and publication of government statutes and other legislative documents in that language) was upheld. The current status of the French language remains short of the official status which had been proposed in the May 1983 provisional agreement. Moreover, the level of government services in the French language, which would have been much enhanced had the NDP government's proposals been passed, was not affected by the Supreme Court decision. In fact, as a result of the Supreme Court ruling, there may be a reaction against the small Francophone community, and progress towards increased services even further frustrated.

In summary, members of minority language communities in Canadian provinces do not enjoy a high level of protection. Only in three provinces have they any constitutional protection at all (other than the guarantees to education provided for in the Charter). Of these, only one offers protection greater than the guarantees related to the courts and legislature (the 'section 133' guarantees). In two of the provinces, there exists a slow and incremental, albeit progressive, process of increasing services to Francophones. These are largely affected by the economic circumstances and there is no constitutional obligation driving on these processes. In Quebec, there was an effort by the provincial government, primarily in the late 1970s, to curb the use of the minority language. That has been greatly modified, partly due to changes in public attitudes and, in large measure, as a result of the courts upholding the province's own Charter of Human Rights and Freedoms.

Efforts to substantially increase the level of services or to implement constitutional protection of minority language rights, especially during the first part of the 1980s, have been met with hostility. Incrementalism seems to be the only plausible policy for a government wishing to increase minority language services.

The result is that any services which a provincial government, other than New Brunswick, may provide for the minority linguistic community, beyond those accruing from section 133-type provisions, are subject to the whims of provincial legislatures. There is no constitutional protection of these services.

The recent task force report in New Brunswick suggests that even though the right to communicate and receive services from the New Brunswick government in either official language is guaranteed in the Canadian Charter of Rights and Freedoms, this right may not always exist in practice.

This lack of congruence between constitutional obligation and practice also exists in the area of minority language education. Section 23 of the Canadian Charter of Rights and Freedoms guarantees any member of an official language minority the right to an education in his or her own language. This applies in all provinces. Legislation in both Quebec and Ontario has been tested in the courts. Both Bill 101 in Quebec and the Education Act in Ontario have been found wanting.

Why is there such a reluctance to protect minority language rights in the constitution and why is it often necessary for the courts to be used in order to enforce the few rights which do exist? While there is no one explanation, a number of factors may shed some light on these phenomena. In particular, these factors may help to explain why there seems to have been a strong reaction against provincial language policies during the early part of the 1980s.

First, bigotry and xenophobia cannot be dismissed as factors bearing on the controversies in at least three of the provinces. Resentment towards the minority Francophone communities has been expressed at the public level in both Manitoba and New Brunswick. Fear of a negative backlash has dictated Ontario's prudent position with respect to French-language rights. Much of the media coverage and commentary on the language situation in Manitoba and, to some extent, in New Brunswick has been focused on the element of bigotry, often ignoring other reasons people may have for opposing increased governments support of minority languages.

One such reason is the economic recession and the costs associated with the language proposals. The fear of costs to the Anglophone community, as expressed primarily by segments of the Manitoba and New Brunswick populations, suggests that the extension of minority language rights is more difficult in a period of economic restraint. Costs may be either the financial costs associated with increased government services or the negative employment effects which arise when policies to increase minority representation in the civil service coincide with restraint measures aimed at reducing the size of the civil service.

It is easier to extend services and rights to a disadvantaged minority if the policy has little or no ill-effect on the people that comprise the majority. Federal bilingual policies may serve as an example. Although the passage of the federal Official Languages Act in 1969 initially met a considerable amount of opposition, the subsequent increase in the Francophone component of the federal civil service during the 1970s occurred with few negative repercussions. This is not to suggest that there have not been complaints, cases of 'blocked promotions' and some dissatisfaction with the pace of the policy implementation. Generally, though, rather significant shifts in the proportions of the linguistic communities in the civil service have occurred with a minimal amount of controversy. An important factor is the rapid growth of the civil service during this period. As such, the change in the relative proportions of the two linguistic communities did not entail an absolute decline in the number of Anglophones.

Another factor which may help explain the recent controversies is the apparent fear of putting entrenched rights beyond the reach of politicians. Although

Bruce G. Pollard

this argument may be couched in terms of respect for the parliamentary tradition and responsible government, it is often rooted in a fear that a minority group will make unrealistic and crippling demands at some future date. (The reverse argument is that only by entrenching the guarantees in the constitution can the rights of the minority be secured.) Constitutional entrenchment makes the court system, rather than the elected legislators, the final arbiter in the protection of minority rights.

One final factor is the attitude of Canadians towards the federal government. Some of the opposition to proposals extending the rights and services for minority Francophone communities, especially in Western Canada, can be seen as a reaction against federal policies generally and against the government of Pierre Trudeau specifically. This negative feeling was especially pronounced during 1983 and 1984, the last years of the Trudeau government.

This feeling has been expressed by Patrick O'Callaghan, publisher of the Calgary Herald, who has suggested that the resentment expressed by Manitobans is not an anti-French feeling as such. Rather, it is a result of the way federalism works in Canada, holding little comfort for Westerners. It 'flows from an improper assumption on the part of Manitobans that their province, because of its minor-league status within confederation, is having the duality of language forced on it, while the two major founding provinces, Ontario and Quebec, go their merry ways, each still unilingual.'[37] Mr. O'Callaghan argued that the language proposals implied to westerners that provincial rights can always be overridden by intervention of a central government in Ottawa. At the heart of the matter was the belief that western provinces are not full partners in confederation. An advertisement, placed in the 7 January 1984 edition of the Winnipeg Free Press by Manitoba Grassroots, opposed the provincial government's proposal because it was not a 'Made in Manitoba' solution.

The pro-western stance and anti-French sentiments were inextricably linked in the rise of a new party in western Canada: the Confederation of Regions Party (COR). The party's raison d'être was a proposal dividing Canada into four equal regions: the West, Ontario, Quebec, and the Atlantic region. Each region would be represented by an equal number of elected parliamentarians. The party wanted to establish the western provinces as a power bloc in Canada.[38]

Although the party's platform included a number of typically western demands, such as a new system of freight rates, opposition to the extension of bilingualism was its major plank during the 4 September federal election campaign. The party fielded 55 candidates in the four western provinces, including 10 in Manitoba. In that province, the COR party captured 8.5 per cent of the popular vote and placed second in three rural ridings.

Of all of his government's policies, Prime Minister Trudeau was probably most closely identified with the passage of the Official Languages Act, and with his efforts to achieve a level of bilingualism in the federal civil service. The Trudeau government was also very concerned about provincial policies toward minority language groups. Mr. Trudeau believed that the federal government, as the national government, was responsible for ensuring that the official minority language communities were protected. As such, the federal government offered substantial resources to help the Manitoba government provide services to its Francophone community under the terms of the 1983 provisional agreement, to which the federal government was party. Furthermore, the federal Parliament made two impassioned resolutions asking the Manitoba legislature to accept the agreement. Mr. Trudeau also made several attempts to convince the Ontario government of the need to constitutionally entrench the rights of its minority Francophone community.

This position on minority language rights has been shared by Brian Mulroney, leader of the federal Progressive Conservative party and, after 4 September 1984, prime minister of Canada. In an address made in Winnipeg on 29 March 1984, Mr. Mulroney suggested that the great challenge for Manitoba and Canada was to reconcile 'two different views of history – one which sees Canada as a compact between English and French, a duality, the other which sees Canada as a cultural mosaic, a land of diversity.'[39] Mulroney argued that Canada can have both: the acceptance of linguistic duality need not mean the rejection of cultural diversity.

The role of the federal government in provincial language policies has always been a crucial issue for Canadian federalism. It became a political issue in the spring of 1984, when controversial comments were made by candidates running for the leadership of the federal Liberal party. The timing of the leadership campaign coincided with the federal government's decision to refer the Manitoba language issue to the Supreme Court of Canada.

The issue was personified in John Turner and Jean Chrétien, the two main combatants in the 'battle for the rose' to replace Pierre Trudeau as leader of the federal Liberal party. Jean Chrétien, having essentially the same sentiments as his former leader, strongly felt that the national government was compelled to support the rights of the linguistic minority everywhere in Canada.

John Turner, however, favoured the resolution of the Manitoba language issue within the province. On 20 March, he stated that 'provincial services for the French language within a province should be a matter of provincial initiative and should be negotiated within the province and should be a matter for provincial political resolution, and not a matter imposed by judicial decision.'[40]

In a statement two days later, in an attempt to clarify his position, Turner made a distinction 'between the extension of French services by a province and the respect of fundamental minority rights to language and education.' He asserted that 'the extension of services, as opposed to the recognition of fundamental rights, is a matter for provincial initiative .... In dealing with the extension of services by a province, the responsibility remains provincial, although Parliament may exercise strong moral suasion.'[41]

Bruce G. Pollard

Mr. Turner's remarks hit on a key difficulty of bilingual policies in a federation. There is an inherent contradiction between respect for language rights as a matter of fundamental national interest and the provision of provincial services by a provincial government. Where do the jurisdictions end? As Michel Roy, editor of La Presse, wrote, 'the federal government cannot remain indifferent when minority language rights, recognized by the Constitution, confirmed by the Supreme Court, are still denied by the majority.'[42]

Notes

1. Quoted in Ramsay Cook, *Canada and the French-Canadian Question* (Toronto: Macmillan of Canada, 1966) p. 183.
2. Premier Richard Hatfield at a news conference, 4 January 1985. Reproduced in *The Week-in-Review*, Vol. 7, No. 1, 10 January 1985.
3. *Towards Equality of the Official Languages in New Brunswick. Report of the Task Force on Official Languages* (Fredericton: Government of New Brunswick 1984) p. 137.
4. *Ibid*, p. 429.
5. Reported in *Saint John Telegraph-Journal*, 7 January 1984.
6. Provincial Advisory Committee on Official Languages, *The Task Force Report on Official Languages. A Summary* (1984) p. 9.
7. Government of New Brunswick, *The Week-in-Review*, 11 October 1984.
8. *Saint John Telegraph-Journal*, 19 October 1984.
9. Camille Laurin, then Minister of State for Cultural Development, in 1977, when introducing Bill 101. Quoted in *Ottawa Citizen*, 5 January 1985.
10. See S. Dunn, *The Year in Review 1982: Intergovernmental Relations in Canada* (Kingston: Institute of Intergovernmental Relations, 1982).
11. *Ottawa Citizen*, 19 December 1984.
12. Reported in *The Globe and Mail*, 27 July 1984.
13. *Draft Agreement on the Constitution: Proposals by the Government of Québec*, May 1985, p. 17.
14. Reported in *The Gazette*, Montreal, 26 March 1984.
15. Reported in *The Gazette*, Montreal, 5 September 1984.
16. *The Gazette*, Montreal, 24 September 1984.
17. *The Gazette*, Montreal, 6 March 1985.
18. *Ottawa Citizen*, 8 June 1984.
19. Among those who have asked the Ontario government to adopt official bilingualism are Jean-Luc Pepin, while he was co-chairman of the Task Force on National Unity, Claude Ryan, while Quebec Liberal leader, Richard Hatfield, and three successive Commissioners of Official Languages, *Vancouver Sun*, 11 August 1984.
20. Letter from Premier Davis to Prime Minister Trudeau, 12 June 1984.
21. *Ottawa Citizen*, 3 April 1984.
22. *Toronto Star*, 8 November 1984.
23. In *The Globe and Mail*, 22 November 1984.
24. In letter from Prime Minister Trudeau to Premier Davis, 23 March 1984.
25. *Winnipeg Free Press*, 12 May 1984.
26. Minister of Justice, *News Release*. 20 May 1983.

27. Attorney General of Manitoba, 'Constitutionally Speaking', July 1983, and *Winnipeg Free Press*, 11 February 1984.

28. Announced on 6 September 1983 by Attorney General Roland Penner before a standing committee of the Manitoba legislature. See B. Pollard, *The Year in Review 1983. Intergovernmental Relations in Canada*, pp. 36-7.

29. *House of Commons Debates*, 6 October 1983, p. 27816.

30. Quoted in *The Globe and Mail*, 4 April 1984.

31. Including Attorney General Roland Penner, *Winnipeg Free Press*, 6 April 1984.

32. For example, *Calgary Herald* editorial, 7 April 1984.

33. An article in the *Winnipeg Free Press*, 12 May 1984, was helpful in constructing this summary of positions.

34. Frances Russell, 'Manitoba Case Most Difficult', *Winnipeg Free Press*, 15 June 1984.

35. Quoted in *Ottawa Citizen*, 26 April 1984.

36. From Supreme Court of Canada decision concerning section 23 of *Manitoba Act, 1870*, 13 June 1985, p. 6.

37. 'Official Languages: A Western Perspective. Patrick O'Callaghan's Remarks', in *Language and Society*, No. 14, 1984, pp. 9-11.

38. *Edmonton Journal*, 11 July 1984.

39. Brian Mulroney, *Speech*, Winnipeg, 29 March 1984.

40. CTV Network, *Canada AM*, 20 March 1984.

41. Statement by John Turner to members of the federal Liberal caucus, 22 March 1984. Printed in *Ottawa Citizen*, 23 March 1984.

42. Quoted in Jeffrey Simpson, 'Mr. Turner's Remarks', *The Globe and Mail*, 20 March 1984.

List of Titles in Print

Peter M. Leslie, *Politics, Policy, and Federalism: Defining the Role of the Institute of Intergovernmental Relations*, 1984. ($7)

Catherine A. Murray, *Managing Diversity: Federal-Provincial Collaboration and the Committee on Extension of Services to Northern and Remote Communities*, 1984. ($19)

Peter Russell *et al*, *The Court and the Constitution: Comments on the Supreme Court Reference on Constitutional Amendment*, 1982. (Paper $7, Cloth $15)

The Year in Review

Bruce G. Pollard, *The Year in Review 1983: Intergovernmental Relations in Canada*. ($16)

Revue de l'année 1983: les relations intergouvernementales au Canada. ($16)

S.M. Dunn, *The Year in Review 1982: Intergovernmental Relations in Canada*. ($12)

Revue de l'année 1982: les relations intergouvernementales au Canada. ($12)

S.M. Dunn, *The Year in Review 1981: Intergovernmental Relations in Canada*. ($10)

R.J. Zukowsky, *Intergovernmental Relations in Canada: The Year in Review 1980, Volume I: Policy and Politics*. ($8) (*Volume II not available*)

D. Brown, *Intergovernmental Relations in Canada: The Year in Review 1979*. ($7)

Queen's Studies on the Future of the Canadian Communities

Keith Banting, *The Welfare State and Canadian Federalism*, 1982. (Published with McGill-Queen's University Press. Distributed by University of Toronto Press.)

Allan Tupper, *Public Money in the Private Sector: Industrial Assistance Policy and Canadian Federalism*, 1982. ($12)

William P. Irvine, *Does Canada Need a New Electoral System?*, 1979. ($8)

Discussion Paper Series

22. Robert L. Stanfield, *National Political Parties and Regional Diversity* (forthcoming, 1985).
21. Donald Smiley, *An Elected Senate for Canada? Clues from the Australian Experience*, 1985. ($8)
20. Nicholas Sidor, *Consumer Policy in the Canadian Federal State*, 1984. ($8)
19. Thomas Hueglin, *Federalism and Fragmentation: A Comparative View of Political Accommodation in Canada*, 1984. ($8)
18. Allan Tupper, *Bill S-31 and the Federalism of State Capitalism*, 1983. ($7)
17. Reginald Whitaker, *Federalism and Democratic Theory*, 1983. ($7)
16. Roger Gibbins, *Senate Reform: Moving Towards the Slippery Slope*, 1983. ($7)
15. Norman K. Zlotkin, *Unfinished Business: Aboriginal Peoples and the 1983 Constitutional Conference*, 1983. ($10)
14. John Whyte, *The Constitution and Natural Resource Revenues*, 1982. ($7)
13. Jack Mintz and Richard Simeon, *Conflict of Taste and Conflict of Claim in Federal Countries*, 1982. ($7)
12. Timothy Woolstencroft, *Organizing Intergovernmental Relations*, 1982. ($8)
10. Anthony Scott, *Divided Jurisdiction over Natural Resources*, 1980. ($6)

Bibliographies

Federalism and Intergovernmental Relations in Australia, Canada, the United States and Other Countries: A Bibliography, 1967. ($9)

A Supplementary Bibliography, 1975. ($10)

A Supplementary Bibliography, 1979. ($5)

Aboriginal Peoples and Constitutional Reform

Background Papers

1. Noel Lyon, *Aboriginal Self-Government: Rights of Citizenship and Access to Governmental Services*, 1984. ($10)
2. David A. Boisvert, *Forms of Aboriginal Self-Government*, 1985. ($10)
3. NOT AVAILABLE
4. Bradford Morse, *Aboriginal Self-Government in Australia and Canada*, 1985. ($10)
5. Douglas E. Sanders, *Aboriginal Self-Government in the United States*, 1985. ($10)
6. Bryan P. Schwartz, *First Principles: Constitutional Reform with Respect to the Aboriginal Peoples of Canada 1982-1984*, 1985. ($15)

Discussion Paper

David C. Hawkes, *Aboriginal Self-Government: What Does It Mean?*, 1985.
   ($10)
Set ($60)

Publications may be ordered from:

Institute of Intergovernmental Relations
Queen's University
Kingston, Ontario, Canada
K7L 3N6

DATE DUE
DATE DE RETOUR